RIGHTS AND RETRENCHMENT

This groundbreaking book contributes to an emerging literature that examines responses to the rights revolution that unfolded in the United States during the 1960s and 1970s. Using original archival evidence and data, Stephen Burbank and Sean Farhang identify the origins of the counterrevolution against private enforcement of federal law in the first Reagan Administration and then (1) measure the counterrevolution's trajectory in the elected branches, court rulemaking, and the Supreme Court, (2) evaluate its success in those different lawmaking sites, and (3) test key elements of their argument. Finally, the authors leverage an institutional perspective to explain a striking variation in their results: although the counterrevolution largely failed in more democratic lawmaking sites, in a long series of cases little noticed by the public, an increasingly conservative and ideologically polarized Supreme Court has transformed federal law, making it less friendly, if not hostile, to the enforcement of rights through lawsuits.

STEPHEN B. BURBANK is David Berger Professor for the Administration of Justice at the University of Pennsylvania Law School. He is editor (with Barry Friedman) of *Judicial Independence at the Crossroads: An Interdisciplinary Approach* (2002) and the author of numerous articles drawing on interdisciplinary perspectives. He served as Chair of the Board of the American Academy of Political and Social Science. Burbank was a member of the National Commission on Judicial Discipline and Removal and a principal author of its report.

SEAN FARHANG is Professor of Law and Associate Professor of Political Science and Public Policy at the University of California, Berkeley. He is the author of *The Litigation State: Public Regulation and Private Lawsuits in the US* (2010), which received the Gladys M. Kammerer Award from the American Political Science Association for the best book in the field of US national policy, as well as the C. Herman Pritchett award for the best book on law and courts.

RIGHTS
AND
RETRENCHMENT

The Counterrevolution against Federal Litigation

STEPHEN B. BURBANK

University of Pennsylvania

SEAN FARHANG

University of California, Berkeley

CAMBRIDGE
UNIVERSITY PRESS

CAMBRIDGE
UNIVERSITY PRESS

University Printing House, Cambridge CB2 8BS, United Kingdom

One Liberty Plaza, 20th Floor, New York, NY 10006, USA

477 Williamstown Road, Port Melbourne, VIC 3207, Australia

4843/24, 2nd Floor, Ansari Road, Daryaganj, Delhi – 110002, India

79 Anson Road, #06-04/06, Singapore 079906

Cambridge University Press is part of the University of Cambridge.

It furthers the University's mission by disseminating knowledge in the pursuit of education, learning, and research at the highest international levels of excellence.

www.cambridge.org
Information on this title: www.cambridge.org/9781107136991
DOI: 10.1017/9781316480229

First published 2017

Printed in the United States of America by Sheridan Books, Inc.

A catalogue record for this publication is available from the British Library.

Library of Congress Cataloging-in-Publication Data

Names: Burbank, Stephen B., author. | Farhang, Sean, 1966- author.
Title: Rights and retrenchment : the counterrevolution against federal litigation / Stephen B. Burbank, Sean Farhang.
Description: New York : Cambridge University Press, 2017. | Includes bibliographical references and index.
Identifiers: LCCN 2017006680 | ISBN 9781107136991 (hardback)
Subjects: LCSH: State action (Civil rights)—United States. | Actions and defenses—United States. | Federal government—United States. | Political questions and judicial power—United States. | Law—Political aspects—United States. | Conservatism—United States.
Classification: LCC KF1325.C58 B87 2017 | DDC 342.7308/5—dc23 LC record available at https://lccn.loc.gov/2017006680

ISBN 978-1-107-13699-1 Hardback
ISBN 978-1-316-50204-4 Paperback

For Our Families:
Ellen Coolidge Burbank and Peter Burbank
Ingrid McKenney, Silas and Miles Farhang

CONTENTS

List of Figures   ix
List of Tables   xiii
Preface and Acknowledgments   xvii
Table of Cases   xxi

1 Retrenching Rights in Institutional Context:
   Constraints and Opportunities   1

2 Legislative Counterrevolution: Emergence,
   Growth, and Disappointment   25

3 Rulemaking Counterrevolution: Birth, Reaction,
   and Struggle   65

4 Counterrevolution in the Supreme Court:
   Succeeding through Interpretation   130

5 Subterranean Counterrevolution: The Supreme Court,
   the Media, and Public Opinion   192

6 Rights, Retrenchment, and Democratic Governance   217

Bibliography   249
Index   267

FIGURES

1.1 Number of federal statutory plaintiff's fee-shifting and damages enhancement provisions enacted, 1933–2014   13

1.2 Cumulative federal statutory plaintiff's fee-shifting and damages enhancement provisions, and federal private statutory litigation rate, 1933–2014   14

2.1 Annual number of private enforcement retrenchment items: damages, attorney's fees, class actions, sanctions, offers of judgment, 1973–2014   38

2.2 Republican and Democratic support for private enforcement retrenchment, 1973–2014   39

3.1 Proportion of judges, practitioners, and academics on Advisory Committee, 1960–2014   78

3.2 Practitioner types on the Advisory Committee, 1960–2014   80

3.3 Aligned versus unaligned practitioners, 1960–2014   82

3.4 Population adjusted ratio of Republican to Democratic appointees serving on the Advisory Committee, 1971–2014   85

3.5 Number and direction of Advisory Committee proposals affecting private enforcement, 1960–2014   93

3.6 Probability of pro-plaintiff Advisory Committee proposal, 1960–2014   95

A.3.1 Probability of pro-plaintiff Advisory Committee proposal, item level and rule level, 1960–2014   128

4.1 Number of private enforcement issues per term, and probability of dissent, 1960–2014   148

4.2 Probability of pro-private enforcement outcomes and justice votes in private enforcement issues, 1960–2014   153

4.3 Probability of pro-private enforcement outcomes and justice votes in private enforcement issues with dissents, 1960–2014   155

4.4 Probability of pro-private enforcement outcomes and justice votes in issues with dissents, separately for government and business defendants, 1960–2014   156

4.5 Balance between government and business defendants in Court's private enforcement issues, 1960–2014   157

4.6 Probability of pro-private enforcement outcomes and justice votes in all federal statutory and constitutional rights issues with dissents, 1960–2014   159

4.7 Average annual number of amicus briefs filed per case in Supreme Court's private enforcement cases, and in all cases, 1960–2014   161

4.8 Proportion of cases with Chamber of Commerce Amicus Briefs, and with Washington or Pacific Legal Foundation Amicus Briefs, 1970–2014   163

4.9 Number of Federal Rules private enforcement issues per term, and probability of dissent, 1960–2013   172

4.10 Probability of pro-private enforcement outcomes and justice votes in all Federal Rules private enforcement issues, 1960–2014   175

4.11 Probability of pro-private enforcement outcomes and justice votes in Federal Rules private enforcement issues with dissents, 1960–2014   176

4.12 Balance between government and business defendants in Federal Rules private enforcement cases, and non-Federal Rules private enforcement cases, 1960–2014   177

A.4.1 Probability of pro-private enforcement outcomes
       and justice votes in parallel policy sample cases with
       dissents, 1960–2014   190

  5.1 Media coverage index of private enforcement issues,
       1960–2013   204

  6.1 Rate of private civil rights litigation in federal court,
       1961–2014   229

TABLES

2.1 Types of private enforcement issues in bills   36

2.2 Policy distribution of bills   37

2.3 Negative binomial model of legislator support for anti-private enforcement provisions, with Congress fixed effects, 1973–1980   42

2.4 Negative binomial model of legislator support for anti-private enforcement provisions, with Congress fixed effects, 1981–2014   45

2.5 Negative binomial coefficients and marginal effects for legislator party in models of legislator support for anti-private enforcement provisions, with Congress fixed effects, by presidential administration   47

3.1 Logit model of committee service and committee appointments for Article III judges, with year fixed effects, 1971–2014   87

3.2 Logit model of chair service and chair appointments for Article III judges, with year fixed effects, 1971–2014   90

4.1 Types of private enforcement issues   145

4.2 Policy distribution of private enforcement issues   145

4.3 Party types in private enforcement issues   146

4.4 Percentage of pro-private enforcement votes in private enforcement cases with dissenting votes   151

4.5 Logit model of justice votes in private enforcement
     cases, with case fixed effects, 1960–2014   166

4.6 Logit model of justice votes in private enforcement
     cases, government versus business defendant models,
     with case fixed effects, 1960–2014   167

4.7 Logit model of justice votes in all federal statutory and
     constitutional issues (Spaeth data), with case fixed
     effects, 1960–2014   168

4.8 Types of Federal Rules issues   171

4.9 Percentage of pro-private enforcement votes in
     Federal Rules cases with at least one dissenting
     vote   174

4.10 Logit model of justice votes in Federal Rules
     private enforcement cases, with case fixed effects,
     1960–2014   178

A.4.1 Percentage of pro-private enforcement votes in all
     private enforcement cases, including unanimous
     decisions   183

A.4.2 Percentage of pro-private enforcement votes in Federal
     Rules cases, including unanimous decisions   184

A.4.3 Logit model of justice votes in private enforcement
     cases, and in Federal Rules cases, with case fixed
     effects, and 2000 break   185

A.4.4 Logit model of justice votes in private enforcement
     cases, government versus business defendant models,
     with 2000 break, and case fixed effects   186

A.4.5 Marginal effects from models substituting Segal-Cover
     scores for Martin-Quinn scores   188

A.4.6 Logit model of justice votes in parallel policy sample,
     with case fixed effects, 1960–2014   191

5.1 Mean values of newspaper coverage of Supreme Court
     decisions: private enforcement versus merits issues   201

5.2 Negative binomial model of newspaper coverage of
     Supreme Court decisions   202

5.3 Marginal effects of negative binomial count
     models of newspaper coverage of Supreme Court
     decisions   203

5.4 Logit model of Supreme Court case outcomes/justice
     votes, 1961–2012   208

5.5 Logit model of Supreme Court case outcomes/justice
     votes, 1995–2012   213

PREFACE AND ACKNOWLEDGMENTS

The genesis of this project lay in our shared recognition that Farhang's book, *The Litigation State* (2010), while chronicling the revolution that started in the late 1960s as a result of congressional choices to stimulate private enforcement of federal rights through statutory attorney's fees and damages provisions, only lightly touched its aftermath. Focused elsewhere, *The Litigation State* did not explore retrenchment of private enforcement by any of the lawmaking institutions of the federal government. Thus it also did not consider the possibility that the judiciary enjoys a privileged position to use procedure for the purposes of retrenchment.

In this book, we report the results of a multi-year project that we designed to map the aftermath of the revolution in private enforcement that is the focus of *The Litigation State*. In thinking about the definition and scope of our project, we decided early on that we would not study either efforts to reduce federal judicial power through court-curbing (e.g., jurisdiction stripping) bills or cases involving judicial review of administrative action (or inaction). Although court-curbing has been described in terms of retrenchment (of judicial power) (Staszak 2015), it can be designed either to promote or retard private enforcement of federal rights. Similarly, although decisions on administrative agency power may affect the enforcement of federal law, they bear no necessary connection to private enforcement.

Instead, we sought to identify issues that are widely acknowledged as critical to the infrastructure of private enforcement of federal rights. Among the cases raising such issues that we decided to study, those involving private rights of action, damages and attorney's fees involve only federal claims. Standing cases are potentially broader, but very few cases triggering Article III or prudential standing issues arise under state law,[1] and the doctrine applies to all cases in federal court – that is, the doctrine

---

[1] Of the standing issues in the dataset we created, which we discuss in Chapter 4, only 2 of 112 (1.8%) involved state law claims.

is transsubstantive. Cases interpreting Federal Rules of Civil Procedure that predictably affect private enforcement (e.g., Rule 23, the class action rule) often involve state law claims, but, again, the resulting interpretations apply equally to federal claims. Finally, we restricted the arbitration cases we studied to those in which the claimant sought to litigate federal claims, a choice that reflected not only our definition of scope but also awareness that different legal standards apply as between federal and state claims when the question is whether an arbitration agreement can be disregarded consistently with the Federal Arbitration Act (FAA).

Thus circumscribing our study's domain, we were conversant with a large literature concerning attacks on lawyers and litigation, and we knew that other authors had chosen different parts of the litigation landscape, and different statutes, cases, or Federal Rules, to illustrate their claims about those attacks. We were also aware that little of the anti-litigation literature was grounded in systematically collected data, with the result that readers could not determine whether the picture of litigation painted by an author was representative. We believed that a systematic approach combining both qualitative and quantitative analysis – a multi-method research strategy – was overdue.

Although inclined to restrict this project to the phenomenon chronicled in *The Litigation State*, and thus to study only legal issues pertinent to the private enforcement of federal rights, we considered expanding it to include matters deemed salient by other scholars, both at the beginning of the work and in response to comments or suggestions made by those reading drafts of the articles that we prepared as the foundation of this book. As a result, early on we seriously considered extending our horizons, and our data collection, to include all or part of the landscape of tort reform. Moreover, we considered gathering data on such issues as preemption of state law and state sovereign immunity.

Our decisions not to expand the project in these directions were driven by a number of related concerns. First, there is a limit to the amount of data that can be gathered and analyzed within a reasonable time and at reasonable expense. Second, whether the question was covering tort reform, sovereign immunity, or preemption, we were concerned, at a macro level, about loss of focus, and at a micro level about consistency in the meaning of the data that we aggregated.

We were fortified at the macro level by our archival research, which, as we discuss in Chapter 2, strongly suggests that the counterrevolution gained traction in the first Reagan administration as an ideological campaign against private litigation as a tool of federal policymaking.[2] The choice to restrict the project was also supported by our empirical finding that retrenchment of private enforcement preceded tort reform on the federal legislative agenda during the Reagan years, thereafter merging with the broader national campaign to shield business from the effects of pro-litigation incentives, substantive and procedural, that often flies under the banner of tort reform.

At the micro level, if the goal is to determine whether a bill, rule proposal, or court decision favors or disfavors private enforcement of federal rights, it is essential not to include issues that are not salient for that project, such as preemption (of which FAA cases involving state law claims are a subset), and prudent not to include issues that are predictably overlaid with the baggage of federalism, such as sovereign immunity. We acknowledge, of course, that Supreme Court decisions concerning issues like preemption and sovereign immunity may be driven in part by the justices' preferences concerning litigation, but we are not persuaded either that such views are fungible with attitudes about private enforcement of federal rights or that it would be sensible to aggregate them into the same analysis.

Portions of this book have appeared in articles and a book chapter that have been published during the course of the larger project (Burbank and Farhang 2014, 2015, 2016a, 2016b). We have updated most previously reported data through 2014 and provide empirical analyses not reported in earlier work. We have also supplemented qualitative material with the fruits of additional archival research, notably in the papers of the first Reagan administration (Chapter 2) and the records of the Advisory Committee on Civil Rules (Chapter 3). The major benefit of proceeding in this manner, however, has been the opportunities it has afforded us to consider the suggestions of numerous colleagues who read and commented on drafts. Their comments have enabled us to refine, and hopefully improve, our account of what are, after all, complex phenomena unfolding over a long period of time. To that end, we have presented drafts of parts of this project, and received helpful comments, at workshops, conferences, and symposia held at the University of Pennsylvania Law School, University of California, Berkeley, School of Law, Northeastern Law School,

---

[2] This research also fortified our decision not to include bills or cases whose provisions or holdings were equally applicable to public enforcement of federal law. For the reasons we discuss concerning Rule 23, however, no such decision-rule applies to the Federal Rules of Civil Procedure.

University of California, Hastings College of Law, Stanford Law School, DePaul University College of Law, Boston University Law School, and Hebrew University, Jerusalem.

In addition to participants in the events mentioned in the preceding paragraph, we wish to thank the following individuals for their generosity in providing comments and suggestions that have caused us to think harder, dig deeper, and reconsider both the strengths and weaknesses of our data, methods, and theoretical perspectives:[3] Andrew Bradt*, Jeb Barnes*, Thomas Burke, Cornell Clayton, Barry Friedman, Jonah Gelbach, Deborah Hensler, Robert Kagan, Herbert Kritzer, David Marcus*, Richard Marcus, Joy Milligan, Alan Morrison, Jim Pfander, Ed Purcell*, Kevin Quinn, Shira Scheindlin*, David Shapiro, Cathie Struve, Steve Subrin, Tobias Wolff, and Steve Yeazell. We are also indebted to the anonymous readers who provided comments on the proposal for this book.

In his capacity as Reporter of the first Advisory Committee on Civil Rules, Dean Charles Clark wrote to his colleagues that "listing is always dangerous because of possible omissions" (Burbank 2002: 1044). We are mindful of the magnitude of that risk when seeking to acknowledge the many colleagues who have sought to improve our work over the course of four years, and we ask the indulgence of any who do not appear in this list because of the frailties of our memories or our record-keeping.

We have received invaluable research assistance from numerous students at the University of Pennsylvania Law School and the University of California, Berkeley, including Rishita Apsani, Jessa DeGroote, Joshua Fordin, Noah Kolbi-Molinas, Omar Madhany, Gregory Manas, Mark Mixon, Sonny Pannu, Emily Reineberg, Aadika Singh, and Alex Ussia. Finally, we are grateful to Ed Greenlee and his colleagues at the Biddle Library of the University of Pennsylvania Law School, particularly Ben Meltzer, who have been unfailingly helpful in responding to our requests for assistance, large and small, over the entire period of this project.

---

[3] Individuals whose names are starred read and provided comments on the entire manuscript. To them we owe a special debt of gratitude.

TABLE OF CASES

Amchem Products, Inc. v. Windsor, 521 U.S. 591 (1997).   73, 136, 240

American Express Co. v. Italian Colors Restaurant, 133 S. Ct. 2304
(2013).   142, 220

Ashcroft v. Iqbal, 556 U.S. 662 (2009).   137

Association of National Advertisers, Inc. v. Federal Trade Commission,
627 F.2d 1151 (D.C. Cir. 1979)   164

Bell Atlantic Corp. v. Twombly, 550 U.S. 544 (2007).   137

Boeing Co. v. Van Gemert, 444 U.S. 472 (1980).   75

Bush v. Gore, 531 U.S. 98 (2000).   194

Colgrove v. Battin, 413 U.S. 149 (1973).   135

Conley v. Gibson, 355 U.S. 41 (1957).   118, 135

Crawford-El v. Britton, 523 U.S. 574 (1998).   136

Delta Airlines v. August, 450 U.S. 346 (1981).   134

Hanna v. Plumer, 380 U.S. 460 (1965).   111

Hickman v. Taylor, 329 U.S. 495 (1947).   135

Leatherman v. Tarrant County Narcotics Intelligence & Coordination Unit,
507 U.S. 163 (1993).   136

Ledbetter v. Goodyear Tire & Rubber Co., 550 U.S. 618 (2007).   198

Marek v. Chesny, 473 U.S. 1 (1985).   133

Mistretta v. United States, 488 U.S. 361 (1989).   68

National Welfare Rights Organization v. Mathews, 533 F.2d 637
(D.C. Cir. 1976)   164

Obergefell v. Hodges, 135 S. Ct. 2584 (2015).   196

Ortiz v. Fibreboard Corp., 527 U.S. 815 (1999).   73, 136, 240

Ratner v. Chemical Bank New York Trust Co., 54 F.R.D. 412
(S.D.N.Y. 1972).   43

Shady Grove Orthopedic Associates, P.A. v. Allstate Insurance Co., 559 U.S.
393 (2010).   111

Sibbach v. Wilson & Co., 312 U.S. 1 (1941).   111

Swierkiewicz v. Sorema N.A., 534 U.S. 506 (2002).   136

Wal-Mart Stores, Inc. v. Dukes, 564 U.S. 338 (2011).   142, 198

Retrenching Rights in Institutional Context: Constraints and Opportunities

More than 40 years ago, in his iconic article, "Why the 'Haves' Come Out Ahead: Speculations on the Limits of Legal Change," Marc Galanter emphasized the importance of "attention not only to the level of rules, but also to institutional facilities, legal services and organization of parties" (Galanter 1975: 150).

> If rules are the most abundant resource for reformers, parties capable of pursuing long-range strategies are the rarest. The presence of such parties can generate effective demand for high-grade legal services – continuous, expert, and oriented to the long run – and pressure for institutional reforms and favorable rules. This suggests that we can roughly surmise the relative strategic priority of various rule-changes. *Rule changes which relate directly to the strategic position of the parties by facilitating organization, increasing the supply of legal services (where these in turn provide a focus for articulating and organizing common interests) and increasing the* costs *of opponents – for instance authorization of class action suits, award of attorney's fees and costs, award of provisional remedies – these are the most powerful fulcrum for change.* The intensity of the opposition to class action legislation . . . indicates the "haves'" own estimation of the relative strategic impact of the several levels.
>
> (Ibid.: 150–1) (emphasis added)

As we demonstrate later in this chapter, such insights animated a movement that successfully lobbied for provisions designed to stimulate private enforcement of federal statutes regulating a broad swath of American economic and social activity. Indeed, many of those statutes rely primarily on private enforcement, thereby promoting dramatic growth in the role of lawsuits and courts in the creation and implementation of public policy in the United States, a phenomenon that has stimulated an extensive body of research in political science, law, history, and sociology (Friedman L. 1994; Melnick 1994; Epp 1998; Kagan 2001; Farhang 2010). In the past decade, more than 1.25 million private federal lawsuits were filed to enforce federal statutes, spanning the waterfront of federal regulation.[1] Although Congress has relied on private litigation for this purpose since the rise of the federal regulatory state in the late 1880s, the frequency with which it did so increased dramatically starting in the late 1960s. The rate of private lawsuits to enforce federal statutes increased from about 3 per 100,000 members of the population in 1967 – a rate that had been stable for a quarter-century – to 13 by 1976, 21 by 1986, and 29 by 1996 (Farhang 2010: 15). There was an unmistakable "litigation explosion" of private suits to enforce federal rights during this period.

The consequences and normative implications of the "Litigation State" are the focus of intense current debate, both in scholarly circles (Viscusi 2002; Morriss, Yandle, and Dorchak 2008; Kessler 2011) and in more public fora (Burke 2002).[2] Although existing literature provides a rich picture of the emergence, development, benefits, and costs of the Litigation State, scholars have largely neglected the counterrevolution that ensued. That is our focus in this book.

Recent work has begun to investigate how conservative, anti-regulatory forces responded to these developments in American state regulation. They did not stand still. From this perspective, as Sarah Staszak puts it, scholars who study rights need to pay "attention to a broader historical timeline that incorporates what has come next" and to recognize "that there are always multiple, competing agendas in our complex institutional universe . . . [where] the institutional devices that have transformed the American state may also be the tools for its constriction, or at least for a chipping away at the edges of the rights revolution" (Staszak 2013: 243). In fact, in recent years an increasing number of scholars have examined various aspects of the agenda to diminish or disable the infrastructure for the private enforcement of federal rights (Stempel 2001; Chemerinsky 2003; Karlan 2003; Siegel 2006; Staszak 2015). But a great deal of the story remains untold.

To this emerging literature we add distinctive theoretical perspectives, fresh historical accounts, and substantial new evidence. We use qualitative historical evidence to identify the origins of the counterrevolution. We collect extensive data that allow us (1) to measure the counterrevolution's trajectory over decades in multiple lawmaking sites where retrenchment

---

[1] *See* Administrative Office of the US Courts, Judicial Business of the United States Courts, 2006–15, table C-3, available at www.uscourts.gov/data-table-numbers/c-3

[2] *See* Francis Fukuyama, Decay of American Political Institutions, *The American Interest*, available at www.the-american-interest.com/articles/2013/12/08/the-decay-of-american-political-institutions/

has been attempted, (2) to evaluate systematically how successful it has been in changing law in those different lawmaking sites,[3] and (3) to test key aspects of our argument. We leverage original perspectives founded in institutional theory to explain the striking variation we document in the counterrevolution's achievements across lawmaking sites.

We argue that, in the wake of an outpouring of rights-creating legislation from Democratic Congresses in the 1960s and 1970s, much of which contained provisions designed to stimulate private enforcement, the conservative legal movement within the Republican Party – and more specifically, within the first Reagan administration – devised a response. Recognizing the political infeasibility of retrenching substantive rights, the movement's strategy was to undermine the infrastructure for enforcing them. We show that the project was undertaken in earnest but largely failed in the elected branches, where efforts to diminish opportunities and incentives for private enforcement by amending federal statutory law were substantially frustrated. We also show how, although a number of Chief Justices appointed by Republican presidents hoped to bring about major retrenchment through amendments to the Federal Rules of Civil Procedure, success proved elusive and episodic.

We then document the sharply contrasting success of the counterrevolution in the unelected federal judiciary, where decades of decisions have achieved legal change congenial to many of the counterrevolution's goals. Incrementally at first but more boldly in recent years, over the past four decades, the Supreme Court has transformed federal law from friendly to unfriendly, if not hostile, toward enforcement of rights through private lawsuits. Although the Court's anti-enforcement work has ranged broadly across fields of federal regulatory policy, it has especially focused on civil rights.

In seeking to understand why conservative judges on a court exercising judicial power succeeded where their ideological compatriots in Congress, the White House, and the body primarily responsible for making procedural law for federal courts largely failed, we suggest the importance of institutional differences that are revealed by the cross-institutional theoretical approach that we describe later in this chapter. Moreover, highlighting one such difference, we show that the counterrevolution's legal campaign in the courts – with victories achieved in rulings centered on procedural and other seemingly technical issues – has been little noticed

---

[3] In Chapter 6, we discuss the challenges of assessing the effects that the counterrevolution has had through the legal changes to which it has contributed.

by the American public and thus poses little threat to the perceived legitimacy of the Supreme Court. Ultimately, we raise normative questions
about the desirability of this outcome from the perspective of democratic
governance.

The remainder of this chapter is divided into two parts. In the first part,
we discuss the ideological, partisan, and interest group forces behind the
dramatic growth in private litigation enforcing federal law that began in
the late 1960s. In this part of the chapter we cover terrain that, while useful
as historical background, is indispensable to an adequate understanding of
what animated the counterrevolution's emergence and tactics, failures and
successes, and its relationship to ongoing conflicts over regulatory governance in the United States. One must understand where the Litigation State
came from – the interests that created it, how they did so, and for what
purposes – in order to appreciate the dynamics that ensued when proponents of the counterrevolution sought to dismantle it. One must understand the pervasive role of private enforcement in, and its importance to,
the implementation of federal regulatory policy in order to appreciate
what is at stake in those efforts.

In the second part of this chapter, we articulate our overarching argument, the key pillars of which we support with qualitative and quantitative
evidence in Chapters 2–5.

Emergence of the Litigation State

Liberals' Waning Faith in Administrative Power

During the New Deal liberals were the chief architects of the administrative state-building project, while its principal detractors were business
interests and their allies in the Republican Party. Within the sphere of regulation, liberals' state-building vision and ambition was one of regulation
through expert, centralized, federal bureaucracy. According to James Q.
Wilson, "[t]he New Deal bureaucrats" piloting a centralized federal
bureaucracy "were expected by liberals to be free to chart a radically new
program and to be competent to direct its implementation" (Wilson 1967:
3). By the late 1960s, however, there was mounting disillusionment on the
left with the capacities and promise of the American administrative state.
As Wilson put it, "[c]onservatives once feared that a powerful bureaucracy
would work a social revolution. The left now fears that this same bureaucracy is working a conservative reaction" (ibid.).

The slide toward liberal disillusionment with the administrative state
coincided with, and was propelled by, the proliferation in the number,

membership, and activism of liberal public interest groups starting in the mid-to-late 1960s (Vogel 1981: 155–83; Shapiro 1988: 55–77). A primary focus of these groups was on regulation, mainly of business, in such fields as environmental and consumer protection, civil and worker rights, public health and safety, and other elements of the new social regulation of the period. The political significance of liberal public interest groups to the growth of private litigation to implement public policy is connected to their position within the Democratic Party coalition.

Democratic-Liberal Public Interest Coalition

After about 1968, owing both to liberal public interest groups' increasingly assertive role in American politics and to reforms within the Democratic Party organization, such groups emerged as a core element of the Democratic Party coalition, a position they continue to occupy to the current day (Vogel 1981: 164–75, 1989; Shefter 1994: 86–94; Witcover 2003: ch. 27; Farhang 2010: 129–213). David Vogel shows that within the Democratic Party coalition, "[d]uring the 1970s, the public interest movement replaced organized labor as the central countervailing force to the power and values of American business" (Vogel 1989: 293). The affinity between the Democratic Party and liberal public interest groups is hardly surprising. In the 20th century, a bedrock axis distinguishing the Democratic and Republican parties is Democrats' greater support for an interventionist state in the sphere of social and economic regulation, much of which targets private business (Poole and Rosenthal 1997). An activist state, particularly one prepared to regulate private business, is exactly what the agenda of liberal public interest groups called for, from nondiscrimination on the bases of race, gender, age, and disability to workplace and product safety, to cleaner air and water, to truth-in-lending and transparent product labeling.

Democratic Legislators, Republican Presidents, and Party Polarization

What explains the loss of faith in bureaucracy among liberal public interest groups and their allies in the Democratic Party? A number of charges were leveled. Because regulatory agencies interacted with regulated industries on an ongoing basis, agencies had been "captured" by business – regulators had come to identify with regulated businesses, treating them as the constituency to be protected. Apart from regulated business's extensive access to and influence on bureaucracy, liberal public interest groups believed that they were, by comparison, excluded, disregarded, and ignored by administrative policymakers. Moreover, bureaucrats were by nature timid and establishment-oriented, wishing to avoid controversy and steer clear of the political and economic costs of serious conflict with regulated business. On balance, it was alleged, this added up to an implementation posture hardly likely to secure the transformative goals of the liberal coalition (Wilson 1967; Lazarus and Onek 1971; Stewart 1975: 1684–5, 1713–15; Shapiro 1988: 62–73; Melnick 2004: 93).

As the liberal coalition's growing concerns about the limits of bureaucratic regulation were gathering strength in the late 1960s, an important transformation in the alignment of American government deepened their skepticism toward the administrative state as a regulator. The new dominant governing alignment in the United States combined divided government and party polarization, usually with the Democrats writing laws in Congress and Republican presidents exercising important influence on the bureaucracy charged with implementing them. In the first 68 years of the 20th century, the parties divided control of the legislative and executive branches 21% of the time, and in the subsequent 32 years (from Nixon through Bush II), the figure was 81%. The durability of the condition of divided government that emerged in the late 1960s was exacerbated by another factor contributing to legislative–executive antagonism. Starting around the early 1970s, the growth of ideological polarization between the parties, which increased through century's end, eroded the bipartisan center in Congress and fueled the antagonisms inherent in divided government (Jacobson 2003; McCarty, Poole, and Rosenthal 2006).

Add to this that during the years of divided government between Nixon taking office and the end of the 20th century, Democrats controlled one or both chambers of Congress while a Republican occupied the presidency 77% of the time. Congress – the legislation-writing branch of government – was predominantly controlled by the Democratic Party, with its greater propensity to undertake social and economic regulation, and with liberal public interest groups occupying an important position within the party coalition. This legislative coalition usually faced an executive branch in the hands of a Republican president, the leader of a political party more likely to resist social and economic regulation, and with American business occupying a key position within the party coalition.

This new alignment in American government was unlikely to make anyone happy. Not surprisingly, periods of Democratic Congresses facing Republican presidents were characterized by virtually continuous conflict between the liberal coalition in Congress and the comparatively conservative Republican leadership of the federal bureaucracy. Liberal public interest groups and congressional Democrats regularly attacked the federal bureaucracy under Republican leadership, claiming that it was willfully failing to effectuate Congress's legislative will. They charged that the executive branch adopted weak, pro-business regulatory standards; devoted insufficient resources to regulatory implementation; generally assumed a posture of feeble enforcement, and at times one of abject non-enforcement. Such charges ranged across many policy domains (Aberbach 1990: 27; Melnick 2005: 398–9; Farhang 2010: 129–313, 2012).[4] The convergence of divided government, party polarization, and Democratic legislatures facing Republican presidents sent the liberal legislative coalition in search of new strategies of regulation.

Private Lawsuits as a Statutory Implementation Strategy

The liberal coalition pursued a number of reform strategies to address the problems underpinning its disillusionment with the administrative state, its growing anxiety about presidential ideological influence on bureaucracy, and its concern about non-enforcement of congressional mandates. One set of strategies sought more effective control of the bureaucracy by the liberal coalition. It advocated enlarging opportunities for effective participation in administrative processes – particularly rulemaking – by public interest groups and their allies. It sought to force agency action through legislative deadlines and other means when agencies failed to carry out mandated responsibilities. It pressed for more aggressive congressional oversight and more frequent and stringent judicial review of important agency decisions. These were all strategies of reform through enhanced influence on and control over the bureaucracy, and they have been widely examined by scholars (Lazarus and Onek 1971; Stewart 1975; Vogel 1989; Melnick 2005).

An additional response, which has been less studied but is central to this book, was to advocate statutory rules that circumvented the administrative state altogether by fostering direct enforcement of legislative mandates through private lawsuits against the targets of regulation, such as discriminating employers, polluting factories, and deceptive labelers

---

[4] *See also Hearings on Class Action and Other Consumer Procedures before the Subcommittee on Commerce and Finance of the House Committee on Interstate and Foreign Commerce,* 91st Congress, 2nd Session (1970).

of consumer products (Melnick 1994; Kagan 2001; Burke 2002; Farhang 2010). It is important to differentiate between judicial review of agency action (one of the strategies discussed in the last paragraph) and direct private enforcement lawsuits. Rather than seeking to shape and constrain the behavior of bureaucracy, the direct enforcement strategy instead privatizes the enforcement function. When Congress elects to rely on private litigation by including a private right of action in a statute, it faces a series of additional choices of statutory design – such as who has standing to sue, how to allocate responsibility for attorney's fees, and the nature and magnitude of damages that will be available to winning plaintiffs – that together can have profound consequences for how much or little private enforcement litigation will actually be mobilized (Farhang 2010; Burbank, Farhang, and Kritzer 2013). We refer to this constellation of rules as a statute's "private enforcement regime."

Among the incentives that are available to encourage private enforcement of regulatory laws, especially important are statutory fee-shifting rules that authorize plaintiffs to recover attorney's fees if they prevail (Zemans 1984; Melnick 1994; Kagan 2001). Under the "American Rule" on attorney's fees, which generally controls in the absence of a statutory fee-shift, each side pays its own attorney's fees, win or lose. In light of the high costs of federal litigation, even prevailing plaintiffs might suffer a financial loss as a result of the American Rule, resulting in a disincentive for enforcement. More realistically, unless they were wealthy or could secure representation by a public interest organization, many would not be able to find counsel willing to take their case.

By the early 1970s, in order to mobilize private enforcement, liberal regulatory reformers were urging Congress to include private rights of action and fee-shifting provisions in new statutes across the entire domain of social regulation (Farhang 2010: ch. 5).[5] Monetary damages enhancements that allow a plaintiff to recover more than compensation for injury suffered – such as double, triple, or punitive damages – were also used to stimulate enforcement (21–31). This strategy was designed to facilitate impact litigation by law reform organizations, and, critically, to cultivate a for-profit bar to achieve day-to-day enforcement of ordinary claims – a function beyond the capacity of small non-profit groups. The strategy did

[5] *See also Hearings on Legal Fees before the Subcommittee on Representation of Citizen Interests of the Senate Judiciary Committee*, 93rd Congress, 1st Session (1973) (hereinafter *1973 Hearings on Attorney's Fees*).

not arise from abstract reflection. Rather, it was revealed by unexpected developments in the area of civil rights.

Civil Rights Model

Civil rights groups' embrace of private lawsuits for implementation has ironic origins in the job discrimination title of the foundational Civil Rights Act of 1964. When that law was proposed and debated in 1963–4, liberal civil rights advocates wanted a job discrimination enforcement regime centered on New Deal-style administrative adjudicatory powers modeled on the National Labor Relations Board, with Equal Employment Opportunity Commission (EEOC) authority to adjudicate and issue cease-and-desist orders. The proposal did not provide for private lawsuits. This preference was reflected in the job discrimination bill that liberal Democrats initially introduced with support from civil rights groups. At the time, the Democratic Party, while a majority in Congress, was sharply divided over civil rights, with its Southern wing committed to killing any job discrimination (or other civil rights) bill. In light of these insurmountable intraparty divisions, passage of the CRA of 1964 depended on conservative anti-regulation Republicans joining non-Southern Democrats in support of the bill (Rodriguez and Weingast 2003; Chen 2009: ch. 5; Farhang 2010: ch. 4).

Wielding the powers of a pivotal voting bloc, conservative Republicans stripped the EEOC of the strong administrative powers in the bill initially proposed by civil rights liberals, and they provided instead for enforcement by private lawsuits. Generally opposed to bureaucratic regulation of business, conservative Republicans also feared that they would not be able to control an NLRB-style civil rights agency in the hands of their ideological adversaries in the executive branch, long dominated by Democrats, and which passed from the Kennedy to the Johnson administrations while the bill proceeded through the legislative process. At the same time, in a political environment marked by intense public demand for significant civil rights legislation, some meaningful enforcement provisions were necessary in order for the Republican proposal to be taken seriously. To conservative Republicans and their business constituents, private litigation was preferable to public bureaucracy. Thus, conservative Republican support for Title VII was conditioned on a legislative deal that traded private for public enforcement. As part of the deal, liberals insisted that, if private enforcement was the best they could do, a fee-shift must be included, and thus Republicans incorporated one into their amendments to Title VII.

Civil rights groups regarded the substitution of private lawsuits – even with fee-shifting – for strong administrative powers as a bitterly disappointing evisceration of Title VII's enforcement regime (Farhang 2010: ch. 4).

If civil rights liberals and private enforcement regimes were a forced marriage, they soon fell in love and became inseparable. Civil rights groups mobilized in the early 1970s to spread legislative fee-shifting across the field of civil rights, first to school desegregation cases in the School Aid Act of 1971, to voting rights in the Voting Rights Act Amendments of 1975, and then to all other civil rights laws that allowed private enforcement but lacked fee-shifting in the Civil Rights Attorney's Fees Awards Act of 1976. Why? The two causes discussed earlier in this chapter for declining liberal faith in administrative power were critical: concerns about administrative capture and timidity, greatly exacerbated by Nixon's influence on the federal bureaucracy. Even under the Johnson administration, civil rights liberals regarded the federal bureaucracy's enforcement of civil rights as feeble, lacking in both political will and commitment of resources. When Nixon came to power, open conflict and antagonism broke out between civil rights liberals and the administration across the landscape of civil rights. Perceptions of the federal bureaucracy as lackluster were replaced by perceptions of the federal bureaucracy as purposefully obstructionist, and at times as the enemy (Farhang 2010: ch. 5).

These developments explain civil rights groups' turn away from bureaucracy, not their embrace of private lawsuits with fee-shifting, an enforcement alternative that, when adopted in 1964, they regarded with profound disappointment. Civil rights groups' embrace of private enforcement regimes, and the widespread adoption of private enforcement regimes as a reform strategy by the liberal coalition that shaped the new social regulation, was propelled by several other developments. First, the federal courts during this period took an expansive, pro-plaintiff orientation toward the CRA of 1964, making the judiciary a more hospitable enforcement venue for plaintiffs than anyone expected (Melnick 2014). Second – and more central to our study – private rights of action with fee-shifting proved unexpectedly potent in cultivating a private enforcement infrastructure in the American bar. In this regard, the early 1970s was a critical period of policy learning.

Growth of the Private Enforcement Infrastructure

In the early 1970s, attorney's fee awards contributed resources to existing non-profit public interest groups that prosecuted lawsuits under the new civil rights laws, such as the NAACP Legal Defense Fund and the

Lawyers' Committee for Civil Rights Under Law, adding to their enforcement capacity (O'Connor and Epstein 1984: 241; Derfner 2005: 656).[6] The availability of fee awards also contributed to the formation of significant new civil rights enforcement groups, with foundation seed money, on the expectation that they would be able to draw continuing operating funds from attorney's fees awards (McKay 1977; O'Connor and Epstein 1984: 240). The number of liberal public interest law groups fashioned on the model of these civil rights organizations grew rapidly in the late 1960s and 1970s. Although only seven such groups were in existence prior to 1968, by 1975 the number had grown to 72, spanning the areas of civil rights and civil liberties, environmental, consumer, employment, education, health care, and housing policy (Handler, Ginsberg, and Snow 1978; Vogel 1989: 105). These groups litigated in the fields of the new social regulation, and fee awards contributed revenue to their litigation campaigns.

In addition to increasing enforcement resources available to non-profit civil rights groups, the private enforcement approach in parts of the CRA of 1964 and numerous civil rights laws that followed that model in the ensuing decade fostered the growth of a private for-profit bar to litigate civil rights claims. In the first half of the 1970s, the number of job discrimination lawsuits multiplied 10-fold, growing from an annual total of about 400 to 4,000.[7] Title VII's fee-shifting provision, according to one practitioner in the field, had "led to the development of a highly skilled group of specialist lawyers" to enforce it.[8] This was true of civil rights more broadly. A 1975 *Washington Post* article reported that "[t]he lure of legal fees, paid by the loser, is fertilizing a whole new practice in civil rights disputes,"[9] and a 1977 Ford Foundation report observed that by the mid-1970s "fee-generating private practice has in many areas of the South enabled an indigenous bar, engaged in litigating cases of racial discrimination, to survive" (McKay 1977: 8, 13).

This story of a private for-profit plaintiffs' bar enforcing federal law extended beyond civil rights to the new social regulatory statutes in general. A 1976 study examined private for-profit firms – as contrasted with non-profit public interest organizations – that devoted at least 25% of their practice to "non-commercial" issue areas with the goal of "law reform,"

---

[6] *See 1973 Hearings on Attorney's Fees* (testimony of Armand Derfner).
[7] *Federal Court Cases: Integrated Data Base, 1970–2000*, maintained by ICPSR. The method for arriving at the estimates is explained in Farhang 2010: 271 n. 118.
[8] *1973 Hearings on Attorney's Fees*, at 1113.
[9] Bill Crider, "Civil Rights Turns to Gold Lode for Southern Lawyers," *Washington Post*, April 4, 1976, 59.

including enforcement of civil rights, environmental, consumer, employment, housing, education, and health-care statutes. Two such firms existed in 1966, and the number grew to 55 by 1975 (Handler, Ginsberg, and Snow 1978). The collection of attorney's fees from defendants was an important source of revenue to these firms. In 1977, an advocate of fee-shifting as a strategy of private regulatory enforcement observed that the enactment of such provisions across many policy fields since the Civil Rights Act of 1964 had conjured into existence a for-profit bar prepared to prosecute federal statutory claims on behalf of plaintiffs. Fee-shifting statutes, she explained, made litigating such claims "a financially viable practice," and consequently "public interest laws firms burgeoned" (Derfner 1977).

As civil rights leaders pursued the spread of fee-shifting and observed the remarkable mushrooming of a for-profit civil rights bar in the first half of the 1970s, they were simultaneously active and important participants in collaborative umbrella organizations that brought together groups from across the liberal public interest movement. In these networks, public interest law groups spanning the full range of the new social regulation pooled information, learning from one another's experiences. The question of how to finance public interest law, and the role of fee awards in that calculus, was a matter of extensive attention and discussion within this network in the early-to-mid 1970s (Council for Public Interest Law 1976; Weisbrod 1978; Trubek 2011: 418–19).

The Council for Public Interest Law was formed in the spring of 1974. Succeeded by the Alliance for Justice, the Council was an association of activists in the public interest law movement, including leaders of non-profit public interest organizations spanning civil rights, environmental, consumer, education, public health, good government, and poverty law. Its initial purpose was to develop and disseminate a strategic plan for financing public interest legal representation – a vision for harnessing economic support for the spread and growth of public interest law, with a central focus being the enforcement of rights under the new social regulatory statutes (Trubek 2011). The Council's book-length report, *Balancing the Scales of Justice: Financing Public Interest Law in America* (1976), articulated a coalition-wide, self-conscious, coordinated decision of the leaders of the liberal public interest law movement to embrace the strategy of privatizing the enforcement of regulatory policy.

As expressed in *Balancing the Scales of Justice*, the strategy was to "bring into the marketplace" cases that otherwise would not be prosecuted, making such cases "economically attractive to regular commercial lawyers" in the "commercial legal marketplace." "[T]he passage of legislation authorizing court awards of attorneys' fees," the report argued, "may make it possible for some matters that would now be considered public interest cases eventually to be handled on a contingent commercial basis." The report regarded what it called "private public interest law firms," then beginning to develop under recent fee-shifting legislation, as a model to build on and as "a significant area for growth." Such firms could be "economically viable" in the for-profit arena, could be sustained by fee awards under statutes, and could function as the backbone of the enforcement infrastructure for the new social regulation. In order to "institutionalize" this for-profit private enforcement infrastructure, the liberal public interest movement's reform strategy would need to focus on securing statutory fee-shifting provisions from Congress. The report provided a model fee-shifting statute to be pursued legislatively. *Balancing the Scales of Justice* repeatedly emphasized that this reform strategy was modeled on what had been learned from the success of the civil rights movement in general and experience under Title VII in particular (9–10, 20–1, 37–8, 54, 89–90, 113–14, 134–46, 313–20).

The long-term success of the movement we have been describing is reflected in Figures 1.1 and 1.2. Figure 1.1 displays the total number

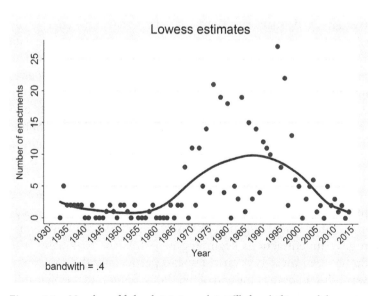

Figure 1.1   Number of federal statutory plaintiff's fee-shifting and damages enhancement provisions enacted, 1933–2014

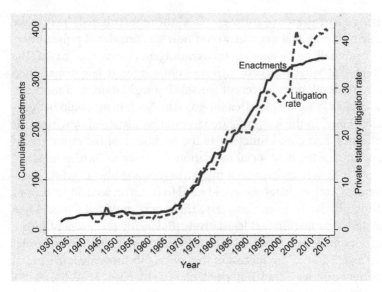

Figure 1.2 Cumulative federal statutory plaintiff's fee-shifting and damages enhancement provisions, and federal private statutory litigation rate, 1933–2014

of plaintiff's fee-shifts and/or damages enhancements (double, triple, or punitive) attached to private rights of action that were enacted by Congress from 1933 to 2014, with a regression curve fit through the data points. The predicted number rose sharply from the late 1960s to the late 1970s, somewhat plateaued until the mid-1990s, and then declined after the Republican Party took control of Congress in 1995. In Figure 1.2, the solid line represents the *cumulative* number of plaintiff's fee-shifts and damages enhancements attached to private rights of action in effect annually, reflecting the structural environment of private enforcement regimes in existence annually. This cumulative count is "net" in that it accounts for exits from federal statutory law due to the underlying law being repealed, expiring, or being declared unconstitutional. The dashed line in Figure 1.2 is the annual rate per 100,000 members of the population of private federal statutory enforcement litigation (it is only possible to distinguish private from government actions beginning in 1942). The strikingly close association between these two variables, and particularly the coincident sharp upward shift in both at the end of the 1960s, reinforces the plausibility of plaintiff's fee-shifts and damages enhancements as measures of the broader phenomenon of private enforcement regimes, and of the efficacy of private enforcement regimes in mobilizing private litigants. It deserves emphasis that about 98% of these suits were prosecuted by for-profit counsel, and only 2% by interest groups.[10]

Even during periods of significant Republican legislative power, while calls for retrenchment were emanating from some quarters of the Republican Party, there was net growth in the private enforcement infrastructure. Republican instigation of the private enforcement regime in Title VII was not anomalous. Indeed, while Republicans controlled the Senate and the presidency from 1981 to 1986, Congress passed and the president signed, per Congress, an average of 12 new private rights of action with fee-shifts and/or monetary damages enhancements. That number was down materially from the Carter years, when 21 per Congress were passed, but it contributed to the continuing growth of opportunities and incentives for private lawsuits enforcing federal law. This basic pattern persisted from 1987 to 2004: Democratic Congresses from 1987 to 1994 passed 20 per Congress, and, although proclaiming an anti-litigation reform agenda, Republican Congresses passed 11 per Congress from 1995 to 2004. In the last decade, as Congress has alternated between Democratic control, Republican control, and divided control, enactments have declined to significantly lower levels, averaging only about three per Congress, with modest partisan variation. It is important to stress that our data do not allow us to assess the extent to which declining levels of enactment of private enforcement regimes are associated with declining levels of regulation by Congress as opposed to declining reliance on private enforcement when Congress does regulate.

We can conclude that under Republican Congresses after 1994, the rate of growth slowed, but material expansion of the private enforcement infrastructure continued. Some examples of Republican Congresses (or chambers) finding private enforcement regimes to be a useful regulatory strategy to serve their constituents are:

- In the Taft–Hartley Act of 1947, a Republican-controlled Congress gave companies a private right of action with economic damages against unions engaged in labor actions proscribed by the Act.[11]
- In the Cuban Liberty and Democratic Solidarity (Libertad) Act of 1996, a Republican-controlled Congress gave United States nationals whose property was confiscated by the Cuban government during or following

---

[10] For a discussion of the data underlying the figures and this paragraph, *see* Farhang (2010: chs. 1 and 3).
[11] Public Law No. 80-101.

the Cuban revolution, a private right of action, with attorney's fees for successful plaintiffs, against "traffickers" in such property.[12]

- In the "Partial-Birth Abortion" Ban Act of 2003, a Republican-controlled Congress created a private right of action with treble damages, and damages for emotional pain and suffering, for fathers (*if* married to the woman on whom the procedure is performed), and for "maternal grandparents of the fetus" if the woman is a minor, against a doctor who performs an abortion in violation of the Act.[13]
- In the Honoring America's Veterans and Caring for Camp Lejeune Families Act of 2012, a Republican-controlled House (and a Democrat-controlled Senate) created a private right of action, with attorney's fees, for injuries resulting from certain protest activity at the funerals of veterans.[14]

Counterrevolution

Although the movement that propelled the growth of the Litigation State was successful, as time went on, it was contested, and ultimately it gave rise to a countermovement that is the subject of this book. The counterrevolution's strategy was to leave substantive rights in place while retrenching the infrastructure for their private enforcement. We divide our investigation of the counterrevolution according to its three main institutional strategies: (1) amend existing federal statutes to reduce opportunities and incentives for private enforcement; (2) amend existing or fashion new Federal Rules of Civil Procedure to do the same; and (3) use litigation to elicit federal court interpretations of private enforcement regimes and Federal Rules that demobilize private enforcers. The counterrevolution's legislative strategy was largely a disappointment, and its efforts to change Federal Rules achieved only modest and sporadic success. In notable contrast, its campaign in the courts – we focus on the Supreme Court – has proved, by far, the most successful for the project of retrenching private enforcement legal infrastructure. We argue in the balance of this chapter that institutional theory provides important insights that help to explain the variation we observe across institutional sites in the success of the campaign to retrench private enforcement. In laying out our institutional argument, we preview the main evidence we rely on in this book – a great deal of which

---

[12] Public Law No. 104-114.
[13] Public Law No. 108-105.
[14] Public Law No. 112-154.

consists of original data and the fruits of archival research – as well as the main empirical results and inferences we draw from the evidence.

Legislative Project

In Chapter 2, we trace the emergence, growth, and substantial failure of a movement in the elected branches to constrict opportunities and incentives for the enforcement of federal rights. We show that the growth of litigation as a central instrument to implement social and economic regulation beginning in the mid-to-late 1960s soon met opposition emanating primarily from the emergent conservative legal movement and the Republican Party. The campaign crystallized in the first Reagan administration, and the strategy it fashioned was to curtail, through legislation, the incentive structure that encouraged the private bar to enforce the rights embodied in the outpouring of rights-creating statutes beginning with the Civil Rights Act of 1964.

Recognizing the political impossibility of actually repealing the substantive rights that underpinned the growing postwar American regulatory state, the strategy was to constrict private enforcement regimes, such as by limiting standing, money damages, and attorney's fee awards for successful plaintiffs. Drawing on original archival research, we show that this legislative strategy included advocacy within the first Reagan administration for a major bill, "The Limitation of Legal Fees Awards Act of 1981," that would have amended over 100 federal statutes to sharply reduce attorney's fee awards to successful plaintiffs under federal statutes. The strategy also included consideration of proposals to amend the Civil Rights Act of 1871 (Section 1983) – among the most wide-ranging and consequential American civil rights laws – by materially restricting opportunities and incentives to enforce it, including by limiting both attorney's fees and damages. We use the archival records of these episodes to uncover the motives and strategy of the counterrevolution's founders and to elucidate the difficulties they encountered.

To investigate retrenchment activity in Congress, we constructed an original dataset of 500 bills that were introduced over the four decades from 1973 to 2014 and that specifically attempted to retrench opportunities and incentives for the enforcement of federal rights. Our congressional bill data allow us to trace over 40 years the emergence, growth, and decline of an attempted legislative counterrevolution; to identify its key advocates; to test hypotheses about the role of ideology and party; and to measure success or failure in effecting legal change. With these data, we show that the movement to retrench rights enforcement initiated in the first Reagan administration quickly spread to congressional Republicans, among whom the introduction of such bills grew steeply beginning in the early 1980s. The movement thereby transformed statutory private enforcement regimes from a relatively non-partisan issue prior to the first Reagan administration into the source of partisan cleavage that we know today. The bill activity peaked in the mid-1990s when Republicans won control of Congress.

Ultimately in Chapter 2, we document the substantial failure of this Republican legislative project in the elected branches and the reasons for that failure. The Reagan administration abandoned private enforcement retrenchment through legislation, having concluded that it was broadly perceived as "anti-rights," threatening unacceptably high political and electoral costs to the administration, and thwarting any realistic prospects of success in the legislative process, apparently even within the Republican Party. Congressional Republican proposals, we show, largely failed as well, even after Republicans achieved unified control of Congress in the mid-1990s. Although some notable retrenchment bills did become law beginning in 1995, they were few in number, usually required years to enact, clustered in a few discrete policy areas, and did not seriously challenge the Litigation State as conservative activists had set out to do. By the present day, we find that retrenchment of private enforcement has largely disappeared from the legislative agenda.

Significant retrenchment of existing private enforcement regimes proved unattainable on the institutional terrain of democratic politics. Why? We argue that, in addition to the inherent stickiness of the status quo arising from America's fragmented legislative institutions, the distinctive political and electoral challenges to retrenching existing rights with broad public resonance proved to be more than the movement could surmount.

Rulemaking

The counterrevolution also pursued retrenchment through court rulemaking. The Supreme Court wields power, delegated to it by Congress, to create and revise the Federal Rules of Civil Procedure (Federal Rules). Court rulemaking occupies intermediate lawmaking space that bridges legislative and judicial power (Burbank 2004a). The Federal Rules govern federal civil litigation, prescribing, for instance, criteria for whether multiple persons with similar claims can proceed in a class action, and what potential evidence parties are able to discover from one another during the pretrial process. Determining both access to court and likelihood of success for those seeking to enforce federal rights through litigation, the Federal Rules can profoundly enable or limit private enforcement.

To exercise these powers, the federal judiciary and Congress have together created an administrative process within the judiciary. In this system, the Advisory Committee on Civil Rules has primary responsibility for drafting the Federal Rules. All members of the Advisory Committee – who are judges, practitioners, and academics – are appointed by the Chief Justice.

In Chapter 3, we first chronicle rulemaking's role in stimulating private enforcement, and we then identify its role in the counterrevolution. Court rulemaking had been a powerful engine driving private enforcement through the 1960s, but it became the focus of retrenchment efforts starting in 1971, under the leadership of Chief Justice Warren Burger, the first of a succession of Chief Justices appointed by Republican presidents who have held that position up to the present. He had hopes for bold retrenchment, which reflected both institutional (docket) concerns and, increasingly as time went by, his own views about litigation as a "mass neurosis" in the United States (Burger 1985: 5).

To investigate how Chief Justices have exercised their appointment power with respect to the Advisory Committee, and to gauge likely Advisory Committee preferences, we compiled original data sets, spanning 1960 to 2014, in which we identified every person who served on the committee. We recorded rulemakers' key characteristics salient to our study, including occupation, party of the appointing president for federal judges, and type of practice for practitioners (e.g., corporate versus individual representation). To investigate the Advisory Committee's output over the same 55-year period, we also collected every amendment to the Federal Rules proposed by the Advisory Committee, evaluated each, and identified those salient to private enforcement and whether they were pro or anti-plaintiff in the direction of their likely effects.

With these original data, we show that under Burger and his successors, the Advisory Committee on Civil Rules came to be dominated by federal judges appointed by Republican presidents and, among its practitioner members, by corporate lawyers. We also demonstrate, however, that few of the Advisory Committee's proposals in the long period we study were pertinent to private enforcement, and that among those that were, ambitious retrenchment efforts have been less frequent than one might have predicted based on salient characteristics of committee members. We show in addition, however, that the proposals affecting private enforcement, although modest in number and usually in ambition, increasingly disfavored it over time. We conclude that notwithstanding the preferences of Republican-appointed Chief Justices, reflected in their committee appointment choices and in other historical evidence, court rulemaking has been a site of only episodic and modest retrenchment.

To explain the limited success we observe in legal retrenchment through court rulemaking, we place particular emphasis on important institutional reforms to the rulemaking process in the 1980s. When influential rights-oriented interest groups and Democratic members of Congress came to believe that the Advisory Committee was embracing the goals of the counterrevolution – in the early 1980s – the Committee's anti-enforcement work product caused a backlash. The resulting changes in the rulemaking process, including some imposed by a Democratically controlled Congress through legislation, required public meetings; widened opportunities for interest group participation; enlarged the Committee's burdens of justification to support rule changes; and enhanced opportunities for legislative veto of rule changes.

Drawing on institutional scholarship on congressional oversight of bureaucracy (McCubbins and Schwartz 1984; McNollgast 1987, 1999), we argue that the effect, and for some proponents the purpose, of these changes was to insulate the (pro-enforcement) status quo. The 1980s reforms ensured that interest groups with a perceived stake in the subject of proposed rulemaking could provide pertinent information to the rulemakers and serve as whistleblowers or fire alarms for members of Congress in the event they thought something was seriously wrong. They also effectively increased the evidentiary burden on the Advisory Committee when seeking to change the status quo, and increased the threat of veto. The reforms were a control strategy designed to ease the legislative costs of monitoring the rulemakers ex post, while at the same time increasing monitoring capacity ex ante. We conclude that the reforms did, in fact, contribute to the stickiness of the rulemaking status quo, making bold retrenchment since the 1980s difficult to achieve, even for those who were ideologically disposed to it.

Supreme Court

In Chapter 4, we show that those wishing to retrench private enforcement of social and economic regulation also waged a campaign in the courts. Their goal was the same: to constrict opportunities and incentives for the enforcement of federal rights, again focusing on such issues as standing, damages, fee awards, and class actions. They learned that retrenching rights enforcement by changing statutory law was politically and electorally perilous and unlikely to succeed, and that an increasingly public and participatory rulemaking process would yield only modest and episodic retrenchment.

They thus pressed federal courts to interpret, or reinterpret, existing federal statues and procedural rules to achieve the same purposes. The federal courts were increasingly staffed by judges appointed by Republican presidents, some of whom had participated in the Reagan administration's failed efforts to retrench rights through legislation. These judges were ideologically sympathetic to the retrenchment project, and, in some cases, they were connected to the conservative legal movement that had given birth to that project. In addition, some of the same Reagan administration officials who were disappointed by failed efforts to retrench private enforcement through legislation, and who advocated a turn to the federal courts as an alternative pathway of retrenchment, also participated in the administration's selection of candidates to fill federal judgeships.

In demonstrating the Supreme Court's dramatic turn against private enforcement, we rely on both quantitative and qualitative evidence. We have created an original dataset of 366 decisions in which the Supreme Court ruled on the same types of issues we examined in our congressional bill data: standing, private rights of action, damages, fees, and arbitration. It also contains decisions on Federal Rules of Civil Procedure issues affecting private enforcement. This dataset allows us to elucidate the changing role of justices' ideology in the adjudication of these issues; to draw out a comparison between the Court's treatment of rules governing enforcement of rights and its treatment of the rights themselves; and to document a striking and uniquely large shift toward constricting opportunities and incentives to enforce rights through lawsuits. In addition, we present qualitative evidence focusing on important procedural issues targeted for retrenchment in Congress and/or through rulemaking before coming to the Court. Such qualitative evidence allows us to observe outcomes in more concrete detail when retrenchment was attempted on the same issue across multiple institutional sites.

In marked contrast to its substantial failure in Congress and modest success in the domain of rulemaking, the counterrevolution against private enforcement of federal rights achieved growing rates of support, especially over the past several decades, from an increasingly conservative Supreme Court. We find empirically that, in cases with at least one dissent, plaintiffs' probability of success when litigating private enforcement issues before the Supreme Court has been in decline for over 40 years, and that by 2014 they were losing about 90% of the time, an outcome driven by the votes of conservative justices. Moreover, we demonstrate that the effect of ideology on justices' votes in private enforcement cases has grown significantly larger over time, especially since about the mid-1990s, during which time the Court's private enforcement docket has come to focus increasingly on business regulation cases. We show that this clear shift in the 1990s toward increasingly ideological conflict on the Court over private enforcement issues in business cases was associated with a roughly contemporaneous, and very large, mobilization of the Chamber of Commerce and conservative law reform organizations on the issue of private enforcement as measured by their amicus filings. With respect to the policy focus of the Court's private enforcement cases, we also observe that it focused disproportionately on civil rights cases relative to their share of the federal civil docket.

This escalation in ideological divisiveness on the Court over private enforcement issues has been particularly striking in Federal Rules cases. Although ideology played a fairly modest role in the justices' votes in Federal Rules cases for many years, there has been a sea change over the past 15 to 20 years toward those cases becoming a distinctively ideological part of the Supreme Court's docket. Remarkably, on the current Supreme Court, justices are more ideologically polarized over apparently techni-cal rules of private enforcement than they are over the actual substantive rights in statutes, and when conflicts arise over these rules, the conserva-tive wing prevails in the vast majority of cases.

The same project of retrenchment that largely failed in other lawmak-ing domains achieved substantial success through the courts. To explain why, we emphasize distinctive institutional properties of the judiciary. First, the Court is governed by a streamlined decisional process and sim-ple voting rules, making it capable of unilateral action on controversial issues (Whittington 2007: 124–34). Second, life-tenured federal judges are largely insulated from the forces and incentives of democratic poli-tics, again affording the Court considerable freedom to act decisively on divisive issues (Graber 1993; Gillman 2002). Third, in eras of divided gov-ernment and party polarization, the Court faces less credible threats of statutory override and correspondingly enjoys more policymaking discre-tion (Eskridge 1991a, b; Whittington 2007: ch. 5; Hasen 2012). Fourth, the law governing or driving private enforcement, perceived by most observ-ers as legalistic and technical, provides the Court a pathway to retrench-ment that is remote from public view, and this subterranean quality is reinforced by the slow-moving, evolutionary nature of case-by-case policy change (Graber 1993; Barnes and Burke 2015). We elaborate this institutional argument in comparative context in this book's conclusion.

In Chapter 5, we undertake an empirical investigation of a key facet of our claim that the Court's private enforcement decisions have been little noticed by the public. The media are the primary source of the public's information about Supreme Court decisions (Davis 1994; Franklin and Kosaki 1995; Hoekstra 2003). We created an original dataset based on content analysis of newspaper coverage of Supreme Court decisions affecting private enforcement, such as decisions on damages, fees, and class actions, and of decisions on merits issues. It allows us to compare the extent of coverage of Supreme Court decisions (1) ruling on substantive rights (e.g., whether conduct was racially discriminatory), and (2) ruling on opportunities and incentives to enforce those rights (e.g., whether a plaintiff has standing to litigate a racial discrimination claim). These data demonstrate that Supreme Court decisions on laws relating to the enforcement of rights receive dramatically less press coverage than their decisions on the rights themselves. The media's role in informing the public about the work of the Supreme Court declines precipitously when one moves from rulings on rights to rulings on their enforcement.

The issue of public attention and understanding matters. The Court recognizes that public standing and perceived legitimacy are important to its institutional power, and it therefore is cautious about straying too far or for too long from public opinion (Stephenson 2004; B. Friedman 2009; Clark 2011). Consequently, the Court's need for broad public support places limits on its ability to scale back highly visible and popular substantive rights directly. When seeking to retrench enforcement of rights that enjoy broad public support, the Court benefits from strategically steering this project onto apparently technical and legalistic terrain, where the public is less likely to learn of the decisions at all. Ultimately, we argue that the Court's decisions on rights enforcement, because of their lower public visibility, are less constrained by public opinion and therefore less tethered to democratic governance.

In this book's concluding chapter (Chapter 6), we elaborate the institutional account that helps to explain the outcome we document: the long-term erosion of the infrastructure of enforcing rights through lawsuits, despite the substantial failure of the counterrevolutions policy project in democratic politics and in the intermediate lawmaking space of court rulemaking. After elaborating our institutional account, we engage the difficulties of measuring the "success" or "failure" of the counterrevolution when attention turns from changing law governing or influencing private enforcement to changing the quantum and quality of private enforcement. We then take up normative concerns that arise when potentially crucial decisions bearing on the fate of broadly popular rights, most of which are conferred by statute, are not the result of public deliberation and democratic politics – indeed, when they are little noticed by the public at all. We also address a number of concrete steps that might be taken to address other normative concerns that our qualitative and quantitative data unearth.

2

Legislative Counterrevolution: Emergence, Growth, and Disappointment

Introduction

By the late 1970s and early 1980s, a deregulatory movement was afoot, primarily catalyzed by businesses, trade associations, state and local officials, and newly emergent conservative public interest groups (Vogel 1981; O'Conner and Epstein 1984; McGarity 1986; Decker 2009). Ronald Reagan came to power on the wave of this movement. It was, of course, quite different from the reform movement that emerged in the late 1960s and early 1970s – and in some sense a reaction to it. That movement was driven by civil rights, environmental, consumer, labor, and other liberal public interest groups. Whereas "fairness," "justice," and "equality" were its central themes, in the late 1970s and early 1980s the themes were "freedom," "efficiency," and "economic growth" (McGarity 1986: 253–4).

Regulatory reform was high on the Reagan administration's policy agenda. However, substantial continuing public support for the aspirational goals of the new social regulation, coupled with lack of cooperation from Congress, effectively ruled out the possibility of retrenching substantive rights by legislation (Greve 1987: 101–4; Vogel 1989: 260–5). Instead, the administration pursued an alternative strategy of deregulation, within the confines of existing statutory mandates, through a combination of withdrawal and redirection of the machinery of administrative implementation. This strategy involved appointing as leaders of agencies people who shared the administration's deregulatory preferences and would exercise discretion to steer the bureaucracy and regulatory policy in the direction desired by the president. Under Reagan-appointed leadership, regulatory agencies in such fields as civil rights, the environment, consumer protection, and public health and safety markedly reduced enforcement activity by numerous objective measures, such as the number of inspections, investigations, citations, civil penalties, administrative enforcement orders, and civil enforcement actions. They

25

also embraced less interventionist regulatory standards through rulemak-
ing, rule rescission, and other forms of regulatory policymaking. Further,
the administration, acting through the Office of Management and Budget
(OMB), sharply reduced agency budgets and, correspondingly, personnel
(Litan and Nordhaus 1983: 119–32; McGarity 1986; Vogel 1989: 246–51;
Farhang 2010: ch.6; Farhang 2012).

Deregulation and the Problem of Private Enforcement Infrastructures

The deregulatory strategy of the Reagan administration has been well documented by scholars. What we wish to stress here is how private lawsuits
to enforce federal statutes impeded Reagan's deregulatory program. Upon
assuming office, leaders of the Reagan bureaucracy well understood that
private enforcement of statutory rights had been growing steeply, and they
saw it as a critical obstacle to their regulatory reform agenda.

By the mid-to-late1970s, conservative activists and leading business
associations had developed considerable antipathy toward the new social
regulation and its encroachment on business and government preroga-
tives. They began to claim that lawsuits under growing federal regulatory
law were having a substantial adverse impact on business interests.
Statutory fee-shifting provisions that, as they saw it, forced business and
government to pay the attorney's fees of plaintiffs' lawyers who prosecuted invasive, disruptive, and costly lawsuits against them, were a particular target of criticism. They also believed that liberal public interest
groups used litigation and courts to shape the substantive meaning of
the new regulatory statutes to their liking, thereby making regulatory
policy that was injurious to the interests of business and government
(O'Connor and Epstein 1984; Greve 1987: 91; Teles 2008: 60–6; Decker
2009: 12–149).

Conservative activists and business associations mobilized and col-
laborated in forming a number of conservative public interest law groups
to pursue an agenda focused, in part, on limiting federal regulation
(O'Connor and Epstein 1984: 483–505; Greve 1987: 91; Teles 2008: 60–6;
Decker 2009: 12–149). Reagan's close associates, including high-ranking
members of his California gubernatorial administration who followed
him to the White House, were instrumental in founding this movement
(O'Connor and Epstein 1984: 495; Teles 2008: 60–1; Decker 2009: 3–5).
Indeed, litigation by liberal public interest groups against the Reagan
gubernatorial administration, obstructing its pursuit of conservative

public policies that Reagan regarded as critical, provoked members of his administration to found the first conservative public interest law group in Sacramento – the Pacific Legal Foundation – which then served as a model for many others (Zumbrun 2004: 42–3; Teles 2008: 62; Decker 2009: 3–5). Reagan himself was openly hostile to liberal public interest lawyers, characterizing them in the early-to-mid 1970s as "a bunch of ideological ambulance chasers doing their own thing at the expense of the poor who actually need help"[1] (Greve 1987: 91), and as "working for left-wing special interest groups at the expense of the public" (Decker 2009: 74).

Upon assuming office, the Reagan administration was acutely aware that private enforcement of federal regulatory law had surged powerfully since the 1960s and that the private enforcement infrastructure presented an important obstacle to its deregulatory agenda. Reagan had appointed numerous leaders and activists from the conservative public interest law movement to important positions in the federal bureaucracy, ranging across Counselor to the President, the White House Office of Policy Development, the OMB, the Equal Employment Opportunity Commission, and the Departments of Interior, Energy, and Justice (Decker 2009). The conservative public interest law movement had been born in opposition to the steep growth in litigation activity undertaken by both the for-profit and non-profit plaintiffs bar under the new social regulatory statutes. They had witnessed the rate of private enforcement lawsuits under federal statutes increase by 352% from Nixon's assumption of office in 1969 to Reagan's in 1981.[2] Now in power, they sought to retrench private enforcement.

According to Michael Greve, a conservative legal activist and founder of the Center for Individual Rights, Reagan administration leadership saw private rights of action with attorney's fee awards as an obstacle to deregulation. Proposals to curtail fee awards under the new social regulatory statutes – along with a constellation of other efforts to reduce sources of funding for liberal public interest groups – were pursued by conservative activists as part of a strategy to "defund the Left" (Greve 1987: 91–106). Greve explains:

> When the Reagan Administration took office in 1981, one of the priorities urged upon it was to cut federal funding for liberal and leftist advocacy groups. Well known conservative activists openly advocated a strategy of

---

[1] Ronald Ostraw, "Legal Services Agency Battles Reagan Attempt to Cut Off Its Funding," *Los Angeles Times*, April 12, 1981, B1.

[2] *See* Chapter 1, Figure 1.1.

"defunding the Left." This was necessary, they argued, for the success of the
conservative social and deregulatory agenda. The incoming administration
shared this assessment. President Reagan . . . sensed that the liberal public interest movement was a primary obstacle to his campaign promises of
"regulatory relief" (91).

Private enforcement litigation was a "primary obstacle" to Reagan's
deregulatory agenda because, with little prospect of actually being able to
repeal or modify legislative mandates, his principal strategy for effectuating the agenda was to demobilize the administrative regulatory enforcement apparatus. The value of withdrawing or reducing administrative
enforcement would be weakened if extensive private enforcement continued, and the strategy would be severely undercut if private enforcement
actually expanded to fill gaps left by withdrawal of administrative machinery. Important members of the Reagan bureaucracy were in full agreement with Greve's characterization. Based on archival research, Jefferson
Decker finds that some were deeply concerned that private rights of action
coupled with fee shifting were producing "a state-sponsored, private governing apparatus" (Decker 2009: 181). Moreover, as we will show, advocates of retrenching private enforcement recognized that the proliferation
of fee-shifting provisions in the 1970s had produced a private enforcement
infrastructure that benefited not just liberal public interest groups, but,
more significantly, the for-profit American bar.

The Reagan administration's efforts to "defund the Left" included a
move to abolish the Legal Services Corporation, or failing that, to reduce
its appropriations (Greve 1987; Quigley 1998). The administration was
openly hostile to Legal Services, antipathy that dated to significant legal
battles between Reagan's gubernatorial administration in California and
Legal Services grantees there (George 1976: 683–7; Quigley 1998: 248–
50). The administration regarded Legal Services as "a program composed
of left-wing lawyers" that "engaged as self-appointed representatives of
the poor in test cases and class actions designed to erode the free enterprise system and to establish a more complete welfare state" (Cramton
1981: 522).

We do not include attacks on Legal Services within our conceptual-
ization of retrenching private enforcement. The private enforcement
infrastructure that we focus on in this book was constructed by creation,
through law, of market incentives to mobilize attorneys as an alternative,
in part, to publicly financed regulatory enforcement (Kagan 2001; Burke
2002; Farhang 2010). The attack on Legal Services was an attack on public

funding for legal assistance to the poor. We acknowledge that the intended effects were to deprive private attorneys (Legal Services grantees) of public resources to represent their clients, and we do not doubt the importance of the effort, just as we do not doubt the importance of public enforcement. But both are outside the scope of this book.

Attacking the Private Enforcement Infrastructure

Attention to private enforcement retrenchment in the first years of the first Reagan administration focused squarely on federal rights, not torts. Tort law was not an issue on the Reagan administration's agenda until 1985, when it made tort reform a policy priority by forming the Tort Policy Working Group. In 1986, the Working Group issued a report calling for a series of reforms, including limits on fees and caps on damages (Farley 1991: 1015–16; Taylor 2012: 358 n. 5). Private enforcement retrenchment with respect to federal rights came first for the Reagan administration, and tort reform followed.

Two legislative initiatives to retrench private enforcement were considered. The first was a cross-cutting bill that would have amended over 100 statutes by limiting attorney's fee awards to successful plaintiffs in suits against government. The second involved amending the Civil Rights Act of 1871 with the goal of diminishing opportunities and incentives for private civil rights actions against state officials for violating federal rights. We explore both episodes with archival documents from the Reagan Library and the National Archives.

Starting in 1981, the OMB, with David Stockman as Director and Michael Horowitz as general counsel, developed a fee-cap bill that focused on suits against federal and state government defendants. Horowitz, who played a leading role in developing and advocating the bill, was an important figure in the conservative legal movement (Teles 2008: ch. 3). Advocates of the fee-cap bill believed that the extensive fee-shifting legislation since the Civil Rights Act of 1964 was a critical part of the incentive structure generating excessive litigation, and the goal of the fee-cap proposal was to "drive a stake through that incentive structure" (Decker 2009: 177). Initially titled "The Limitation of Legal Fees Awards Act of 1981," the proposed bill would amend over 100 federal statutes allowing recovery of attorney's fees in successful suits against government, ranging across suits under, for example, civil rights, environmental, antitrust, public health and safety, and freedom of information statutes, among many others. The initiative went through a number of permutations from 1981 to 1984. Some core attributes of the initial version were:

- A fee cap of $53 per hour for private attorneys representing paying clients (a figure derived from the annual salaries of government lawyers and one drastically below what courts had been awarding).
- No fee awards for public interest organizations with staff attorneys, legal services organizations receiving federal funds, or for-profit attorneys representing plaintiffs on a *pro bono* basis.
- The $53 per hour fee award would be reduced by 25% of any money judgment.
- The $53 per hour fee award would be reduced if it was disproportionate to the actual damages suffered by the plaintiff.
- Fee awards would apply only with respect to issues on which the plaintiff actually prevailed that were necessary for resolving the dispute.[3]

Shortly after work on The Limitation of Legal Fees Awards Act of 1981 began, a related proposal emerged in the Department of Justice (DOJ), in some ways narrower and in other ways broader. In the summer of 1982, John Roberts (then Special Assistant to the Attorney General) and Kenneth Starr (then Counselor to the Attorney General) made a request to the Office of Legal Policy (OLP) in DOJ for "a memorandum outlining the range of legislative changes that could be considered" to the Civil Rights Act of 1871, commonly known as Section 1983.[4] Section 1983 is the broadest federal civil rights statute and among the most consequential. It provides a private cause of action against any person who, "under color of" state law, causes the deprivation of rights secured by the "Constitution and laws" of the United States.[5] As is clear on the face of the statute, Section 1983 covers all federal rights, not only rights of non-discrimination and others traditionally associated with civil rights policy. The statute can only be enforced by private lawsuits; it contains no government right to sue or other public enforcement provisions.

---

[3] Mike Horowitz to David Stockman and Edwin Harper, June 22, 1982, Reagan Library, John G. Roberts, Jr. Files, box 5, Attorney's Fees (folder 1 of 3) (attachments B and C); Fred Barbash, ". . . And Uncle Sam Wants to Save on His Legal Fees," *Washington Post*, February 10, 1982, A25; Mary Thornton, "Plaintiffs' Legal Fess Attacked by OMB," *Washington Post*, August 12, 1982, A21; Percival and Miller (1984).

[4] Jonathan C. Rose to Edward C. Schmults, August 6, 1982 (cover memo), National Archives, John G. Robert, Jr. Files, box 125, Section 1983.

[5] 42 U.S.C. § 1983 (2012).

In the internal administration debate that John Roberts and Kenneth Starr helped to ignite, there emerged a consensus (judging from archival documents) that on the policy merits Section 1983 required substantial amendments to limit the growth of private lawsuits enforcing it. The statute was narrowly construed and rarely invoked during its first 90 years on the statute books (Note 1969). That changed in the 1960s, and even more in the 1970s, when Section 1983 actions began to grow significantly alongside other types of civil rights litigation and private federal statutory filings in general.

As internal Justice Department memoranda put it, explaining the need for Section 1983 amendments, civil rights litigation in general had "mushroomed" and "ballooned" in the past two decades, with the surge concentrated in private civil rights suits. One memo observed: "The number of 'private' civil rights suits filed in the federal district courts totaled 280 in 1960; 3,586 in 1970; 11,485 in 1980; and 13,534 in 1981. . . . Thus, since 1960 there has been an increase of almost 5,000%."[6] Administration officials questioned the merits of much of the growing civil rights litigation, with one memo opining that "[n]o grievance seems too trivial to escape translation into a § 1983 claim."[7] Amendments to Section 1983 were necessary "to stanch the flood of litigation it has engendered."[8]

The potential amendments to Section 1983 that were ventilated within DOJ were wide-ranging. They included:

- Entirely abolishing, or limiting, attorney's fees awards in Section 1983 cases (under the Civil Rights Attorney's Fees Awards Act, which expressly applies to such claims), with limitations accomplished, for example, by capping hourly rates, eliminating the use of multipliers, or limiting awards to plaintiffs who decline a settlement offer and do not achieve a better result at trial.
- Barring the award of punitive damages under Section 1983.
- Immunizing state and local officials from money damages under Section 1983 if there is a sufficient remedy in state law.
- Restricting the range of substantive statutory rights protected by Section 1983, such as to only constitutional and not statutory rights, or limiting protected statutory rights to those providing guarantees of non-discrimination.

[6] Rose to Schmults 8/6/1982; Jonathan C. Rose to William French Smith, June 15, 1983, National Archives, Carolyn B. Kuhl Files, box 15, Section 1983.
[7] Rose to Schmults 8/6/1982.
[8] Rose to Smith 6/15/1983.

- Creating a good-faith defense for municipalities under Section 1983, so that no action would lie against local government officials if they acted in good faith with a reasonable belief that their actions were lawful.
- Requiring that state remedies be exhausted as a precondition to filing a Section 1983 action, following the model of habeas corpus cases.
- Restricting the scope of Section 1983 to regulate only conduct arising from state law or official policy, excluding from coverage acts by officials that violate state law but are not undertaken pursuant to state law or official policy.
- Excluding acts of negligence by state and local officials from Section 1983 coverage.[9]

Although both the fee bill and the potential Section 1983 amendments appear quite extreme, they are notable for the fact that they applied only in suits against government. The initial private enforcement retrenchment movement in the Reagan administration did not attempt to restrict fees in suits against the private (business) sector. This dimension of the retrenchment project came later.

Demobilizing the Private Bar

The archival record makes clear that those seeking private enforcement retrenchment were concerned about, and responding to, the growing scale of enforcement activity by the private bar. As already discussed, conservative activists had long been critical of litigation by liberal public interest groups, but their focus now turned to for-profit plaintiffs' attorneys as well. Greve observes that when the Reagan administration sought to curtail fee awards, "a sizeable portion of attorneys' fees [was] collected not by public interest groups but by big, for-profit law firms" (Greve 1987: 103). This became an important theme and concern among Reagan White House advocates for retrenching private enforcement, articulated repeatedly in support of the fee bill. In a 1983 memo discussing the problem that the fee bill sought to address, Horowitz explained: "Not only the 'public interest' movement but, *more alarmingly*, the entire legal profession is becoming increasingly dependent on fees generated by an open-ended 'private

---

[9] *See* Rose to Schmults 8/6/1982; Rose to Smith 6/15/1983; Michael Robinson to Geoffrey Stewart, April 20, 1983, National Archives, Carolyn B. Kuhl Files, box 15, Section 1983; Michael Robinson to Geoffrey Stewart, June 14, 1983, National Archives, Carolyn B. Kuhl Files, box 15, Section 1983.

Attorney General' role that is authorized under more than 100 statutes,"[10] a large portion of which had been enacted since the Civil Rights Act of 1964.

Writing to OMB Director Stockman, Horowitz characterized the fee-cap bill as "designed in part to bar fee awards to entrepreneurial attorneys who now engage in contingency litigation"[11] under federal statutes. "A literal industry of public interest law firms has developed," he continued, "as a result of the legal fee awards with such groups regarding attorney's fees as a permanent financing mechanism," and one central to their commercial viability and business model.[12] When Stockman transmitted a version of the fee-cap bill to Speaker of the House Tip O'Neill in 1982, he repeated Horowitz's lamentation that a "literal industry" had developed of plaintiffs' lawyers dependent on statutory fee awards.[13] In the same vein, a Justice Department memo to Counselor to the President Edwin Meese, reporting on the content of the fee-cap bill, stated that it was meant to address the problem of the "growing industry of attorneys capitalizing on civil fee awards."[14]

Reagan administration advocates of retrenching private enforcement were surely right, from the standpoint of a deregulatory agenda, that the statutory enforcement activity of the for-profit bar, mobilized by fee awards, was more alarming than the activity of the non-profit bar. The year Reagan took office, about 90% of actions enforcing federal statutes were privately prosecuted, and the fraction was rising.[15] Non-profit groups prosecuted a tiny fraction of the cases. One study found that non-profits prosecuted 2% of a sample of federal statutory actions that spanned from 1960 to 2004 (Farhang 2010: 11). To the extent that the "regulatory relief" sought by Reagan involved, in part, less aggressive enforcement of existing statutory mandates, and the private enforcement infrastructure posed a problem to presidential control, the problem was emanating overwhelmingly from the for-profit bar responding to market incentives.

John Roberts, an initiator of the proposals to amend Section 1983, was also an active participant in deliberations over the fee-cap bill.

---

[10] Mike Horowitz to Dick Hauser and Bob Kabel, June 16, 1983, Reagan Library, James W. Cicconi Files, box 23, Department of Justice (folder 1) (emphasis in original).
[11] Horowitz to Stockman and Harper 6/22/82.
[12] Ibid.
[13] David Stockman to Thomas P. O'Neill, July 22, 1982, Reagan Library, John G. Roberts, Jr. Files, box 5, Attorney's Fees (folder 1 of 3).
[14] Joseph R. Wright, Jr. to Edwin Meese, III, July 25, 1983, Reagan Library, box 9094, Attorney Fee Reform Legislation.
[15] Judicial Business of the United States Courts, Administrative Office of the United States Courts, 1981, Table C-2.

Notwithstanding differences of opinion within the administration about the political wisdom of pursuing the bill, Roberts joined those advocating it. In explaining why, he stated, "This legislation will, of course, be opposed by the self-styled public interest bar, but the abuses that have arisen in the award of attorney's fees against the government clearly demand remedial action." Antonin Scalia endorsed the fee bill as well. Writing as a University of Chicago law professor and editor of the American Enterprise Institute's *Regulation* magazine (just months before his appointment to the D.C. Circuit), he argued that recent D.C. Circuit pro-fee award decisions were a "bad dream" in need of the administration's legislative remedy and that the bill would surely be opposed by the "private attorney general industry."[16] As we shall see, after their legislative advocacy failed, Roberts and Scalia were to become among the most anti-private enforcement justices to serve on the Supreme Court in a period spanning more than 50 years.

The Reagan administration's private enforcement retrenchment initiatives failed. Examining the reasons why provides insights into the political and institutional dynamics of litigation retrenchment. Before turning to the reasons for failure, we first explore private enforcement retrenchment efforts in Congress and how they fared.

Private Enforcement Retrenchment
Proposals in Congress

In order to map the legislative movement for private enforcement retrenchment and its partisan configuration in Congress, we identified all bills that sought to amend federal law so as to (1) reduce the availability of attorney's fees to plaintiffs or increase plaintiffs' liability for defendants' fees; (2) reduce the monetary damages that plaintiffs can recover; (3) reduce opportunities and incentives for class actions; (4) strengthen the operation of sanctions against counsel; and (5) strengthen the operation of offer of judgment rules.[17] These provisions fall into two groups. The fees and damages provisions seek to reduce directly the economic recovery available to successful private enforcers and thereby to reduce economic incentives for enforcement by would-be plaintiffs and their attorneys. We discussed the

---

[16] "The Private Attorney General Industry: Doing Well by Doing Good," *Regulation*, May/June 1982, at 5–7; Horowitz to Stockman and Harper 6/22/82 (including ex. H).

[17] We excluded bills that sought to affect incentives for asserting rights in administrative proceedings or for judicial review of administrative action. Our focus is on private lawsuits to enforce federal rights against the objects of statutory regulation.

significance of attorney's fees and monetary damages to private enforcement in Chapter 1.

The class action, sanctions, and offer of judgment provisions seek to modify the Federal Rules in ways that disadvantage private enforcers. More specifically, we included these three procedural issues in our measure of legislative retrenchment efforts for the following reasons:

1. *Class actions*. Under Federal Rule of Civil Procedure 23, a plaintiff can sue on behalf of a class of absentees, typically alleging that a defendant injured a large number of people in the same way. In the context of federal rights, the device has been used extensively to enforce civil rights, environmental, consumer, antitrust, and securities laws. The device has great regulatory power and has been a target of retrenchment efforts in rulemaking and litigation, which we discuss in Chapters 3 and 4. We included in our data bills that proposed to amend existing law to curtail the operation of the class action rule.

2. *Sanctions*. Federal Rule of Civil Procedure 11 confers power on district judges to impose sanctions, under specified conditions, on attorneys or parties. Rule 11 applies equally to counsel for plaintiffs and defendants. As we discuss in Chapter 3, however, advocates of retrenchment have often attributed cost and delay to frivolous lawsuits and have advocated strengthening Rule 11 sanctions with the goal of targeting an allegedly frivolous complaint and thus the plaintiff's attorney who drafts it. We included in our data bills that proposed to amend existing law to broaden the scope of, or increase the sanctions under, Rule 11.

3. *Offer of Judgment*. Federal Rule of Civil Procedure 68 provides that a prevailing party who has rejected an offer of judgment – an offer to settle the case – more favorable to that party than the judgment ultimately obtained must pay the "costs incurred after the offer was made." The rule seeks to promote settlements through financial incentives that are keyed to a comparison of a rejected offer and a subsequent judgment. As we discuss in Chapters 3 and 4, advocates of retrenchment have sought to strengthen the incentive for settlement by, among other things, adding reasonable attorney's fees to the post-offer costs that become non-recoverable in the circumstance just described, a move that threatens to undermine one-way statutory fee-shifting provisions that Congress included in legislation in order to stimulate private enforcement (Burbank 1986; Burbank 1989a; Burbank 1989b). We included in our data bills that proposed to amend existing law to increase penalties in this scenario.

Table 2.1. *Types of private enforcement issues in bills*

Private enforcement issues	Percentage of total bills in data*
Damages	61
Attorney's fees	47
Class actions	14
Sanctions	10
Offers of judgment	6

*This column sums to more than 100% because one bill can seek to amend existing law with respect to multiple private enforcement issues.

Our search captured 500 bills from 1973 (when the Library of Congress bill database starts) to 2014. Table 2.1 shows the percentage of these bills containing each of our five anti-private enforcement items. Table 2.2 reflects the distribution of policy areas covered by the bills (for policy areas comprising 2% or more of the data). The largest share (25%) is represented by bills targeting civil rights and civil liberties issues, prominently including bills focused on policing, prisoners, discrimination, religion, and abortion. Multiple civil rights bills sought to amend Section 1983 and the Civil Rights Attorney's Fees Awards Act of 1976 so as to reduce litigation under them. Other important policy areas included antitrust, environmental, labor, securities, and consumer policy.

Twenty-nine percent of these bills contained more than one private enforcement-retrenchment item, with an average of 1.4 items per bill. The bills had an average of 11 co-sponsors, yielding a total of 6,133 instances of legislators sponsoring or co-sponsoring a bill with at least one retrenchment item in it. There were 3,608 episodes of legislators supporting a bill with a provision limiting damages, 2,913 with an attorney fee provision, and 2,149 with procedural provisions. Summing across all items, there were 9,022 instances of a legislator supporting our five retrenchment items. Fifty-seven percent of the members of Congress who served from 1973 to 2014 supported one of our retrenchment provisions at least once.

In order to analyze the relationship between legislators' party and the likelihood that they would support anti-private enforcement proposals, we constructed the following dataset. Separately for each of our items and for each legislator who served in Congress from 1973 to 2014, we calculated the total number of episodes of sponsorship or co-sponsorship per Congress. That is, the unit of analysis is a Congress-legislator count

Table 2.2. *Policy distribution of bills*

Policy area		Percentage of cases
Civil rights and liberties		25
Policing	(5)	
Prisoner	(2)	
Equality	(5)	
Religion	(3)	
Abortion	(4)	
Other	(6)	
Civil rules*		12
Antitrust		11
Environmental		6
Suits against government**		6
Labor and employment		5
Intellectual property		5
Securities		4
Consumer		4
Transportation		4
Public health and safety		3
Other		15

*Civil rules include proposals to amend existing general rules governing federal civil actions. These include primarily amendments to Federal Rules of Civil Procedure, but also other proposals to create transsubstantive rules to govern all federal civil actions, such as a loser pays fee rule.

**Suits against government include rules which specify that they govern suits against government in general, such as a rule cutting across all policy areas to cap legal fees or damages available in actions against government.

of the total number of times that each legislator in each Congress sponsored or co-sponsored one of our five items. Figure 2.1 fits a curve to the count, per Congress, of the total number of episodes of legislator support for anti-private enforcement provisions; the aggregation of proposals to reduce damages and fees (monetary recoveries); and the aggregation of proposals to change class action, sanctions, and offer of judgment rules (procedural rules). Years on the horizontal axis designate Congresses seated in that year.

Two things stand out in these data. First, support for anti-private enforcement bills grew strongly in the Reagan years. Because the regression curve smooths over year-to-year fluctuations, it does not reveal sharp breaks in the data, and thus the raw underlying data are instructive. During the Carter presidency, there was an average of 71 episodes

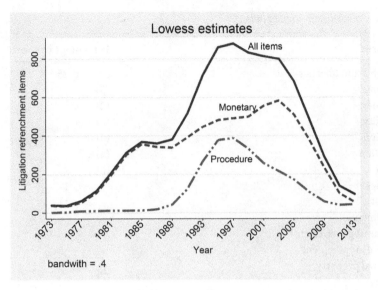

Figure 2.1   Annual number of private enforcement retrenchment items: damages, attorney's fees, class actions, sanctions, offers of judgment, 1973–2014

per Congress of legislative support for one of our anti-private enforcement items. In Reagan's first term, the figure rose to 240 per Congress, and in his second term it rose to 457 per Congress – 544% higher than in the Carter years. Though growth was beginning in the late 1970s, it increased dramatically in the Reagan years and peaked at 1074 in the 104th Congress (1995–6), when Republicans took control. It has since declined considerably, continuing its downward slope to the present, with estimated values in the last two Congresses comparable to the late-1970s.

Second, in the first half of the 1980s, episodes of support for procedural proposals were negligible in number and flat, while fee and damages proposals exploded. Procedural proposals, however, grew significantly starting in the early 1990s. The raw Congress-level counts again tell the story. In Ronald Reagan's first term in office, there was an average of 4 episodes per Congress of support for anti-private enforcement procedural proposals, and in his second term the number was 17. In George H.W. Bush's term in office, the number rose to 28 per Congress, and in Bill Clinton's first term the figure grew to 371, for more than a 35-fold increase over the Reagan years. It peaked at 589 in the 105th Congress (1997–8) and subsequently declined, a trend continuing to the present.

Figure 2.2 provides an initial sense of the significance of ideology and party affiliation by presenting separate regression curves for the number of Democratic and Republican sponsors and co-sponsors in the top panel, and sponsors only in the bottom panel. Until Reagan took office, Democrats provided more support for these proposals than Republicans,

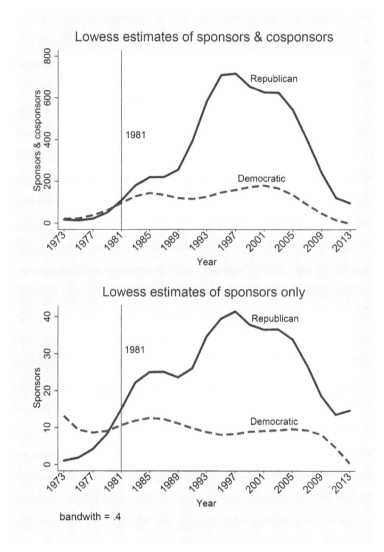

Figure 2.2   Republican and Democratic support for private enforcement retrenchment, 1973–2014

and there was an even larger partisan disparity in sponsorship. Again, smoothed regression estimates are not useful for locating year-to-year changes. The raw data reveal that in each of the four Congresses from 1973 to 1980, while the volume of proposals was very low, Democratic support exceeded Republican support modestly when sponsors and co-sponsors are aggregated, and did so to a greater extent in sponsorship. The 97th Congress (1981–2) is the first in our dataset in which Republican support for anti-private enforcement measures exceeds Democratic support, and this is true both when sponsors and co-sponsors are aggregated and when sponsorship alone is examined. Once Reagan took office, Republican members emerged as the chief advocates of retrenchment, and the partisan gap on this issue exploded, peaking in the 105th Congress (1995–6). As the number of Republican proposals declined after this peak, so also did the absolute size of the gap between the two parties.[18]

We collected bills containing the same set of five retrenchment items applied to state tort law. As with the Reagan administration's retrenchment proposals, our bill database shows that proposals in the field of federal rights led the way and tort reform followed. From 1973 through 1984 (the end of Reagan's first term), the total number of bills containing such items targeting federal rights outnumbered those targeting tort by a margin of more than three to one, and episodes of sponsorship and co-sponsorship of provisions targeting federal statutory rights outnumbered those targeting tort by a margin of about four to one. Only in the 99th Congress (1985–6), corresponding exactly to Reagan's embrace of tort reform, did tort reform surge in Congress to levels rivaling, and subsequently sometimes surpassing, proposals targeting federal rights.

In order to test systematically the relationship between legislator party and support for anti-private enforcement proposals, we use negative binomial count models. We code 0 for Democrats and 1 for Republicans. We employ Congress fixed effects to address the possibility of potential confounding factors, including the political and public salience of the private enforcement issue, the lobbying priorities of business and state governments that may wish to reduce private enforcement pressures, and election cycles. This approach leverages only variation in the relationship between legislators' party and their votes *within* Congresses to estimate the effects of party. This approach allows us to estimate the effects of party most effectively because it holds constant

---

[18] Note that Figure 2.2 is based on raw figures of support and does not attempt to make adjustments for the share of seats controlled by each party. This is addressed in our statistical models.

the influence of any variables that would take the same value for each legislator in a given Congress, and in this sense these estimates of the effects of party are net of the effects of any such variables (Greene 2003: ch. 13).

We suggest earlier in this chapter that the Reagan administration's fee bill appeared to mark an important juncture in the Republican Party's anti-private enforcement campaign. The session of Congress corresponding to Reagan's first two years in office was the first session of Congress in our dataset in which Republican support for anti-private enforcement proposals exceeded Democratic support. In our statistical models, we subset the data by time periods in order to assess the effect of party before and after Reagan's assumption of office.

We estimate separate negative binomial count models for (1) the pooled number of episodes of support for all five types of anti-private enforcement provisions; (2) the aggregation of proposals to reduce damages and fees (monetary recoveries); and (3) the aggregation of proposals to change class action, sanctions, and offer of judgment rules (procedural rules). In our measure of legislator support in the models, we use counts that include both sponsorship and co-sponsorship. We do so because we are interested in the degree of legislative support for litigation retrenchment proposals. To neglect co-sponsors would be to treat a bill that a legislator introduces only for herself as equivalent to one that dozens of other members of Congress wish to support. We discuss modeling choices, interpretation, and alternative specifications in the appendix.

In Table 2.3, we estimate the effects of legislator party on support for anti-private enforcement provisions for the period from 1973 to 1980. We find no statistically significant party effect in the model for pooled episodes or the model for monetary recoveries. We do find a statistically significant effect with respect to procedural provisions, and the sign on the coefficient reflects that *Democrats* were more likely to support such bills. We are not inclined to make much of this result because only about 4% of members of Congress sponsored such a bill during this period – procedure had not yet emerged as a locus of significant bill activity.[19] Yet, it is worth exploring possible reasons why, although private enforcement

---

[19] Examining the pre-1981 portion of Figure 2.2 suggests that we may detect a party effect by using dependent variables constituted by sponsorship only. We examined such models. In the model of all items we did find a statistically significant party effect ($p = .06$), with the move from Republican to Democrat associated with a 118% increase in the number of provisions sponsored. In these models there was not a significant party effect when the dependent variable was decomposed into monetary and procedural items. With only 41 bill introductions in the data for this period, we interpret these results cautiously.

Table 2.3. *Negative binomial model of legislator support for anti-private enforcement provisions, with Congress fixed effects, 1973–1980*

All bills

	Coefficient	Marginal
Party	−.24	−27%
	(.18)	

Monetary recoveries

	Coefficient	Marginal
Party	−.11	−12%
	(.18)	

Procedure

	Coefficient	Marginal
Party	−1.43***	−318%
	(.53)	

(Congress fixed effects in all models not displayed)
$N = 2154$
Adj. Dev. R^2 = .10 (All bills), .06 (Monetary recoveries), .24 (Procedure)

***.01; **<.05; *<.1
Standard errors in parentheses, clustered on legislator

retrenchment was an area of scarce legislative activity prior to Reagan, to the extent that it was an issue, it was not a Republican issue. In order to do so, we focus on legislative reactions to experience in class actions brought under the 1966 amendments to Federal Rule of Civil Procedure 23.

In an environment of proliferating regulatory statutes and greater competition within the legal profession, the potential of the 1966 amendments both to serve the purposes of their drafters and to enable attorneys to do well by doing good (or, depending on one's perspective, to enrich themselves) was quickly realized. So also was the potential of the (b)(3) class action, the provision in Rule 23 most used by those seeking damages, to promote inefficient over-enforcement of substantive law. This problem surfaced quickly and dramatically in litigation under the Truth in Lending Act (TILA), a complex regulatory statute enacted in 1968 that promotes private enforcement by authorizing minimum and maximum statutory damages (in addition to actual damages, if any, which are difficult to prove) and attorney's fees.[20] Statutory damages are damages of an amount,

[20] *See* 15 U.S.C. § 1601 et seq. (2012). The provisions on individual and class damages are contained in ibid. at § 1640.

or within a range, specified in the statute rather than being based on harm actually suffered by the plaintiff.

Although such provisions make sense as part of a private enforcement regime to induce individual litigation, minimum statutory damages can lead to devastating liability for technical statutory violations when aggregated in a class action.[21] Troubled by this evident misfit, some federal district courts refused to certify (b)(3) class actions in TILA litigation,[22] prompting Congress to cap the statutory damages recoverable in a class suit at the lesser of 1% of the creditor's net worth and, first (in 1974), $100,000,[23] and a few years later (in 1976), $500,000.[24] Indeed, of the eight bills to reduce the opportunities or incentives for class actions that were introduced in Congress from 1973 (when the Library of Congress bill database starts) through 1980, four were targeted at this specific problem.[25] Another bill would have made class actions unavailable in cases asserting claims valued at less than $10,[26] suggesting that interest extended beyond the phenomenon of over-enforcement to the very concept of using class litigation to vindicate small claims, prevent unjust enrichment, or deter illegal conduct.

The existence of such interest on the part of the Executive Branch was made clear in ambitious proposed legislation developed by the

---

[21] "The legislative history of the TIL Act makes no mention of the class action; apparently, the drafters simply failed to consider it" (Comment 1976–7: 418). For the views of a federal judge "whose experience was that many, if not the great majority, of [TILA] cases were brought on the basis of allegations of hypertechnical violations of an extremely complicated law where *logical* arguments could be made by lawyers on either side of the case," see *Qui Tam and Federal Reserve Board Procedures; Hearing on S. 3008 Before the Subcommittee on Consumer Affairs of the Senate Committee on Banking, Housing and Urban Affairs*, 94th Cong., 2d Sess. 342 (1976) (statement of Judge Sidney O. Smith, Jr.).

[22] *See, e.g., Ratner v. Chemical Bank New York Trust Co.*, 54 F.R.D. 412 (S.D.N.Y. 1972). "Between February 14, 1972, the date of the *Ratner* decision, and November 29, 1972 . . . the courts denied twenty-one class actions alleging Truth in Lending violations while allowing only two." (Note 1974: 1412). Problems ensued even after Congress capped the damages available in a TILA class action, some of which derived from the possibility that the cap might lead to a smaller recovery by class members than they could obtain in individual actions (Comment 1976–7: 425–32, 447–8).

[23] *See* Act of October 28, 1974, Pub. L. No. 93–495, tit. IV, § 408(a), 88 Stat. 1500, 1518.

[24] *See* Consumer Leasing Act of 1976, Pub. L. No. 94–240, § 4, 90 Stat. 257, 260. In 1980, Congress also made the cap applicable to a series of class actions arising out of the same failure to comply by the same creditor. *See* Act of March 31, 1980, Pub. L. No. 96–221, § 615(a)(1), 94 Stat. 180.

[25] *See* S. 3690, 93rd Cong. (1974); H.R. 4270, 96th Cong. (1979); H.R. 1289, 96th Cong. (1979); H.R. 3553, 96th Cong. (1979).

[26] *See* H.R. 7683, 95th Cong. (1977).

Office for Improvements in the Administration of Justice in the Carter Administration's DOJ. In August 1978 Senator DeConcini (for himself and Senator Kennedy) introduced this proposed legislation as S. 3475.[27] The accompanying commentary set out the case for a legislative approach, observing that "revision of class damage procedures should be accomplished by direct legislative enactment rather than through the rule-making process," because "deterrence of widespread injury is of substantial public interest, and Congress should devote extensive consideration to any proposal." The commentary also argued that, because such revision "would have significant economic ramifications," there were "serious questions as to whether [it] is appropriately within the scope of the rule-making authority granted by the Rules Enabling Act."[28]

The proposed legislation would have repealed Rule 23(b)(3), replaced the small-claims class action with a public action (brought by or on behalf of the United States),[29] and restructured large-claims class (compensatory) actions[30] to "increase the fairness of the procedure and to make it less expensive and time consuming."[31] The commentary asserted that the "use of the Rule 23(b)(3) compensation-oriented procedures for actions brought to remedy pervasive small harm has posed major problems for plaintiffs, defendants and the courts."[32] The bill responded to problems created by Rule 23 and Supreme Court decisions interpreting it (in particular those concerning notice) for plaintiffs and the federal courts, as well as to problems created for defendants.[33] A similar bill was introduced in the House in 1979.[34]

---

[27] *See* S. 3475, 95th Cong. (1978). In floor remarks, both Senators indicated that the bill was intended to start a conversation, and thus that they were not wedded to its provisions. *See* 124 Cong. Rec. 27,859 (1978) ("Neither Senator Kennedy nor I are wedded to its provisions.") (Senator DeConcini); ibid. at 27,869 (bill "will begin the debate on revision of one of our most important procedural rules") (Senator Kennedy). For contemporaneous commentary, *see* Note 1979.

[28] 124 Cong. Rec. 27,860 (1978).

[29] *See* S. 3475, 95th Cong. §§ 3001–7 (1978).

[30] *See* ibid. at §§ 3011–4.

[31] 124 Cong. Rec. 27,859 (1978). *See* ibid. at 27,859–61; Burbank and Wolff 2010: 58–9.

[32] 124 Cong. Rec. 27,861 (1978).

[33] "The present notice requirement of Rule 23(c)(2) and certification prerequisites of Rule 23(b)(3) are designed for actions brought predominantly for compensatory, rather than deterrent purposes. The burden of these requirements can thwart entirely the maintenance of an action where the individual injury is small, even though the case may be meritorious and the harm widespread." 124 Cong. Rec. 27,861 (1978) (Proposed Revisions in Federal Claims Damages Procedures – Bill Commentary).

[34] *See* H.R. 5103, 96th Cong. (1979).

Nothing came of this legislative initiative.[35] The Carter administration's proposal is notable precisely because it was led by Democrats. Indeed, of the eight class action bills in this period, seven were introduced by Democrats, and of 31 total sponsors, 27 were Democrats. One interpretation of this fact is that, once the catalytic regulatory potential of amended Rule 23 became clear, as the primary architects of the Litigation State, Democrats took the lead in attending to its supervision and calibration prior to the emergence of the counterrevolution.

Returning to discussion of the empirical models, in Table 2.4 we estimate the model for the 1981–2014 period. The results change dramatically. The party variable is statistically significant in the expected direction in all three models: all types of provisions pooled, those reducing monetary recoveries only, and those affecting procedural issues only. In the model of all anti-private enforcement provisions, moving from Democrat

Table 2.4. *Negative binomial model of legislator support for anti-private enforcement provisions, with Congress fixed effects, 1981–2014*

All bills

	Coefficient	Marginal
Party	1.25***	249%
	(.05)	

Monetary recoveries

	Coefficient	Marginal
Party	1.19***	229%
	(.05)	

Procedure

	Coefficient	Marginal
Party	1.49***	344%
	(.08)	

(Congress fixed effects in all models not displayed)
$N = 9190$
Adj. Dev. R^2 = .31 (All bills), .27 (Monetary recoveries), .47 (Procedure)

***.01; **<.05; *<.1
Standard errors in parentheses, clustered on legislator

[35] For other Carter Administration civil litigation reform initiatives, *see* Yeazell 2013: 1774–5. "Nothing happened, and no subsequent Democrat has taken up that banner." Ibid.

to Republican is associated with an increase in legislators' predicted count by 249%. The figure is 229% in the model of fees and damages and 344% in the model of procedural provisions. Interestingly, the effect of party on the level of support is highest among the procedural provisions.

Our model pools data over about 30 years, raising two obvious questions: First, is the relevant effect present throughout this period? Second, has its magnitude changed over time? In order to answer these questions, we summarize the results from a series of models over time in Table 2.5. We aggregated the two Congresses associated with each presidential administration from 1981 to 2014, with the exception that we aggregated three Congresses under Obama since the fourth has yet to conclude. The marginal effects column reflects the percent increase in legislators' predicted count of support for private enforcement retrenchment proposals moving from Democrat to Republican. Table 2.5 shows that, with respect to the fee and damages bills, the party effects are significant in each regression. The magnitude of the party effect grew over the Reagan–Bush years and peaked in Clinton's first term. It subsequently declined, while remaining large, and then spiked during the Obama Congresses. In contrast, the effect of party on legislators' support for anti-private enforcement procedural items took slightly longer to emerge. There was no statistically significant effect in Reagan's first term. By his second term, however, the party effect emerged as durably statistically significant. Its growth has been more continuous than for the monetary recovery items, reaching its highest levels in the most recent Congresses. The large party effect across all of our bill data during the Obama years may seem odd when juxtaposed with Figure 2.2, which shows a declining absolute distance between Republican and Democratic support for the anti-private enforcement provisions. This is explained by the fact that our count models estimate the growth factor in Republican support relative to Democratic support, and Democratic support has declined to extremely low levels in recent years. To appreciate the salience of retrenching private enforcement in Congress, one must examine both Figure 2.2 (to gauge the volume of activity), and Table 2.5 (to gauge how partisan that activity is).

Failure of Private Enforcement
Retrenchment in Congress

The legislative project of private enforcement retrenchment mounted by the Republican Party was largely a failure. Reagan's fee bill was unable to gain traction even in the Republican-controlled Senate (Percival and

Table 2.5. *Negative binomial coefficients and marginal effects for legislator party in models of legislator support for anti-private enforcement provisions, with Congress fixed effects, by presidential administration*

All bills

	Coefficient	Marginal
Reagan I (1981–4)	.47***	60%
Reagan II (1985–8)	.81***	125%
H.W. Bush (1989–92)	1.05***	186%
Clinton I (1993–6)	1.85***	536%
Clinton II (1997–2000)	1.21***	235%
W. Bush I (2001–4)	1.08***	194%
W. Bush II (2005–8)	1.60***	395%
Obama (2009–14)	2.09***	708%

Monetary recoveries

	Coefficient	Marginal
Reagan I (1981–4)	.46***	58%
Reagan II (1985–8)	.80***	123%
H.W. Bush (1989–92)	1.07***	192%
Clinton I (1993–6)	2.08***	700%
Clinton II (1997–2000)	1.19***	229%
W. Bush I (2001–4)	.83***	129%
W. Bush II (2005–8)	1.52***	357%
Obama I (2009–14)	1.90***	569%

Procedure

	Coefficient	Marginal
Reagan I (1981–4)	1.35	
Reagan II (1985–8)	.98**	166%
H.W. Bush (1989–92)	.91***	148%
Clinton I (1993–6)	1.54***	366%
Clinton II (1997–00)	1.22***	239%
W. Bush I (2001–4)	1.80***	505%
W. Bush II (2005–8)	2.02***	654%
Obama I (2009–14)	2.68***	1359%

*** .01; ** <.05; * <.1

Miller 1984). Numerous proposals by congressional Republicans fared little better in the ensuing years, even when they controlled both chambers of Congress. Some of the fees and damages proposals were transsubstantive bills that would have cut across the whole landscape of the Litigation State, such as bills requiring federal courts to award attorney's fees to prevailing defendants in all civil actions[36] or to impose a general loser pays fee-shifting rule.[37] Another transsubstantive proposal would have capped punitive damages in all civil actions in federal court against small businesses, while increasing the burden of proof for establishing entitlement to such damages.[38]

Many other Republican proposals targeted particularly active areas of federal civil litigation and sought to reduce economic incentives: A 1981 bill proposed full immunity from civil damages suits for police officers who conducted illegal search and seizures in violation of the Fourth Amendment.[39] A 1982 bill proposed to repeal the attorney fee-shifting provision in the Civil Rights Attorney's Fees Awards Act of 1976.[40] A 1987 bill proposed to amend the Clayton Act to reduce the amount recoverable in many private antitrust actions from treble to actual damages.[41] A 1992 bill proposed to eliminate class actions under the Truth in Lending Act.[42]

Although a substantial majority of the Republicans' procedural proposals would have amended specific statutes, some were transsubstantive, and these were overwhelmingly bills amending Rules 11 and 23. Of the Rule 11 bills, a substantial majority sought to reverse the 1993 amendments by making sanctions mandatory rather than discretionary.[43] Of transsubstantive bills targeting Rule 23, a substantial majority were precursors to the Class Action Fairness Act of 2005.[44]

Republican successes were few in number. Three are well known: the Private Securities Litigation Reform Act of 1995,[45] the Prison Litigation

---

[36] *See, e.g.*, Frivolous Suit Reduction Act of 1995, H.R. 64, 104th Cong.; Frivolous Suit Reduction Act of 1994, H.R. 5189, 103rd Cong.

[37] *See, e.g.*, Loser Pays Legal Fee Fairness Act of 2005, H.R. 3497, 109th Cong.; Loser Pays Act of 1993, H.R. 2880, 103rd Cong.

[38] *See, e.g.*, Small Business Lawsuit Abuse Protection Act of 1998, H.R. 3382, 105th Cong.; *see also* Small Business Liability Reform Act of 2001, S. 865, 107th Cong.

[39] House Resolution 4259 proposed to amend titles 18 and 28 of the United States Code to eliminate, and provide an alternative to, the exclusionary rule in federal criminal proceedings. H.R. 4259, 97th Cong. (1981).

[40] Judicial Reform Act of 1982, S. 3018, 97th Cong.

[41] Trade, Employment, and Productivity Act of 1987, H.R. 1155, 100th Cong.

[42] Community Bank Regulatory Relief Act of 1992, S. 2794, 102nd Cong.

[43] *See, e.g.*, Small Business Growth Act of 2007, H.R. 1012, 110th Cong.; Civil Justice Fairness Act of 1995, S. 672, 104th Cong.

[44] *See, e.g.*, Class Action Fairness Act of 2004, S. 2062, 108th Cong.; Class Action Fairness Act of 2000, S. 353, 106th Cong.

[45] Pub. L. No. 104–67, 109 Stat. 737 (codified as amended in scattered section of 15 U.S.C.).

Reform Act of 1996,[46] and the Class Action Fairness Act of 2005 (CAFA).[47] We do not deny the significance of these laws. However, excluding the jurisdictional provisions of CAFA, which themselves do not directly affect federal rights,[48] the three are narrowly focused.

Beyond these major laws, only eight more Republican-proposed private enforcement-retrenchment bills in our database passed. More telling than their number is how limited the bills were in substantive scope. They included three antitrust bills limiting multiple damages: one in 1982 applying only to actions by foreign governments,[49] one in 1984 applying only to narrowly defined "joint research and development venture[s],"[50] and one in 2004 applying only to antitrust violators who report their own cartel activity to the Justice Department and cooperate in its ensuing investigation.[51] They also included three bills limiting fee awards to disabled students or their families suing schools: two of these capped only fee awards paid from monies appropriated for the District of Columbia in each of two years, without permanent limits,[52] and the third limited fee recovery by (or imposed some fee liability on) plaintiffs' counsel for frivolous or unreasonable litigation behavior.[53] In 1995, a Republican-proposed bill passed, imposing a five-month moratorium on certain consumer class actions, again with no permanent effects.[54] In 1996, a Republican proposal

---

[46] Pub. L. No. 104–134, 110 Stat. 1321–66 (codified as amended in scattered sections of 11, 18, 28, and 42 U.S.C.).

[47] Pub. L. No. 109–2, 119 Stat. 4 (codified as amended in scattered sections of 28 U.S.C.).

[48] As we discuss in Chapter 4, CAFA significantly increased the number of state law class actions that were governed by a transsubstantive and ever-more-conservative federal class action jurisprudence. It therefore may have encouraged anti-private enforcement class action jurisprudence that also governs enforcement of federal rights.

[49] Act of December 29, 1982, Pub. L. No. 97–393, 96 Stat. 1964 (codified at 15 U.S.C. § 15 (2012)).

[50] National Cooperative Research Act of 1984, Pub. L. No. 98–462, § 2(a)(6), 98 Stat. 1815, 1815 (codified as amended at 15 U.S.C. § 4301 (2012)).

[51] Standards Development Organization Advancement Act of 2004, Pub. L. No. 108–237, §§ 106–107, 118 Stat. 661, 664–65 (codified at 15 U.S.C. §§ 4304–4305 (2012)).

[52] Transportation, Treasury, Housing and Urban Development, the Judiciary, the District of Columbia, and Independent Agencies Appropriations Act, 2006, Pub. L. No. 109–115, 119 Stat. 2396 (2005); District of Columbia Appropriations Act, 2005, Pub. L. No. 108–335, 118 Stat. 1322 (2004).

[53] Individuals with Disabilities Education Improvement Act of 2004, Pub. L. No. 108–446, § 615(i)(3), 118 Stat. 2647, 2724–25 (codified at 20 U.S.C. § 1415 (2012)).

[54] Truth in Lending Class Action Relief Act of 1995, Pub. L. No. 104–12, § 2, 109 Stat. 161, 161 (codified as amended at 15 U.S.C. § 1640 (2012)).

passed, foreclosing fee awards in Section 1983 actions against judges for actions taken in a judicial capacity.[55]

In sum, Republican successes across the issues in our database, over the three and a half decades from the emergence of the issue on the Republican agenda in 1981 until 2014, nibbled around the edges of the Litigation State. They did not challenge it seriously.

Why Private Enforcement Retrenchment by Legislation Failed

The story of the failure of the Reagan administration's fee-cap bill and initiative to amend Section 1983 teaches some important lessons about the long-run resilience of the private enforcement infrastructure against retrenchment through democratic policymaking processes. It is also important, in itself, because the failure helped to drive the retrenchment project into the federal courts, where, as we demonstrate in Chapter 4, quite significant changes in law have been effected. To appreciate the lessons, it is useful first to highlight several institutional factors that make retrenchment of rights difficult.

An institutionally fragmented legislative process empowers many actors to block legislation, making legislative change difficult on contentious issues and leading to the stickiness of the status quo. Legislative processes characterized by many "veto points" make moving the legal status quo difficult (Immergut 1992: 63–4). The American separation of powers system, giving a considerable degree of constitutional independence, autonomy, and legitimacy to separate executive, legislative, and judicial branches, coupled with the strong norm of judicial review, is characterized by multiple veto points (Sundquist 1988; Shugart and Carey 1992; Weaver and Rockman 1993). Adding to the stickiness created by these veto points, the lawmaking process within Congress is particularly fragmented. Bicameralism, an elaborate committee system that gives disproportionate powers to committee members and chairs, and the filibuster in the Senate, combine to create a multitude of players with the power to kill or radically reshape legislation that would easily command a solid majority if only it could reach a floor vote (Landes and Posner 1975; Steinmo 1994; Brady and Volden 2005). This line of institutional theory has also emphasized that the relative weakness of parties in the United States encourages pivotal lawmakers to respond to important, even if very narrow and

---

[55] Federal Courts Improvement Act of 1996, Pub. L. No. 104–317, § 309(c), 110 Stat. 3847, 3853 (codified as amended at 28 U.S.C. § 2412 (2012)).

particularized, constituencies and interest groups when deciding whether and how to exercise their veto powers. The net result is a very sticky status quo. In this lawmaking system, as Moe puts it, "Whatever is formalized will tend to endure" (Moe 1990: 240).

This is especially true when the legal change sought involves divesting groups of existing rights, and even more so when those rights enjoy a broad base of support. In his work on welfare state retrenchment, Paul Pierson observes that rights-retrenching reforms confront serious political hurdles. The legal rights and interests that retrenchers seek to remove often have already given rise to "resources and incentives that influence the formation and activity of social groups . . . [and] create 'spoils' that provide a strong motivation for beneficiaries to mobilize in favor of programmatic maintenance or expansion" (Pierson 1994: 40). In the context we investigate in this book, rights-oriented interest groups – which propelled the growth of private enforcement, see it as critical to their policy missions, and rely on fee awards to support litigation campaigns – together with private plaintiff's bar groups, can be counted on to mobilize against efforts to retrench private enforcement, in which they have a direct interest.

Pierson also emphasizes that the phenomenon of "negativity bias" (or an "endowment effect") leads people to be substantially more likely to mobilize to avoid the imposition of losses of existing rights and interests, as compared to securing new ones. It also leads voters to be more likely to punish politicians who have impaired their interests than to reward politicians who have benefited them, and politicians know this (Pierson 1994: 17–19, 39–46; see also Eskridge and Ferejohn 1995: 1560). Thus, retrenchment of rights is difficult because: (1) institutional fragmentation facilitates blocking policy reforms; (2) existing rights often contribute to group capacity to defend them; and (3) "negativity bias" enlivens group mobilization to block rights retrenchment, heightening the electoral threat to retrenching politicians. These forces produce a policy status quo that is durable against change through democratic lawmaking processes.

Political Costs of Retrenchment

Ultimately, Justice Department leadership elected not to proceed with sponsoring a bill to amend Section 1983. Department officials concluded that Section 1983 amendments to limit opportunities and incentives for private civil rights enforcement, through desirable, were a losing proposition. They believed that a bill simply could not pass Congress, would taint the administration as anti-civil rights, and was electorally disadvantageous.

A memo by the head of the OLP, after embracing the desirability of Section 1983 amendments, recommended against pursuing a bill, explaining: "any effort by the administration to reform Section 1983 will become enmired in controversy and labeled as yet another assault upon the civil rights laws. Of course, it goes without saying that legislation to amend the Section will stand virtually no chance of success in Congress, particularly with a presidential election around the corner."[56] In the same vein, another OLP memo stated:

> Section 1983 clearly needs an extensive overhaul to correct its many inadequacies . . . However, more modest proposals in the 97th Congress met with considerable opposition from affected groups, particularly those in the civil rights community. More important, the public perception of this Administration's record on civil rights may make it politically unwise for the Administration to sponsor any legislative proposals to restrict what most people would consider key provisions of civil rights laws.[57]

Although the fee-cap bill made it further in the legislative process, it ultimately failed for the same reasons. A number of high-ranking members of the Reagan administration regarded the bill's likely political and electoral costs as much too high. To be sure, advocates of the bill within the administration did not propose publicly advocating for the bill as a means to curtail enforcement of rights. Rather, they sought to frame it as a means of: (1) protecting scarce federal and state tax revenue from middle class lawyers; (2) compensating "private attorneys general" at the same rate as actual government lawyers rather than big law firm lawyers; and (3) protecting state and local autonomy from overzealous private enforcement of federal mandates against states.[58] These themes linked fiscal responsibility and federalism, which were two broad aspects of the administration's core identity. Indeed, several DOJ memoranda on potential Section 1983 amendments advanced the view that the generality of the fee-cap bill – attacking "abuses" in fee awards in general – made it more politically viable, and less politically dangerous, than "singling out civil rights statutes as the place to start cutting back attorneys' fees."[59]

[56] Rose to Smith 6/15/1983.
[57] Robinson to Stewart 6/14/1983.
[58] Mike Horowtiz to Lee Verstandig and Rick Neal, October 19, 1983, Reagan Library, JL007 Case File 20054, Attorneys' Fees Reform Bill.
[59] Rose to Schmults 8/6/1982; Robinson to Stewart 4/20/1983.

However, important administration leaders were extremely doubtful that the terms of the debate over the fee-cap bill could be controlled with this rhetorical strategy. Instead, they foresaw opponents successfully turning the battle into one over the preservation of substantive rights protected by the statutes to be amended – rights to be free of racial and gender discrimination, to be shielded from predatory business practices, to drink clean water, and to breathe clean air. That is, they knew that the administration would be attacked by liberal public interest groups and the plaintiff's bar, and be perceived by a material segment of the voting public as seeking to take popular rights away from vulnerable groups.

They were correct. Liberals regarded the proposal as "designed expressly to discourage public interest litigation by reducing the incentive effect of fee shifting statutes" (Percival and Miller 1984: 244). National media coverage conveyed such groups' dismay to the public. The *Washington Post* alone ran at least three articles on the fee bill in 1982. Leaders of the ACLU, the NAACP, the Wilderness Society, Public Citizen, and the Alliance for Justice – an umbrella organization representing a wide range of liberal public interest law groups – were among those that attacked the proposal in the pages of national newspapers. They emphasized its impact in the areas of civil rights, the environment, consumer welfare, labor, and social welfare benefits. They characterized its likely consequences as "crippling," "choking off," and "devastating" to the enforcement of rights in these fields. The losers, they maintained, would be racial minorities, environmentalists, workers, and the poor. The winners would be the wealthy.[60]

Following this reporting and as if he had been reading it, Attorney General William French Smith observed that striking too severely at attorney's fee awards risked "excessive controversy." He emphasized that in the public relations battle the administration would be cast as "anti" rights. "Attorney's fee cap proposals," Smith wrote, "are thought by public interest litigating organizations to strike at a vital source of their financial support. Accordingly, these groups have characterized fee cap proposals

---

[60] Fred Barbash, ". . . And Uncle Sam Wants to Save on His Legal Fees," *Washington Post*, February 10, 1982, A25; Mary Thornton, "Plaintiffs' Legal Fess Attacked by OMB," *Washington Post*, August 12, 1982, A21; Mary Thornton, "Administration Readies Legislation to Cut Down Legal Fees Set by Courts," *Washington Post*, November 20, 1982, A3; Stuart Taylor, "Fees of Public Interest Lawyers Under Attack," *New York Times*, February 19, 1982, A14; "Cutting Off Lawyers, and Law," *New York Times*, December 31, 1983, 1.22. The *Wall Street Journal* provided favorable editorial coverage. "Ambulance Chasers?," *Wall Street Journal*, February 26, 1981, 26; "Lawyers on the Dole," *Wall Street Journal*, September 8, 1982, 32.

as 'anti-civil rights' or 'anti-environmental' proposals."[61] Opponents of
the proposal would be able to beat it back with "the rhetoric of rights and
justice," as one supporter put it (Greve 1987: 104). Smith also observed
that the timing of the bill seemed particularly bad with an election on the
horizon.[62] When the bill was sent to the president's staff to be cleared in
December 1983, Counsel to the President Fred Fielding echoed Attorney
General Smith's deep concern as to both the bill's political risks and its
questionable electoral timing:

> The circumstances in which attorneys' fees are awarded to parties prevail-
> ing against the government . . . typically involved civil rights litigation, wel-
> fare entitlement suits, environmental litigation, and the like. Since the "fee
> cap bill" would have its greatest impact in these areas, I remain deeply con-
> cerned that it will be viewed and portrayed as yet another Administration
> effort to limit the delivery of legal services to minorities, the poor, and the
> aged . . . I am not convinced that this is the time to open another front in the
> ongoing battle over our record in these areas.[63]

Lack of Moderate Republican Support in Congress

In light of this political calculus, it is not surprising that the fee-cap bill
was ultimately unable to attract the support of moderates in Congress,
even among Republicans. As the administration surveyed the bill's legislative prospects, Democratic control of the House caused many to seriously
doubt that the bill could pass that chamber. But the problem was not only
with the Democrats. Administration officials assessing the bill's prospects
also recognized that it would require the support of moderate Republicans
and conservative Democrats, and they expressed little optimism that
the bill could even pass the Republican-controlled Senate (Decker 2009:
184).[64] Indeed, despite its efforts, the administration was unable even to

---

[61] William French Smith to Cabinet Council on Legal Policy, June 15, 1983, Reagan Library,
James W. Cicconi Files, box 23, Department of Justice (folder 1).
[62] Ibid.
[63] Fred F. Fielding to Richard G. Darman, December 16, 1983, Reagan Library, John G.
Roberts, Jr. Files, box 31, Legal Fees Reform Act (folder 2 of 3). For additional expressions
of this concern, see Fred F. Fielding to Richard Darman, September 21, 1983, Reagan
Library, John G. Roberts, Jr. Files, box 31, Legal Fees Reform Act (folder 1 of 3); Edward
C. Schmults to Michael Horowitz, June 1, 1983, Reagan Library, JL007 Case File 20054,
Attorneys' Fees Reform Bill.
[64] Edward C. Schmults to Edwin Meese III, October 31, 1983, Reagan Library, James W.
Cicconi Files, box 23, Department of Justice (folder 1); Jonathan C. Rose to Edward C.
Schmults, October 27, 1983, Reagan Library, James W. Cicconi Files, box 23, Department
of Justice (folder 1).

find a Republican sponsor for The Limitation of Legal Fees Awards Act of 1981, which died without one (Percival and Miller 1984: 234 n. 8).[65] Some conservative activists recognized, with disappointment, that support within Congress for civil rights, environmental, and consumer groups was very broad, including many moderate Republicans, either because of their sincere preferences or because they feared being cast as an enemy of rights that enjoyed broad public support (Greve 1987: 101–2). Ultimately, the views of William French Smith and Fred Fielding seemed to be shared by many Republicans in Congress. Even if they had any inclination to join the administration's attack on the private enforcement infrastructure, the political calculus was against it.

Lack of Interest Group Support

In causing its (modified) fee-cap bill to be introduced in Congress, the administration appears to have underestimated the degree of opposition that it would face, and to have overestimated the degree of support the bill would enjoy. Prior to announcing the bill, the administration initiated contacts with "interested groups," which it deemed to be State attorneys general, municipal law enforcement officers, mayors, business, and liberal public interest organizations. The administration, of course, anticipated strong opposition from liberal public interest organizations and from the for-profit plaintiffs' bar, both of which stood to lose if the fee-cap bill succeeded.[66] As we have noted, the threat or reality of such opposition weakened support for the fee-cap bill within the Republican Party. However, the administration anticipated support from states and business. As it turned out, both were internally divided.

With respect to state officials – attorneys general, local government attorneys, and mayors – the administration anticipated support because the bill would preserve state and city tax resources against fee awards and reduce incentives for private federal lawsuits against cities and states.[67] However, of these groups only the National Association of State Attorneys General promised support. The National Institute of Municipal Law Officers (an organization of local government attorneys) declined to take a

---

[65] *See* Mary Thornton, "Plaintiffs' Legal Fess Attacked by OMB," *Washington Post*, August 12, 1982, A21.

[66] Rose to Schmults 10/27/1983; Smith to Cabinet Council 6/15/1983; Fred Barbash, ". . . And Uncle Sam Wants to Save on His Legal Fees," *Washington Post*, February 10, 1982, A25.

[67] Horowtiz to Verstandig and Neal 10/19/1983; Rose to Schmults 10/27/1983.

public position, and the United States Conference of Mayors would at best remain silent, but threatened possible public opposition. Representatives of local government attorneys explained that they actually regarded fee awards as being of marginal significance relative to overall liability and that they would take no position on the legislation. They did not explain why, even if liability was larger than fees, they would still not support capping fees, which would reduce incentives for lawsuits and liability exposure at least somewhat.[68] The position of the Conference of Mayors provides possible illumination of their motivation.

A representative of the Conference of Mayors explained to administration officials that most members of the Conference (which represents larger cities) "would react negatively" to the bill and would oppose it. Despite the frequency of lawsuits against cities, he explained, "the mayors themselves were more likely to be sympathetic to the interests of the plaintiffs." The representative indicated that any policy that would reduce incentives for enforcement of civil rights and environmental legislation, in particular, would be especially likely to provoke opposition given the broad popularity of such policies. The calculus for position-taking by mayors was not so straightforward as simply supporting the bill because cities are the targets of lawsuits and fee awards. Rather, the calculus also included weighing the popularity of rights-protecting federal regulation among the constituents of big city mayors, not to mention their potential sincere support for the laws. The Conference of Mayors representative also indicated that the issue of attorney's fees had arisen in the past and proven "so controversial that it has not been able to come to the floor of the Conference." He advised that if the Conference managed to muster any public position on the administration's fee-cap bill it would be negative. Thus, of the three state groups from which the administration sought support, State AGs would support the administration, local government attorneys would not, and the Conference of Mayors might publicly oppose.[69]

To the administration's surprise, business was divided as well, although for different reasons. The administration anticipated that business interests would be served by reducing fee awards to plaintiffs' counsel litigating against governments under federal statutes, since such litigation includes challenges by liberal groups to administrative regulatory policymaking calculated to move regulatory law in a liberal direction. Reducing the influence of liberal public interest organizations on federal and state

[68] Rose to Schmults 10/27/1983.
[69] Ibid.

policymaking, the administration thought, would capture business support for the fee-cap bill. Further, a victory for the fee-cap bill as applied to litigation against government could be the thin end of a wedge, opening the possibility of retrenching private enforcement as applied to the private sector. After the administration gauged the preferences of business leaders, it concluded that big business could be counted on for support. Small business, however, looked like a big problem. Administration strategy memos on the bill suggested, with disappointment, that it threatened to provoke the "wrath of the small business community."[70]

The reason was that, ironically, small businesses had themselves developed an interest in preserving fee awards under the Equal Access to Justice Act, and that interest was threatened by the administration's bill. With Republicans and business as legislative catalysts, in 1980 Congress had enacted the Equal Access to Justice Act, which provided for attorney's fee awards for small businesses, individuals, and organizations that prevail against the federal government in administrative or judicial proceedings in which they challenge the legitimacy of federal regulatory actions. The law, passed as part of a small business assistance statute, was primarily intended to aid small businesses in challenging excessive and unreasonable regulation by the federal government, including prosecutions of small businesses accused of violating regulatory laws. In the absence of fee shifting, it was argued, small businesses often had limited capacity or incentive to resist the abuse of federal regulatory power. The fee shift would help to level the playing field and curb excessive and unreasonable regulation (Ragozin 1986: 219–21; Mezey and Olson 1993: 13–20; Sisk 1994: 220–9, 280 n. 396).[71] When the Reagan administration's fee-cap bill became public, small business groups made clear that they would not give up their new weapon quietly and that any effort to take it away would be regarded as "break[ing] faith with the small-business community," as one business association leader declared in an interview published in the *Wall Street Journal*.[72]

After the initial versions of Reagan's fee-cap bill failed to find a congressional sponsor even within the president's own party, the administration developed a more moderate version of the proposal. In 1984, hearings were held on this bill in a Senate subcommittee chaired by Orrin Hatch

[70] Horowitz to Hauser and Kabel 6/16/1983; Horowitz to Stockman and Harper 6/22/1982; Rose to Schmults 10/27/1983.
[71] H.R. 1418, 96th Cong., 2nd Sess., 1980, 12; S. 253, 96th Cong., 1st Sess., 1979, 7.
[72] "Small-Business Groups Protest Reagan's Veto of Bill for Legal Fees," *Wall Street Journal*, November 12, 1984, 3.

(R. UT), who championed the bill, known as the Legal Fee Equity Act of 1984, as a much needed corrective to the proliferation of statutory fee-shifting rules in the 1970s, creating "exorbitant windfalls for lawyers," leading to an "explosion of litigation" which had "clogged the courts."[73]

Hatch had sponsored bills in 1981[74] and 1983[75] that differed in many respects from the Reagan administration bill, most prominently for present purposes because they targeted civil rights cases. Like the Legal Fee Equity Act of 1984, however, the Hatch bills contained a provision denying fees incurred after a prevailing party rejected an offer of judgment if the relief obtained was not more favorable than the offer.[76] Despite Hatch's alignment with conservatives in the administration who sought to retrench the private enforcement infrastructure, he was unable to muster support for the Legal Fee Equity Act of 1984 in his own Republican-controlled committee, where the bill died.

Alternative Pathway of Courts

Many scholars have observed that the Reagan administration's law-reform objectives were profoundly inhibited by Democratic control of one or both chambers of Congress (Litan and Nordhaus 1983: 119–32; McGarity 1986: 260–70; Greve 1987: 101–4; Vogel 1989: 246–65; Farhang 2010: 172–213; Farhang 2012). One particular strand of work is relevant to the long-run inter-institutional story of private enforcement retrenchment. That strand argues, we believe persuasively, that the Reagan administration saw the federal judiciary as an important alternative avenue to effect legal change that could not be accomplished through Congress. As Mark Graber put it, "[t]he Reagan administration sought to achieve its social agenda primarily by staffing the Justice Department and judiciary with movement conservatives" (Graber 1993: 63; see also O'Brien 1988: 60–7; Murphy 1990: 219–21; Goldman 1997; Pickerill and Clayton 2004: 241–2; Whittington 2007: 226-7). It sought thereby to lay the foundation for law reform through federal litigation and federal judges – without the aid of legislators. Although this claim has generally focused on the administration's constitutional

---

[73] *Hearings on the Legal Fee Equity Act (S. 2802) Before the Subcommittee on the Constitution of the Senate Judiciary Committee*, 98th Cong., 2nd Sess., 1984, 1–3.

[74] S. 585, 97th Cong. (1981).

[75] S. 141, 98th Cong. (1983). Senator Thurmond co-sponsored this bill.

[76] *See* S. 585, 97th Cong., § 2(c) (added in 1982 mark up); S. 141, 98th Cong., § 2(c) (1983); S. 2802, 98th Cong., § 8(2) (1984).

commitments, we argue that the strategy played out on the issue of private enforcement retrenchment as well.

In the OLP memorandum concluding that Section 1983 amendments "will become enmired in controversy and . . . stand virtually no chance of success in Congress, particularly with a presidential election around the corner," Jonathan Rose, head of OLP, went on to propose the alternative pathway of courts. What could not be accomplished by statutory amendment could be accomplished by statutory interpretation.

> I would . . . suggest that the Department study the possibility of pursing changes to the Section through a program of *amicus* participation in Section 1983 actions in the courts of appeals and the Supreme Court . . . I believe that the Department's participation in selected Section 1983 cases might have an important influence on the outcome of these cases and provide significant interim relief to states and cities until Congress enacts a legislative solution.[77]

The Rose memo went on to identify, as an example for amicus participation, a case pending before the Supreme Court "involving several important issues concerning the availability and means of calculating attorneys' fee awards in Section 1983 actions."[78] At the time he wrote this memo in 1983, Rose was head of the OLP, whose responsibilities included screening potential judicial nominees. As head of the screening committee, Rose has been credited as an important and successful advocate for the Reagan administration's emphasis on careful scrutiny of potential judicial nominees' ideological alignment with administration policy priorities (Goldman 1997: 291; Lyles 1997: 144; Murphy 2014: 96). Rose had worked with Scalia both in the firm Jones Day (with a notable corporate defense practice), and in the Nixon and Ford administrations, and he championed Scalia's appointment to the D.C. Circuit shortly after Scalia's public endorsement of the Reagan fee-cap bill in the American Enterprise Institute's *Regulation* magazine (Murphy 2014: 96).[79] Rose was recently Secretary of the Standing Committee on Rules of Practice and Procedure and Chief of the Rules Committee Support Office in the Administrative Office of the US Courts.

In the same vein, writing to then-Counselor to the President Edwin Meese, Deputy Attorney General Edward Schmults expressed both his skepticism that Congress could achieve private enforcement retrenchment

---

[77] Rose to Smith 6/15/1983.
[78] Ibid.
[79] *See supra* note 16 and accompanying text.

via statutory amendment, and his optimism that the Supreme Court could achieve the underlying goals via statutory interpretation. About the Reagan fee bill, he wrote:

> From a political standpoint . . . it is probable that a serious fee reform bill would sharply divide Congress . . . [and] like other controversial legislation, it is unlikely that the bill would be enacted into law . . . As in the past, real progress in curtailing abuses in the award of attorneys' fees is likely to be gained through the Supreme Court, where we have enjoyed considerable success in recent years . . . An administration fee reform bill will bring to the public eye many of the policies we have been espousing before the courts.[80]

Schmults went on to detail successful efforts by the Justice Department to curtail statutory fee awards in civil rights, employment, and environmental litigation in federal courts, including the Supreme Court. Schmults had been a partner in the firm of White & Case (with a notable corporate defense practice), had worked in the Nixon and Ford administrations, including as Deputy Counsel to President Ford and co-chair of his Domestic Council Review Group on Regulatory Reform, and was a member of the Council of the Administrative Conference of the United States.[81] After leading the team to vet vice presidential candidates for then-Governor Reagan, he was appointed to his DOJ leadership position.[82] Schmults' duties at DOJ included working with Rose to identify judicial candidates and secure their appointment to the federal bench (Goldman 1997: 287–8, 308, 325).

Data on amicus filings confirm that the Reagan administration undertook an amicus campaign in earnest on private enforcement issues. We coded counts of the number of amicus briefs filed in each of our private enforcement cases (discussed in Chapter 4) that contained only the private enforcement issue, so that we can know that the briefs actually addressed the private enforcement issues (279 of 365 cases). In this body of cases, the Nixon–Ford administrations and the Carter administration filed five, six, and four amicus briefs in their three successive presidential terms. In

---

[80] Schmults to Meese 10/31/1983.
[81] "Nomination of Edward C. Schmults to Be Deputy Attorney General," January 23, 1981, *The American Presidency Project* (Gerhard Peters and John T. Woolley), available at www.presidency.ucsb.edu/ws/?pid=43713
[82] Michael K. Deaver, Edwin Meese III, and Richard B. Wirthlin, "The Accidental Vice President," October 2, 2000, *New York Times Magazine*; Edwin Meese III, "How Reagan Helped to Build the House of Bush," January 30, 2001, *Hoover Digest*, available at www.hoover.org/research/how-reagan-helped-build-house-bush

the three presidential terms comprising the Reagan–Bush years, the numbers were 19, 17, and 18. No subsequent administration through 2014 has equaled this level.

Rose and Schmults were keen observers of American politics and government. They were optimistic that the federal judiciary, which they worked hard to staff with ideological allies, would prove the most promising terrain for a private enforcement retrenchment campaign that had proven politically divisive and electorally risky, and that had no chance of success in Congress. We show in Chapter 4 that they were right.

Conclusion

The first Reagan administration's fee-cap bill was among the most aggressive attacks on the private enforcement infrastructure in federal regulation ever undertaken, and the Section 1983 amendments that it seriously considered were comparably ambitious. They marked the beginning of a movement to retrench private enforcement, and that movement quickly spread to congressional Republicans, among whom the introduction of such bills grew steeply beginning in the early 1980s. Statutory private enforcement regimes were thereby transformed from a relatively nonpartisan issue prior to the first Reagan administration into the source of partisan cleavage that we know today.

In this chapter we have documented the substantial failure of this Republican legislative project in the elected branches and the reasons for that failure. Archival materials from the Reagan administration provide a rich and clear picture of why its initiatives failed, and we believe that the episode teaches some important lessons about the resilience of the Litigation State in the domain of legislative politics. First, as a matter of political framing, it was difficult for advocates of retrenching private enforcement to separate the legal structures of private enforcement (like fee shifts) from the substantive rights to which they were attached. Their attempt to retrench enforcement provisions elicited public attention and a political response little different than if they had sought to repeal substantive rights. This rights focus of the debate caused divisions within the Reagan White House and the Republican Party, with the risk of electoral and reputational costs a key motivation for those who successfully opposed the retrenchment initiatives.

Second, over the course of time the interests tied to private enforcement deepened and widened, making private enforcement more difficult to uproot. Liberal law reform organizations became invested in retaining their own access to fee awards, and even more so in protecting the life-blood of the private enforcement infrastructure that they had so assiduously cultivated. Moreover, the private for-profit bar thereby cultivated sought to protect its own interests, adding heft and capacity to the coalition defending the private enforcement status quo when the retrenchment movement emerged in the early Reagan years.

The interests tied to private enforcement spread even to some quarters of business, which is typically regarded as an opponent. In Chapter 1 we note the irony in conservative Republicans – over the objections of liberals – insisting on Title VII's private enforcement regime. The irony was compounded when conservative Republicans pressed for small business to participate in the bounty of fee awards through the Equal Access to Justice Act, thereby helping to cement the whole system in place by extending its benefits into the Republican base. The costs of that move – and the difficulty of retrenching private enforcement regimes, no matter who the beneficiary – became apparent when small business interests refused to support the Reagan fee-cap bill.

APPENDIX

In our bill data models, the dependent variables are counts of the number of legislators sponsoring or co-sponsoring litigation retrenchment bills. Because the distribution of event counts is discrete, not continuous, and is limited to non-negative values, it is best modeled assuming that the errors follow a Poisson distribution rather than a normal distribution. A negative binomial count model is appropriate for data with this structure in the presence of overdispersion of the dependent variable, which is the case with the data analyzed here. Overdispersion is present where the variance exceeds the mean, violating an assumption of a standard Poisson model (Cameron and Trivedi 2013).

We cluster standard errors on legislator because standard regression models (without clustering) treat each legislator's support for a bill as independent from his/her support for other bills, but episodes of bill support by the same legislator are not independent from one another. Non-independent observations add less information to regression estimates than independent observations. Clustering standard errors on legislator adjusts standard errors to account for this and thereby avoids standard errors that are too small (Wooldridge 2013: ch. 14).

For the models of the 93rd to 96th Congresses (Table 2.3), and the 97th to the 113th Congresses (Table 2.4), we ran alternative specifications substituting common space NOMINATE scores for party. These scores are continuous measures of legislator ideology based on a spatial model of roll call voting behavior, and thus they are a granular ideology measure as compared to the dichotomous party variable (Poole and Rosenthal 1997). With this ideology measure substituted for party, we obtained results parallel to those reported in Tables 2.3 and 2.4 in terms of statistical significance, direction of effect, and rough magnitude.

In the models of the 93rd to 96th Congresses (Table 2.3), we had in excess of 90% zeros in our dependent variables, suggesting the potential need for zero-inflated models (Cameron and Trivedi 2013: 139–42). We replicated the models in Table 2.3 with zero-inflated negative binomial count models and obtained very similar results: statistical insignificance in the "All bills" and "Monetary recovery" models, and a significant negative coefficient of comparable size in the "Procedure" model.[83]

The coefficients of a count model are not directly interpretable. In order to transform them into interpretable form, an x-unit increase in an independent variable translates into a factor change in the rate of the dependent variable given by $\exp(x\beta)$. For example, for a coefficient of .655, the factor change in the expected count for a one-unit change in the associated independent variable is given by exponentiating $((1)(.655))$, which equals 1.93. This means that when the independent variable is increased by one unit, holding other variables constant, the expected number of enactments increases by a factor 1.93. This is the equivalent of saying that the expected number of enactments increases by 93%. This is how all marginal effects were computed.

[83] These models were run using Stata's zinb command.

3

Rulemaking Counterrevolution: Birth, Reaction, and Struggle

Introduction

In Chapter 2 we show that the counterrevolution against private enforcement of federal law became a partisan project in the elected branches during the first Reagan administration and that its sponsors did not have notable success in the ensuing decades. Victories were few and usually hard-fought; they clustered in discrete policy areas, and, viewed in isolation, they left the Litigation State largely intact.

The federal judiciary can frustrate or enable legislative policy concerning private enforcement in many ways. In order to understand and measure the extent of that phenomenon, one of the legal domains we explore comprises matters on which the judiciary was long ceded the first, and essentially the final, word: federal procedural law. The federal judiciary's procedural lawmaking is not confined to creating and interpreting rules while deciding cases in the exercise of judicial power under Article III of the Constitution. In the Rules Enabling Act of 1934 and its statutory successors,[1] Congress has delegated to the Supreme Court the power to promulgate prospective, legislation-like rules of procedure to govern proceedings in the federal trial courts – the Federal Rules of Civil Procedure (Federal Rules). Moreover, in order to fashion them the Court has increasingly relied on other bodies within, and members of, the federal judiciary. Court rulemaking occupies intermediate lawmaking space that bridges legislative and judicial power (Burbank 2004a).

Some Federal Rules effectively determine access to court and likelihood of success in court for those seeking to enforce federal rights through litigation. Rulemaking was an ally of private enforcement from 1938, when the original Federal Rules became effective, through the 1960s. It became

---

[1] Act of June 19, 1934, Pub. L. No. 73-415, 48 Stat. 1064. For the current statutory authority, *see* 28 U.S.C. §§ 2072–74 (2012).

a focus of retrenchment efforts starting in 1971, a decade before the counterrevolution took off, and became a partisan project, in the elected branches. In this chapter, using qualitative and quantitative evidence, we first chronicle rulemaking's role in stimulating private enforcement, and we then identify its role in the counterrevolution. In Chapter 4, where we focus on Supreme Court decisions implicating private enforcement, we complete the picture of procedure's role by assessing the work of the Court in cases that call for interpretation of Federal Rules.

In this chapter, we show that under Chief Justice Warren Burger and his successors, all of whom were appointed by Republican presidents, the Advisory Committee on Civil Rules, which has primary responsibility for drafting the Federal Rules, came to be dominated by federal judges appointed by Republican presidents and, among its practitioner members, by corporate lawyers (and in recent years by corporate defense lawyers). We also demonstrate that, although few of the Committee's proposals in the long period we study were salient to private enforcement, those that were increasingly disfavored it. Finally, we explore reasons why, given these trends, court rulemaking has been a site of only episodic and modest retrenchment, and we raise the question whether intensely controversial 2015 amendments to the discovery rules signal a more robust role for rule-making in the counterrevolution going forward.

Chief Justice Burger was successful in stanching the 1960s' flow of Federal Rules that favored private enforcement. He had hopes for bold retrenchment, however, which reflected both institutional (docket) concerns and, at least as time went by, his own views about litigation as a social problem. Those hopes were largely frustrated. Notwithstanding Burger's encouragement, the Advisory Committee, which he wholly reconstituted in 1971, sent forward few proposed amendments during the 1970s. Their recommendations were much less ambitious than proposals advanced in the 1960s, and the only two proposed amendments that were salient to private enforcement favored it. Moreover, once influential interest groups and members of Congress thought that the Advisory Committee was embracing the goals of the counterrevolution – in the early 1980s – the Committee's work-product caused a backlash. The changes in the rule-making process that ensued had the effect, and for some advocates of change the purpose, of impeding retrenchment by Federal Rule. To that extent, the changes insulated the (pro-enforcement) status quo.

Burger's inability to control the judge-dominated committee he appointed in the 1970s may have influenced him to rely more heavily on selecting judges appointed by Republican presidents and corporate practitioners whose known or presumed views favored retrenchment. He thus intensi-fied a partisan slant in the appointment of judges, and a pro-corporate slant in the appointment of practitioners, that continued under Chief Justices Rehnquist and Roberts. Still, the stickiness of the rulemaking status quo since the 1980s has made bold retrenchment difficult to achieve, even for those who are ideologically disposed to it. This record of modest success in retrenchment by the Advisory Committee sets in relief the phenomenon we document in Chapter 4: the ability of a conservative majority of the Supreme Court to make potentially significant inroads in private enforcement when deciding cases, including cases that call for interpretation of Federal Rules.

Our evidence also demonstrates, however, that, notwithstanding a designedly sticky process, the Chief Justice and the leaders of the rule-making committees can exercise important influence on the ambition or restraint of proposed reforms. Viewed in that light, the 2015 amendments to the discovery rules may suggest that the prior period of relative restraint by the rulemakers was an interlude in an ongoing struggle. Among those disposed to the goals of the counterrevolution, it is a struggle in which con-cerns about the perceived legitimacy of the Enabling Act process vie with the desire to exercise power. Another plausible view of those amendments, however, sees them as confirming the difficulty of ambitious retrenchment through rulemaking, with the struggle moved to the domain of interpreta-tion by the federal courts.

Building a Litigation Highway

The original Federal Rules of Civil Procedure became effective in 1938, four years after the successful conclusion of a decades-long campaign that culminated in the Rules Enabling Act of 1934. The leaders of the cam-paign sought to have Congress delegate to the Supreme Court legislative power to make prospective rules for the conduct of all civil actions. They dismissed the notion that procedure's potential impact on the enforce-ment of substantive law was cause for concern. They assured their audi-ences not only that procedure is technical and requires expert knowledge to fashion – which certainly may be true – but also that it is "details" or "adjective law," subsidiary in importance to, and operating independently of, substantive law – which very often is not true. Such rhetoric, deployed by those favoring judicial over legislative control of procedure, helped the federal judiciary to secure a virtual monopoly over procedural lawmaking and to retain it for decades following the promulgation of the 1938 Federal Rules (Burbank 1982; Burbank 1985; Burbank 2004a).

More recently, informed observers have acknowledged the power of procedure to affect substantive rights. Indeed, the Supreme Court has acknowledged it as well, observing in 1989:

> [T]his Court's rulemaking under the enabling Acts has been substantive and political in the sense that the rules of procedure have important effects on the substantive rights of litigants ... Rule 23 of the Federal Rules of Civil Procedure, for example, has inspired a controversy over the philosophical, social, and economic merits and demerits of class actions.[2]

The partisan valence of bills seeking to affect private enforcement through changes to procedural law that we discuss in Chapter 2 confirms that members of Congress, too, understand the regulatory power of procedure. Legislators tapping into procedure's power to implement regulatory policies may hope that the traditional rhetoric still persuades – that procedure can be a wolf in sheep's clothing.

The market in which the judiciary secured a virtual monopoly under the Enabling Act was the market for "general rules."[3] The original Federal Rules were general in the sense that they were applicable in all federal trial courts throughout the country. In addition, the Advisory Committee that drafted them interpreted the term "general" to require that the rules be applicable in all types of cases, that is to say, transsubstantive (Burbank 1989a; Burbank 2009). Whatever the normative case for transsubstantive procedure (D. Marcus 2010; D. Marcus 2013a), it facilitates rulemakers' claims of lawmaking neutrality. Transsubstantive scope makes it inevitable that many Federal Rules are written at a high level of indeterminacy, according substantial discretion to the courts interpreting and applying them (Burbank 1989a). This feature serves the institutional interests of the federal judiciary. It permits rulemakers to bury policy choices that federal judges will ultimately have to make in the context of case-by-case interpretation. As explained later in this chapter, if those policy choices were made explicitly in a Federal Rule, Congress would have an opportunity to veto them before they became effective (Burbank 1987). In this sense, the transsubstantive scope of Federal Rules helps to insulate judicial policymaking from congressional review. It also accords federal judges, at the interpretive stage, broad policymaking discretion.

---

[2] *Mistretta* v. *United States*, 488 U.S. 361, 393 & n. 19 (1989).
[3] For the text of the 1934 Act, *see* Burbank 1982: 1097–8. The pertinent current language remains the same.

Pleading and Discovery under the Federal Rules

The 1938 Federal Rules were litigation-friendly. In this they reflected the jurisprudential and social commitments of the individuals who were responsible for drafting them.[4] The way that those individuals approached pleading and discovery in the 1938 Federal Rules made these procedural features critical pillars of the regime they created, and it is thus not surprising that, as we discuss later in this chapter and in Chapter 4, they have been important sites of contestation.

Pleading rules regulate the process by which, and the specificity with which, parties must assert their claims and defenses at the outset of litigation. The drafters of the Federal Rules repudiated "fact pleading," which required that a plaintiff's complaint state all facts necessary to establish each cause of action. Instead, they opted for what would become known as "notice pleading," under which a plaintiff is required to state a claim that is legally tenable on any set of facts, and to do so only in sufficient detail to give the defendant fair notice of what that claim is. Thus, Federal Rule 8 requires that a complaint include only "a short and plain statement of the claim showing that the pleader is entitled to relief." The drafters had little use for rules that obstructed a clear view of the facts and prevented resolution of disputes on their merits. They believed that pleadings are an inferior method to find out what actually happened (Subrin 1987).

Implementing the view that pleading should play a minor role in litigation required other means to ascertain facts prior to trial. To that end, the architects of the 1938 Federal Rules wrote rules that afforded parties pre-trial authority to demand information from other parties (and non-parties) much greater than had been available under prior systems (Sunderland 1939; Burbank 2004b). Such broad discovery appealed to the commitments of the Progressive movement in American law, of which Edson Sunderland, the chief architect of the Federal Rules on discovery, had long been a proponent (Burbank 2004b). Progressives contended that effective regulation was impossible without access to the facts concerning the regulated enterprise (Kersch 2002). As Sunderland wrote in 1925:

> The spirit of the times calls for disclosure, not concealment, in every field – in business dealings, in governmental activities, in international relations, and the experience of England makes it clear that the courts need no longer permit litigating parties to raid one another from ambush (116).

---

[4] Of course, those who drafted the original Federal Rules were not free agents. On the non-academic members of the original Advisory Committee, *see* Burbank 2004a: 1718.

The legal profession alone halts and hesitates. If it is to retain the esteem
and confidence of a progressive age, it must itself become progressive (129).

Discovery under the 1938 Federal Rules conferred on private litigants
and their attorneys the functional equivalent of administrative subpoena
power (Carrington 1997; Higginbotham 1997).

Advisory Committee

The system that the Court devised to exercise the power that Congress
delegated in the Enabling Act remained essentially the same until 1956.
An Advisory Committee appointed by the Court prepared draft Federal
Rules and amendments, with some (albeit, by modern standards, limited) input from the bench and bar, for consideration by the Court and, if
acceptable, reporting to Congress. Once so reported proposed rules went
into effect if not vetoed by Congress in legislation signed by the president
within a specified period.[5] The Advisory Committee became a continuing
body in 1942.[6] Because there were no prescribed terms, its membership
remained remarkably stable thereafter. Indeed, it may be that a reason for
the Committee's peremptory discharge "with thanks" in 1956[7] was the perception that it consisted primarily of old men.[8]

The Committee's discharge prompted concerns about the "void" that
resulted (Clark 1969). To address those concerns, the judiciary sought,
and in 1958 Congress enacted, legislation revamping the rulemaking process. The 1958 legislation directed the Judicial Conference of the United
States, through which the federal judiciary formulates and supervises the
implementation of institutional policy, to "carry on a continuous study of
the operation and effect of" the various rules of practice and procedure
promulgated under the Enabling Act. It further directed the Conference to
recommend to the Court "[s]uch changes in and additions to those rules
as the Conference may deem desirable to promote simplicity in procedure,
fairness in administration, the just determination of litigation, and the

---

[5] For the order appointing the original Advisory Committee, see 295 U.S. 774 (1935). Note
that the statutory arrangements governing the Enabling Act's "report and wait" system
changed in 1950. See Act of May 10, 1950, ch. 174, § 2, 64 Stat. 158; Burbank 1982: 1077 n.
268. As we discuss later in this chapter, they changed again in 1988.

[6] See Continuance of Advisory Committee, 314 U.S. 720 (1942).

[7] See Order Discharging the Advisory Committee, 352 U.S. 803 (1956).

[8] See "A Self-Study of Federal Judicial Rulemaking: A Report from the Subcommittee on
Long Range Planning to the Committee on Rules of Practice, Procedure and Evidence of
the Judicial Conference of the United States," 168 F.R.D. 679, 685 (1995).

elimination of unjustifiable expense and delay."[9] The Judicial Conference promptly decided to exercise its statutory duties through a system of advisory committees reporting to a single Standing Committee, which in turn reported to the Conference.[10]

As provided by the Conference's 1958 resolution, the Chief Justice, as Chair of the Conference, appoints the members of all Conference rule-making committees, thereby preserving them from the "degradation" that was feared if those committees were not closely linked to the Court (Clark 1969: xix). Chief Justice Warren appointed the members of the reconstituted Advisory Committee on Civil Rules in April 1960. The original (1935–8) Advisory Committee consisted exclusively of practicing lawyers (9 or 69%) and academics (4 or 31%)[11] – with two members having previously held judicial office. The fifteen-member committee appointed by Chief Justice Warren comprised seven practitioners (47%), four academics (27%), three judges (20%), and one ex officio government official (7%).

In remarks to the reconstituted Advisory Committee at its first meeting in 1960, Chief Justice Warren confided that "the responsibility of keeping these rules up to date – and the fact that we were not doing it – weighed very heavily on us." Reasoning that under the new system "all the legal profession can have the satisfaction of knowing that [the Federal Rules] are current," Warren added that the Court did not "expect great changes to be made in the rules." "On the contrary," he continued, "we feel that in the main our rules work very well. We don't advocate any radical changes, or even any considerable departure from . . . the Civil Rules as they exist."[12]

No one familiar with federal court rulemaking would characterize the work of the reconstituted Advisory Committee in the 1960s as merely keeping the Federal Rules up-to-date. Starting with a review and reworking of its predecessor's 1955 proposals, on which the Court had taken no action, the Advisory Committee produced substantial packages of

---

[9] Act of July 11, 1958, Pub. L. No. 85-313, 72 Stat. 356.
[10] Report of the Proceedings of the Regular Annual Meeting of the Judicial Conference of the United States, September 1958, at 6–7, available at www.uscourts.gov/about-federal-courts/reports-proceedings-1950s
[11] We do not count Reporters, who are always academics, as members of the Committee for this purpose.
[12] Minutes of the December 1960 Meeting of the Advisory Committee on Civil Rules, at 2–4, available at www.uscourts.gov/rules-policies/archives/meeting-minutes/advisory-committee-rules-civil-procedure-december-1960.
      These minutes contain hand-written edits, all in the same handwriting. Since they include changes to the Chief Justice's transcribed remarks, we assume that they were the work of the Chairman, Dean Acheson. The quotations in the text reflect the edits.

proposals leading to amendments that became effective in 1961, 1963, 1966, 1970, and 1971. While sitting for 19% of the study period (1960–2014), the 1960s Advisory Committee produced 80 proposals (at the Rule level),[13] comprising 31% of all proposals to amend the Federal Rules that the Committee sent forward over the period. Twelve of these proposals predictably implicated private enforcement, comprising 36% of all such proposals that we identified for the study period.

1966 Class Action Amendments

The 1966 amendments to Rule 23 (class actions) alone constituted "great changes," and many would call them "radical." We discuss these amendments in some detail for two reasons. They provide important historical context for understanding the power of the Federal Rules to mobilize private enforcement. In addition, they highlight why those leading the counterrevolution – in Congress, on the Advisory Committee, and on the Court – have set their sights on the Federal Rules in general, and class actions in particular, as potentially fertile terrain for retrenchment.

Prior to the Federal Rules, class actions were permitted in a limited set of circumstances marked out by the practice of courts of equity in England. The class action rule that the Court promulgated in 1938 divided the world of group litigation into three parts, colloquially called true, hybrid, and spurious class actions. The distinctions among them turned on an analysis of the abstract nature of the rights involved that often verged on the metaphysical. For this and other reasons, class actions did not play a major role in federal litigation prior to the 1960s (Kalven and Rosenfield 1941; Yeazell 1987; Hazard, Gedid, and Sowle 1998; Burbank and Wolff 2010).

The 1960s Advisory Committee's stated agenda in revising Rule 23 was largely uncontroversial.[14] They sought to turn federal jurisprudence from abstract inquiries to functional analysis that considered the practical effects of litigation. To that end, in Rule 23(a) the Committee specified four requirements applicable to all litigation if it was to proceed as a class action, colloquially called numerosity, commonality, typicality,

---

[13] Later in this chapter, we discuss alternative ways to measure the volume of proposals.

[14] The stated goals of the Advisory Committee can be found in the Advisory Committee Note that accompanied the 1966 amendments. Benjamin Kaplan, the Reporter, elaborated his views on those goals in articles published after the amendments became effective. *See* Kaplan 1966; Kaplan 1969. In addition to these sources, this account draws on our reading of records of the Committee's deliberations and on the recent work of David Marcus, which confirms our reading.

and adequacy of representation. They also reformulated the categories appropriate for class action treatment and specified different procedural requirements depending on the category.

The first category (Rule 23(b)(1)), capturing the core of traditional practice, allowed class actions in situations where separate lawsuits might either establish incompatible standards of conduct for the opposing party or necessarily affect the interests of non-party claimants.[15] The second category (Rule 23(b)(2)), conceptually close to the first, allowed class actions where class-wide injunctive or declaratory relief was appropriate. The Advisory Committee's primary purpose in this category was to provide prospective relief to classes of civil rights plaintiffs, helping to give practical meaning to emerging constitutional and statutory rights. As David Marcus has noted, "other than desegregation, no substantive concern surfaced in committee deliberations" (D. Marcus 2013b: 605).

It was the third category (Rule 23(b)(3)) that marked the 1966 amendments to Rule 23 as a break from the past. Here, a court may certify a case as a class action if it finds that "the questions of law or fact common to the members of the class predominate over any questions affecting only individual members, and that a class action is superior to other available methods for the fair and efficient adjudication of the controversy." If the court does so certify, Rule 23 requires notice to the members of the class, together with the opportunity to opt out of the action, avoiding its preclusive (binding) effects.

Although the Advisory Committee could not have foreseen all of the effects of their handiwork in Rule 23(b)(3), the members were aware that they were breaking new ground. "Class actions were a litigation backwater when they began work, but they seemed to have some sense that their obscure rule would assume far greater importance going forward" (D. Marcus 2013b: 608). Thus, they recognized that Rule 23(b)(3) would enable people with small claims for whom individual litigation would be economically irrational (those with "negative value claims") to band together in litigation against a common adversary.

Contrary to the view espoused by the Supreme Court[16] (and many commentators), however, this was not the Advisory Committee's main

---

[15] See Ortiz v. Fibreboard Corp., 527 U.S. 815 (1999).

[16] Amchem Products, Inc. v. Windsor, 521 U.S. 591, 617 (1997) ("While the text of Rule 23(b) (3) does not exclude from certification cases in which individual damages run high, the Advisory Committee had dominantly in mind vindication of 'the rights of groups of people who individually would be without effective strength to bring their opponents into court at all.' Kaplan, Prefatory Note 497.").

purpose in 23(b)(3).[17] The Court's interpretation is difficult to square with the Advisory Committee Note, which foregrounds the goal of "achiev[ing] the economies of time, effort, and expense, and promot[ing] uniformity of decision as to persons similarly situated." Class actions packaging negative value claims create litigation; they do not make existing or prospective litigation more efficient or consistent.[18] It is even more difficult to square with Rule 23(c)(2)'s requirement of individual notice to members of (b)(3) classes who can be identified with reasonable effort. For most people with small claims, notice and an opportunity to opt out are hardly important, while paying for notice may present insuperable financial obstacles for those representing the class.[19] Finally, the record of the Committee's deliberations does not support the Court's assertion in *Amchem*.[20]

Long before the 1966 amendments to Rule 23 – in the 19th century – federal courts carved out an exception to the American Rule (according to which each party pays its own attorney's fees, win or lose) in order to ensure that those who created a "common fund" could be reimbursed from that fund. This exception to the American Rule recognizes that a

---

[17] David Marcus reached the same conclusion (2013b: 599–600, 605–06), as did John Coffee (2015: 61–3).

[18] The only reference to small claims in the section of the Note explaining (b)(3) came toward the end. In discussing the interest of individuals in conducting separate lawsuits (one of the factors pertinent to predominance and superiority), the Committee observed that such interest may be "theoretic rather than practical . . . [because] the amounts at stake for individuals may be so small that separate suits would be impracticable."

[19] The unpublished record reveals that these aspects of the revised rule were added late in the drafting process to meet concerns that the subdivision might be used by defendants, in league with class counsel, to bind those with *large* individual claims through group litigation inimical to their interests (Burbank 2008; D. Marcus 2013b).

[20] The *Amchem* court relied heavily on Kaplan's articles. The small-claims class action loomed larger among Kaplan's goals than it did among those of the Advisory Committee as a whole. Moreover, it only became prominent in his remarks to the Committee late in the process of developing the rule, when the argument that (b)(3) was the "small man's rule" was useful in response to repeated efforts by John Frank to delete the entire subsection. *See* Minutes of the May 15, 1965 Meeting of the Advisory Committee on Civil Rules, at 14, in Records of the US Judicial Conference: Committees on Rules of Practice and Procedures, *microformed on* CI-8002-83 (Cong. Info. Serv.). Indeed, at the meetings in late October/early November, 1963, Kaplan was still describing (b)(3) primarily as a vehicle for antitrust and fraud claims. *See* Transcript of Meeting of the Advisory Committee on Civil Rules, October 31–November 2, 1963, at 4, in Records of the US Judicial Conference: Committees on Rules of Practice and Procedures, *mircroformed on* CI-7104-53 (Cong. Info. Serv.). Shortly thereafter, Judge Wyzanski remarked that "one aspect which isn't emphasized . . . is the claim of a particular individual which is very small and unlikely to be litigated." Ibid. at 7. We are grateful for insight on this subject to J. Taylor Gooch, Penn Law Class of 2013.

lawyer "who recovers a common fund for the benefit of persons other than himself or his client is entitled to a reasonable attorney's fee from the fund as a whole."[21] The exception made it possible for class representatives to confine the risk of having to pay the entire legal bill for the class to the event of defeat. Later, if the litigation was covered by a contingency fee agreement, that risk belonged to class counsel, and the exception became a potent economic incentive to use the class form of litigation (Burbank, Farhang, and Kritzer 2013: 652, 654).

Thus, the 1966 amendments to Rule 23 did not just create new types of class actions potentially available across the entire landscape of American law. Through the addition of Rule 23(b)(3) for cases seeking monetary relief, they greatly expanded the territory in which the common fund exception to the American Rule could operate. Moreover, amended Rule 23 immediately overlaid pre-1966 statutory private enforcement regimes and became part of the background against which subsequent regimes were constructed. Inserted into a legal landscape that had previously known them only in the wings, class actions soon occupied center stage, functioning as a kind of private enforcement "wild card . . . divorced from the statutes and administrative regulations that are the authorized sources of regulatory policy" (Burbank, Farhang, and Kritzer 2013: 660).

The legislative responses to amended Rule 23 in the 1970s that we discussed in Chapter 2, which reflected concerns about the potential for inefficient over-enforcement of substantive law and about small-claims classes more generally, demonstrate that it did not take long to recognize that the small-claims class action presents a difficult public policy dilemma. On one view, that dilemma is how to provide sufficient access to court in a society that relies heavily on private litigation for the enforcement of important legal norms, while ensuring fidelity to those norms and the regulatory policies underlying them, avoiding unfairness to defendants and others affected by litigation, and respecting the limited capacity of the courts. The puzzle is that this dilemma was not apparent to the group that drafted the amendments or the other bodies that considered them before they became effective.

One possible explanation, already suggested by our discussion of Rule 23(b)(3), is that, far from being pre-occupied with negative value claims, the Committee did not give them adequate attention. That would have required considering the costs as well as the benefits of animating them. Another is that the Committee did not anticipate developments in

---

[21] *Boeing Co. v. Van Gemert*, 444 U.S. 472, 478 (1980).

substantive law, statutory private enforcement regimes, and the legal profession that catalyzed the economic incentives of the class action (Miller 1979; Burbank, Farhang, and Kritzer 2013).

Still another possible explanation for the Advisory Committee's failure to engage this and other public policy dilemmas presented by the modern class action lies in the process they followed in fashioning the 1966 amendments. Had that process been more inclusive and transparent, trade-offs that became painfully obvious soon after the amendments were effective might have received adequate attention. In fact, however, a pamphlet containing all of the proposed amendments that became effective in 1966, a group far larger than the proposed amendments to Rule 23, was "widely distributed to the bench, bar and law schools in March 1964," apparently by mail.[22] There were no hearings. The Committee received very few written comments on the entire package of proposed amendments,[23] and of those addressing Rule 23 proposals, many if not most concerned Rule 23.1 (derivative actions). The Reporters tended to treat the few critical comments ("brickbats") about the Rule 23 proposal as naïve, ill-informed, or perhaps immoral,[24] which might have been more difficult if the process had included more participants, or if the critics had been permitted to engage in the give-and-take of a public hearing.

[22] Letter from Warren Olney III to the Supreme Court, October 8, 1965 (transmitting proposed amendments), in Records of the US Judicial Conference: Committees on Rules of Practice and Procedures, *microformed on* CI-6406-02 (Cong. Info. Serv.). We found no evidence that the proposals that became the 1966 amendments were published.

[23] A list of "Communications Received on March 1964 Draft of Amendments to Civil Rules" appears in the Committee's papers in the "Deskbook" that contains the agenda for the May 1965 meetings. It lists 27 "communications" (comments), together with the comments of two bar associations previously distributed. The list is available in the Records of the US Judicial Conference: Committees on Rules of Practice and Procedures, *microformed on* CI-6402-65 (Cong. Info. Serv.).

In a letter to the Reporter, Charles Alan Wright expressed surprise "that these proposals have elicited so little comment from the profession" and noted that he was "disappointed by the quality of the comments which you did receive." Letter from Charles Alan Wright to Benjamin Kaplan, April 24, 1965, at 1, in Records of the US Judicial Conference: Committees on Rules of Practice and Procedures, *microformed on* CI-7005-28 (Cong. Info. Serv.).

[24] The Reporters distributed a memorandum to the Committee "discussing the brickbats received." Memorandum from Benjamin Kaplan and Albert Sacks to the Advisory Committee on Civil Rules (April 21, 1965), in Records of the US Judicial Conference: Committees on Rules of Practice and Procedures, *microformed on* CI-7005-10 (Cong. Info. Serv.). In response to the criticism that (b)(3) should require opting in, rather than permit opting out, the Reporters observed that "[t]he morality of treating such people ["small people with small claims"] as null quantities is very questionable. For them the class action serves something like the function of an administrative proceeding where scattered individual interests are represented by the government." Ibid. at EE-3.

The last possibility may also help to explain why other amendments during this decade that (many would say) went beyond the expectations that Chief Justice Warren articulated in 1960 (no "great changes") quickly became controversial, namely amendments in 1970 that broadened access to discovery (Friedenthal 1975). Like the class action amendments, their tenor was decidedly favorable to private enforcement. Indeed, based on an analysis later in this chapter, we find that this period was one in which the net balance clearly favored plaintiffs, and hence private enforcement. As we also discuss later in this chapter, an inclusive and transparent rulemaking process can make it harder for rulemakers to maximize their preferences. The 1960s Advisory Committee was not constrained by such a process.

An Empirical Examination of Advisory Committee Membership, Appointments, and Output

We have thus far introduced the significance of the Federal Rules as the core infrastructure for private enforcement through civil litigation, emphasized how that infrastructure was initially constructed to pro-mote broad access, and highlighted some important examples of how the 1960s Advisory Committee proposed amendments that facilitated private enforcement. In this part of the chapter, we present data cover-ing the entire period from 1960 to 2014 regarding the membership of the Committee, how Chief Justices have used their appointment power, and the character of the Committee's proposed rule changes that bear on pri-vate enforcement.

Balance of Power on the Advisory Committee

To investigate what institutional, ideological, and other interests have been empowered to influence the Federal Rules, we collected data on commit-tee membership from 1960 through 2014.[25] Each committee member was coded as a judge, practitioner, academic, or ex officio representative of the Federal Government. We then calculated, for each committee-year, the proportion of total membership represented by each category. Because we are primarily interested in the Chief Justice's choices, we do not examine Federal Government representation on the Committee, which is beyond the Chief's control (it averaged 6% over the full period).

---

[25] Our data covers all Advisory Committee members who sat from June 1, 1960, to September 30, 2014.

In order to convey a sense of longitudinal trends, the top panel of Figure 3.1 represents regression curves fit to the annual proportion of judges, practitioners, and academics on the Advisory Committee over time. The data reflect that in the early 1960s, practitioners enjoyed the highest level of representation, followed by academics, with judges

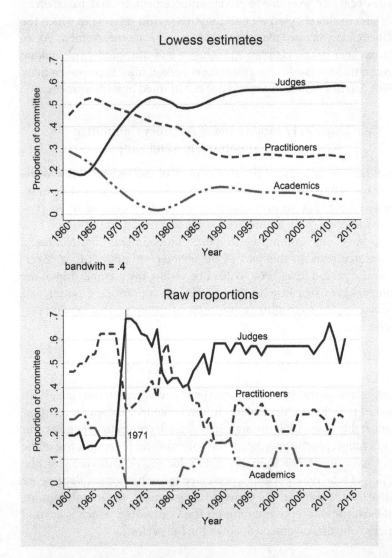

Figure 3.1   Proportion of judges, practitioners, and academics on Advisory Committee, 1960–2014

the least represented. A transformation followed in which, in the 1970s, judges moved from a relatively small minority to a consistent majority on the Committee. Just as precipitous as judges' ascent to majority status was the corresponding decline in the share of committee representation garnered by practitioners and academics.

The smoothed regression lines do not reveal sharp disjunctures in the data. For that purpose, looking at plots of raw proportions for each group is illuminating, and the bottom panel of Figure 3.1 presents that information. These are the data used to estimate the smoothed regression lines in the top panel. These data make clear that the 1971 reconstitution of the Rules Committee under Chief Justice Burger, which we discuss later in this chapter, was a pivotal event. Judges, who represented about 18% of the Committee for the previous decade, overnight became a majority, with their representation rising from 19% immediately before reconstitution to 69% on the new committee in 1971. Practitioners were demoted from solid majority status in the 1960s, and over the long run their position stabilized at a little over 25% of the Committee. Academics disappeared from the Committee for a decade and then rebounded to something on the order of a 10% share of seats. In the last quarter-century, judges have constituted a majority of the Committee in every year.

We also chart practitioner profiles over time along two dimensions: plaintiff versus defendant representation, and individual versus business/corporate representation. In order to assess a practitioner's practice area, we examined multiple sources. We primarily relied on cases in Lexis and Westlaw in which the practitioner appeared as counsel, but we also relied on firm profiles, newspapers, and other historical sources. We acknowledge that these sources have important limits – most significantly, the cases contained in electronic databases may not be representative of each practitioner's client base. Still, we regard the sources, collectively, as informative, albeit not decisive. We describe the coding protocol in detail in the appendix. In general, we classified practitioners as plaintiff or defense lawyers if they represented plaintiffs or defendants in 75% or more of decisions identified, respectively. We classified practitioners who did not represent either plaintiffs or defendants at or above the 75% threshold as representing both client populations. We coded defense practitioners as 0, those representing both sides as 1, and plaintiff practitioners as 2. It is important to note that a practitioner can be designated a plaintiffs' lawyer even when representing predominantly business/corporate clients.

We classified practitioners as individual or business/corporate if they represented individuals or businesses/corporate clients in 75% or more of cases identified, respectively. We include in our conception of individual representation cases in which an attorney represents classes of individuals. We classified practitioners who did not represent either individuals or business/corporate clients at or above the 75% threshold as representing both. We coded practitioners representing business as 0, those representing both as 1, and those representing individuals as 2.

We compiled a dataset in which the unit of analysis is the presence of an individual practitioner on the Committee in each year. From 1960 through 2014, 40 practitioners were members in total, serving an average of 6.7 years, comprising 267 practitioner-committee-year observations. To provide a broad sense of longitudinal patterns, Figure 3.2 presents regression curves with the plaintiff versus defendant scale, and the individual versus corporate/business scale, as dependent variables, and year as the independent variable. The solid horizontal line at the value of 1 represents parity on the plaintiff/individual versus defense/business scales. If, for example, in a particular committee year there were two plaintiff practitioners, one representing both sides, and two defense practitioners, the mean practitioner value for the year would be 1 on the plaintiff versus defense scale. Values above the parity line represent a balance in favor

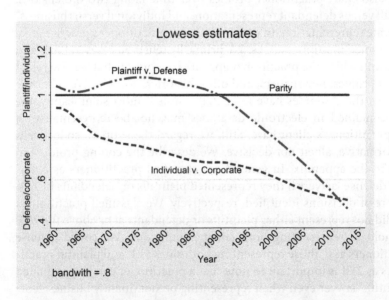

Figure 3.2   Practitioner types on the Advisory Committee, 1960–2014

of plaintiffs/individuals, and values below it represent a balance in favor of defense/business.

The estimated values in the figure reflect that, on the individual versus corporate/business scale, there was a long-run decline over the full period away from near parity and toward corporate/business representation. The estimated values of the individual versus business scale declined from .94 in 1960 to .50 in 2014, falling by 47%. The balance is on the business/corporate side of the parity line throughout.

On the plaintiff versus defendant scale, the estimated values hovered between 1 and 1.08 from 1960 to 1990, and then they declined rapidly to .46 by 2014, for a net decline of 54%. We note, however, that when the scale was on the plaintiffs' side of parity from 1960 to about 1990, only one plaintiffs' lawyer served who represented primarily individual plaintiffs or classes of them. The slight balance in favor of plaintiffs during this period is driven by practitioners representing a mix of business/corporate and individual plaintiffs. By the end of the series, the predicted values for the plaintiff versus defense scale, and the individual versus business scale, converge. This is because by the end of the series Advisory Committee practitioners are composed primarily of two types: plaintiffs' lawyers representing individuals or classes of them, and corporate defense lawyers, with the latter consistently holding the balance of power.

This trend relates to a facet of the client populations represented by Committee practitioners that bears emphasis. At the start of the series, a substantial majority of practitioners on the Committee could not be classified using our 75% rule into any of the four types: plaintiff, defense, individual, or business. Their client populations were sufficiently heterogeneous to place them in the "both" categories on each of the scales. By the end of the series, such unaligned practitioners, once predominant, become nonexistent. To convey this transformation graphically, we coded practitioners 1 if they could be classified into none of the four classifications, and coded them 0 otherwise. We then estimated a regression curve of the probability of such unaligned practitioners serving in each year, and we present the results in Figure 3.3. The probability declines from a high level of 92% in 1960, to essentially zero in 2014.

To some extent these data may reflect the influence of changing professional demographics. For example, 53% of Chicago lawyers' time was devoted to the corporate sector in 1975 (including work for some nonbusiness organizations such as unions and government entities), with 40% devoted to serving individual clients. Twenty years later, the split was 64% to 29% (Heinz et al. 2005). Yet, even assuming Chicago lawyers are

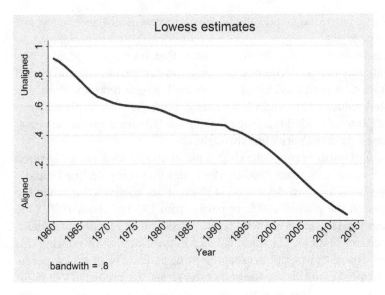

Figure 3.3   Aligned versus unaligned practitioners, 1960–2014

representative of those practicing in large cities, a great deal of federal litigation occurs in other locations, where the demographics of practice may be different. For example, whereas solo practitioners constituted 14% of Chicago lawyers in 1994–5, nationally they constituted 45% of lawyers in 1991 (ibid.). In addition, there have been other potentially relevant changes in legal practice, including growth in the number, size, and budgets of public interest law firms (including firms promoting conservative agendas) (Galanter 2006; Nielsen and Albiston 2006; Rhode 2008; Galanter 2011).

Whatever the cause, we regard the composition of practitioners on the Committee along the individual versus corporate, and plaintiff versus defendant, dimensions as material to assessing their likely preferences. Still, given the small number of practitioners serving on the Committee, limitations in data available to characterize their practices, and the difficulty of specifying the population of attorneys that are or should be regarded as candidates for appointment, our data cannot support strong inferences about a chief justice's goals in making selections. In this respect, Article III judges provide opportunities for more rigorous investigation of ideological bias in the Chief Justices' appointments to the Advisory Committee.

Politics of Appointing Federal Judges to the Committee

The appointment of Article III judges to, and their service on, the Advisory Committee provide unique opportunities to explore in a systematic way the question whether the Committee is selected so as to give it a particular ideological profile. These appointments are made from a readily identifiable pool of candidates, and we have a plausible measure of potential members' presumed preferences that would be visible to the appointing Chief Justice – the political party of the appointing president. This measure is surely imperfect, but empirical evidence establishes that, in at least some fields of law, it is associated with the voting behavior of federal judges in predictable ways (e.g., Segal and Spaeth 2002; Sunstein et al. 2006; Nash 2015).[26]

Judge-members of the Advisory Committee do not exercise Article III judicial power when they participate in rulemaking under the Enabling Act. As we discuss later in this chapter, although being judges may affect their behavior as rulemakers, any close observer of this landscape over time will acknowledge that some of the rulemakers who are judges, some of the time, vote according to their ideological preferences. Nor is this surprising, given that, even in deciding cases, "[w]hen a judge or Justice has to make a legislative decision rather than decide the case just by following clear statutory or constitutional text or clearly applicable precedent, ideology may determine the outcome" (Epstein, Landes, and Posner 2013b: 235).

We do not doubt that most of the Advisory Committee's work is unaffected by members' ideological preferences, including in particular the ideological preferences of members who are judges. As our data confirm, few of the Committee's proposals predictably implicate private enforcement, and a great deal of its work does not map to a left–right ideological dimension. At least since the counterrevolution became a partisan project in the elected branches, however, we believe that the rulemaking proposals most likely to elicit ideological behavior are precisely those that will affect private enforcement.

---

[26] For a study of the Chief Justice's appointments to all Judicial Conference committees in the period 1986–2012, *see* Chutkow (2014). The author finds that the "[o]dds of being selected to any committee increase by about 73% for Republican judges, and the odds of selection to a Law Committee [of which the Civil Rules Advisory Committee is one of nine in the author's disaggregation] more than double" (313). The article has some other findings that parallel those presented here, but because it aggregates data from appointments across nine committees, they do not support inferences about the Advisory Committee.

We focus on the period from 1971 through 2014. The data we collected for the 1960s are too sparse for meaningful analysis in statistical models. Only a handful of federal judges served on the Committee during the entire decade. The large increase in the number of judges on the Committee beginning in 1971 generated sufficient data for analysis. Moreover, because there was a Republican Chief Justice in every year from 1971 through 2014, to assess presumed ideological effects we need only examine whether there was disproportionate reliance on judges appointed by Republican presidents for appointments to the Committee.

If the party of the appointing president were not associated with judges' service on the Advisory Committee, the balance on the Committee would approximate the balance among judges on the federal bench eligible to be appointed. Pooling *judge-years* on the federal bench from 1971 through 2014, the Republican to Democratic-appointee split was 55% to 45%. Pooling *committee-years* of service by Article III judges for the same period, the split was 70% to 30% in favor of Republican appointees. Among 103 *appointments or reappointments* of Article III judges to the Committee, the split was also 70% to 30% in favor of Republican appointees. Of course, these cross-sectional percentages give no sense of how representation on the Committee has changed over time.

We calculated the annual percentage of all sitting judges appointed by Republican presidents who served on the Committee, divided by the same percentage for judges appointed by Democratic presidents.[27] This yields an annual population-adjusted ratio of service. A population-adjusted ratio of one-to-one would occur when appointment to the Committee was not associated with party. A ratio greater than one would occur when Republican appointees constituted a larger fraction of the Committee than they did of eligible judges on the federal bench; and a ratio less than one would occur when Democratic appointees constituted a larger fraction of the Committee than they did of eligible judges on the federal bench. The average value of the annual ratio is 2.5, meaning that judges appointed by

[27] In the years 1994 to 1997, there were six Article III judges appointed by Republican presidents on the committee and none appointed by Democratic presidents. There was one state court judge appointed by a Democratic governor during these years (Christine Durham of Utah). It is impossible to compute a ratio for these years since one cannot divide by zero. In order to avoid discarding data for these years we treated the committee as if there were one Democratic and six Republican appointees. Figure 3.4 therefore modestly understates the size of the Republican slant of Article III judges serving on the Committee in the region of the figure affected by these years.

Republican presidents served at a population-adjusted rate about 150% higher than those appointed by Democrats.

Figure 3.4 represents a regression curve fit through those data points. The horizontal line at the value of one, labeled "partisan parity," indicates where the estimates would cluster if the party of the appointing presidents of federal judges on the Committee reflected that of the federal judiciary. The raw data and regression estimates reflect overrepresentation of judges appointed by Republican presidents on the Committee from the time of its reconstitution under Chief Justice Burger in 1971. There is only one year in the entire period (2004) in which the ratio fell below the parity line, indicating overrepresentation on the Committee of judges appointed by Democrats. Moreover, in terms of absolute numbers, Republican-appointed judges have held a majority of Article III judge seats on the Committee in every year but two from 1971 to 2014 (they were in parity in 1984, and in the minority in 2004). On average, across the full period, they held 70% of Article III judge seats. Thus, at the bivariate level, controlling for the composition of the federal bench, Republican-appointed judges had more than double the estimated probability of serving on the Committee during the period of interest, and in absolute terms, they were a majority of Article III judges in 41 of 43 years.

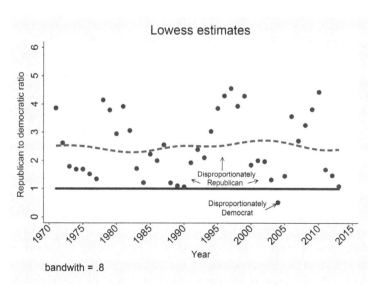

Figure 3.4   Population adjusted ratio of Republican to Democratic appointees serving on the Advisory Committee, 1971–2014

We next assess whether this effect is statistically significant in regression models with controls. We constructed the dataset as follows. For each year, each federal District Court and Court of Appeals judge, both active and senior, is included. The judge-year is the unit of analysis. In the model of committee service (Model 1 below), judges serving on the Committee are coded 1 in each year they serve, and those not serving are coded 0. In the models of committee appointments (Models 2 and 3 below), in years in which appointments were made judges appointed are coded 1, and those not appointed are coded 0. We include independent variables in our models that annually measure the party of the judge's appointing president (Democrat = 1, Republican = 0), whether the judge had taken senior status (active = 0, senior = 1), and whether she was a District or Court of Appeals judge (Court of Appeals = 0, District = 1).

In addition, empirical research has demonstrated that in some types of cases, even controlling for political party, judges' gender and race can be important variables predicting their policy preferences as measured by voting behavior. In particular, a number of studies have found that women and racial minority judges vote more liberally on some important civil rights issues (Farhang and Wawro 2004; Cox and Miles 2008). Civil rights litigation has been central in debates over whether there is excessive litigation in federal courts and the implementation of federal law. As we demonstrate in Chapter 2, it has also been an area frequently targeted by retrenchment proposals, emanating very substantially from the Republican Party, that are calculated to reduce opportunities and incentives for private enforcement litigation. We thus also incorporate variables measuring each judge's gender and race, which the Chief Justice may regard as associated with their likely preferences over the Federal Rules as they bear on opportunities and incentives for litigation. We coded each judge's race (white = 0, non-white = 1) and gender (male = 0, female = 1).

Finally, the models include year fixed effects. With year fixed effects the model estimates the effect of party on appointment and service only relative to the pool of judges sitting in the same year. This is necessary to restrict the model to comparing those appointed or serving on the Committee in any given year only to those eligible to be appointed or serve in that year. Year fixed effects also addresses the possibility of potential confounding factors, such as the identity of the Chief Justice, the political salience of litigation or federal rulemaking, and changes in the regulatory environment. This approach leverages only variation in the relationship between judges' characteristics and selection to, and service on, the Committee *within* years to estimate the effects of those characteristics. It allows us to estimate the effects of party most effectively because it absorbs and holds constant the influence of any variables that would take the same value for each judge sitting in a given year. In this sense, these estimates of the effects of party are net of the effects of any such variables (Greene 2003: ch. 13). Further details about the models, including alternative specifications, are in the appendix.

We first estimate logit models with committee service as the dependent variable. There are 277 years of committee service in the data. Because the probability of service for any judge is extremely low, in order to assess the magnitude of the effects, we focus on the ratio of predicted probabilities between categories of the explanatory dummy variables. That is, we calculate predicted probabilities for the dummy variable at both 0 and 1 and take the ratio of the two predicted probabilities. We report the results in Model 1 of Table 3.1. Appointment by a Democratic president is significantly associated with a lower probability of serving on the Committee.

Table 3.1. *Logit model of committee service and committee appointments for Article III judges, with year fixed effects, 1971–2014*

	Model 1 Committee service	Model 2 Appointment and reappointment	Model 3 Initial appointment only
	Coefficient	Coefficient	Coefficient
Party	−.75**	−.64**	−.57*
	(.34)	(.29)	(.31)
Race	−1.61**	−1.36*	−.98
	(.72)	(.75)	(.72)
Gender	.30	.22	.20
	(.56)	(.42)	(.49)
Senior status	−1.34***	−2.26***	−2.34***
	(.49)	(.58)	(.74)
District Court	−.55*	−.33	−.53*
	(.33)	(.30)	(.31)
Reappointment candidate	⎯⎯⎯	8.42*** (.41)	⎯⎯⎯
(Year fixed effects not displayed)			
N=	42077	42077	32165
Pseudo R²=	.06	.49	.12

***$p < .01$; **$p < 05$; *$p < .1$
Standard errors in parentheses, clustered on judge

The probability of service for judges appointed by Republican presidents is 2.1 times larger than for Democratic appointees. This is comparable to the magnitude we observed when looking at the raw data.

The race variable is significant and negative, indicating that non-white judges are less likely to serve on the Advisory Committee. By comparison, white judges' probability of serving on the Committee is about five times larger. Examining the raw data to assess the plausibility of this very large effect, we observe that although non-white judges account for 11% of the judge-years in the data, they account for only 2% of committee service-years (6 of 277), and 2% of appointments or reappointments (2 of 103).[28] White judges represent 89% of the judge-years and 98% of both committee service-years and appointments or reappointments. Thus, a large race disparity is visible at the descriptive level. Active judges have a probability of service about 3.8 times larger than judges in senior status. Gender and being a District versus Court of Appeals judge are both insignificant.

In Model 2 of Table 3.1, we substitute as the unit of analysis a variable measuring whether the judge was appointed or reappointed in each year. Model 1, focusing on years of service, only describes the association between judge characteristics (party of appointing president, race, etc.) and the probability of serving on the Committee in each year. What the model reveals is critical to understanding the actual composition of the Advisory Committee relative to the federal bench. However, from this we cannot draw direct inferences about appointment decisions. With only 103 episodes of appointment or reappointment, we have limited data to model appointment. In Model 2, we add the additional control variable of reappointment candidate, accounting for whether a judge was already serving on the Committee. Initial appointments cannot be treated in the same way as reappointments because being on the Committee makes one vastly more likely to be appointed and this must be modeled in some fashion. The reappointment candidate variable takes the value of 1 in the year following the conclusion of a term – a year in which a judge can either exit the Committee or transition into the first year of a new term.[29]

In this model, party is again significant. The probability of committee appointment or reappointment of judges appointed to the bench by

---

[28] The two non-white judges are Jose Cabranes, who served one committee term from 2004–6, and Oliver Solomon, who began service on the Committee in 2011.

[29] For appointments from 1971 to 1974, terms were four years. From 1975 to 2013, terms were three years. If a judge went even a single year into a new term, the judge had to be reappointed for that service to occur. Thus, if there was any service beyond a term, we treat the first year of continued service as a reappointment event.

Republican presidents is about 1.5 times larger than that of Democratic appointees. Race remains significant at the .1 threshold, with whites having a probability of appointment or reappointment 2.2 times larger than non-whites. Active judges have a probability of appointment or reappointment 3.9 times larger than judges in senior status; and the gender and District versus Court of Appeals judge variables remain insignificant.

In Model 3, we restrict the dependent variable to initial appointments. We lack information about reappointments that could be material, such as whether a judge sought and was rejected for reappointment, as opposed to choosing to exit service even though the Chief Justice would have accepted or desired the judge's continued service. This model also avoids aggregating initial appointments and reappointments, which are likely quite different decisions. Restricting the dependent variable in this way drops the number of appointing events to 50. The party of appointing president variable remains significant, with judges appointed to the bench by Republican presidents 1.8 times more likely to be initially appointed to the Committee. Race dips below .1 significance, which is likely due to limited data to estimate an effect in the models of initial appointment decisions. Judges in senior status remain substantially less likely to be appointed; gender remains insignificant, and the District judge variable becomes significant with a negative sign, meaning that District judges are less likely than Court of Appeals judges to be initially appointed to the Committee.

Finally, we estimate two additional models, but instead of estimating the probability of service and appointment as a Committee member, we estimate the probability of service and appointment as chair of the Committee. The chair is an especially important appointment, having the capacity to influence, if not control, the Committee's agenda (Cooper 2014: 592). If chief justices have disproportionately selected Republican-appointed judges for the Committee in an effort to influence rulemaking, one would expect the effect to be larger in the selection of the most consequential member of the Committee. This is precisely what we find. We report the results in Table 3.2.

In our models of chair service and appointment, the race variable cannot be included because chief justices have never selected a non-white judge as chair, making it impossible to estimate an effect. In Model 1 we estimate a model with a dependent variable that takes the value 1 for each year of chair service and takes the value 0 otherwise. This model estimates the probability of service as chair. Party of the appointing president is statistically significant, and the magnitude of the effect is dramatically greater than for committee service. Again focusing on the ratio of predicted

Table 3.2. *Logit model of chair service and chair appointments for Article III judges, with year fixed effects, 1971–2014*

	Model 1 Chair service	Model 2 Initial appointment
	Coefficient	Coefficient
Party	−2.91***	−2.18**
	(1.08)	(1.07)
Gender	.23	.19
	(1.12)	(.87)
Senior status	−.40	−.97
	(.84)	(.97)
District Court	−1.50**	−.99*
	(.60)	(.52)
Committee member	—	6.20***
		(.75)
(Year fixed effects not displayed)		
N=	42077	20177
Pseudo R²=	.10	.44

***$p < .01$; **$p < .05$; *$p < .1$
Standard errors in parentheses, clustered on judge

probabilities, the probability of service as chair for judges appointed by Republican presidents is 18.2 times larger than for Democratic appointees.

In Model 2, we estimate a model with a dependent variable that takes the value 1 for the year of initial appointment as chair, and 0 otherwise. Unlike our models of committee service, we do not estimate a model that includes reappointments because, based on inquiries to knowledgeable sources, norms regarding the duration of chair service have evolved over time such that we cannot identify with confidence when reappointments occurred. In this model we include an explanatory variable reflecting whether the judge selected as chair had already been serving on the Committee. Of the twelve chairs from 1971–2014, eight were members at the time of their appointment, and four were new to the Committee. Thus, although service on the Committee greatly increases the probability of being selected as chair, the pool from which appointment to chair is made includes the full federal bench and not only the existing Committee members.

In Model 2, committee membership is statistically significant. Committee members are 331 times more likely to be selected as chair. This, of course, carries with it one pathway of partisan influence. We have established that Republican-appointed judges are about twice as likely to serve on the Committee (Table 3.1, Model 1). As a function of this initial partisan disparity, they are twice as likely to be in the state (committee service) that is 331 times more likely to be selected as chair. Further, even with this effect accounted for in the model, the party variable remains statistically significant. Holding constant the massive effect of committee service on selection as chair, the probability of selection as chair for judges appointed by Republican presidents remains 7.7 times larger than for Democratic appointees.

We examined the raw data to confirm these remarkably large magnitudes and observed that the percentage of Republican-appointed judges on the federal bench serving as chair is 17 times larger than the percentage of Democratic-appointed judges so serving. Eleven of twelve chairs serving from 1971 to 2014 were Republican appointed, accounting for 41 of 43 years of chair service, or 95% of years of chair service.[30] Apparently, chief justices regard the chair position as a distinctively important Advisory Committee appointment.

Committee's Output

In order to track longitudinal trends in the Advisory Committee's posture toward private enforcement, we constructed a dataset of all proposals to change the Federal Rules in a manner predictably affecting private enforcement that the Committee forwarded to the Standing Committee from 1960 through 2014. We coded those proposals for whether they favored or disfavored private enforcement (were pro-plaintiff or pro-defendant) in predictable ways. In order to identify proposals bearing on private enforcement, at least one of the authors read all of the Advisory Committee's proposed revisions to the Federal Rules from 1960 through 2014, including proposals that were not adopted. At the Rule level – counting each proposal to amend a specific Rule in a particular year as a discrete unit – there were 262 proposals over this period.[31] We identified

---

[30]   As we discuss later in this chapter, although the only exception, Judge Frank Johnson, was appointed to the District Court by a Republican president, a Democratic president had appointed him to the Court of Appeals, where he served at the time of his selection as chair of the Advisory Committee.

[31]   The 2007 style amendments and the package of 1987 gender-neutrality amendments are omitted for purposes of the count, as are multiple iterations of substantially similar proposed amendments to the same Rule. Conforming amendments, technical amendments, new Rules proposals, and amendments by way of abrogation are included in the count.

33 of these Rule-level proposals (about 13% of the total) as predictably affecting private enforcement.

We then further broke down the proposals into distinguishable subunits within the Rule level. This had no effect on the count for the 19 Rule-level proposals that sought only a single change bearing on private enforcement. For the remaining proposals, however, disaggregation seemed appropriate. For example, the 1983 proposal to amend Rule 11 included multiple changes to the Rule. Among them we identified two basic types of change: one enlarging the scope of the Rule's application, and one strengthening the sanctions for violations. Thus, we coded the proposal as contributing two units to this measure of proposed changes.

Breaking down the 33 Rule-level proposals into these subunits rendered a total of 44 items. Of these, 41 (93%) passed through the rest of the Enabling Act process and became effective in substantially the language recommended. Three proposals – a 2000 proposal to authorize cost-shifting in Rule 26, and a 1993 proposal to amend Rule 56 (in which we count two items) – were rejected by the Standing Committee or the Judicial Conference.

In the appendix, we show that the basic patterns described below with respect to these data hold if one performs the analysis at the Rule level, or if one breaks the proposals down into even more granular units than we do in our main analysis. Thus, although reasonable people can disagree about the appropriate way to construct the unit of analysis, the same temporal patterns emerge from three alternative plausible strategies. The results we report are not an artifact of our method of counting proposals.

Before discussing our findings, a caveat is in order. Our approach to counting proposals does not distinguish potentially far-reaching proposals from those that appear less consequential. Qualitative analysis and judgment are necessary to assess the relative potential significance of particular proposals, and we offer such analysis and judgments later in this chapter, reserving to Chapter 6 discussion of differences between changes in law and in litigant behavior and the difficulties of measuring the latter. Here our approach is quantitative; we assess change over time in the average direction of proposals on the pro-plaintiff versus pro-defendant dimension. This is a different question than impact, but one that we believe is important to address as we endeavor to understand long-term patterns in the Committee's behavior.

The top panel of Figure 3.5 presents the distribution over time of the 44 proposals affecting private enforcement from 1960 through 2014. The bottom panel of Figure 3.5 presents the net balance, in years in which there were proposals affecting private enforcement, between pro-plaintiff

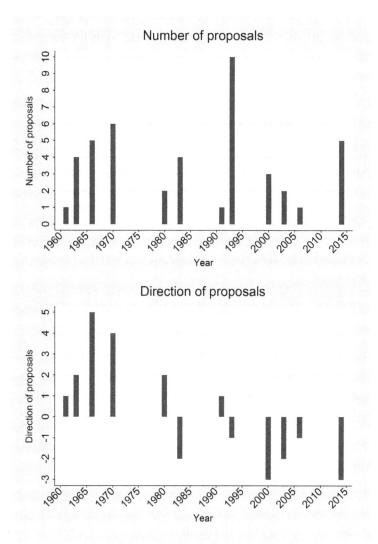

Figure 3.5   Number and direction of Advisory Committee proposals affecting private enforcement, 1960–2014

and pro-defendant proposals. Pro-plaintiff proposals are coded 1; pro-defendant proposals are coded −1, and a single proposal that was evenly divided between pro-plaintiff and pro-defendant elements was coded 0.[32]

---

[32] In the 44 intermediate-level units, we are working with, 40 were wholly pro-plaintiff or pro-defendant and thus straightforward to code. Of the four that were not, three were

The bars in the bottom panel of Figure 3.5 represent the net result from summing across all values of 1, 0, and −1 in each year. There were no years in which all proposals summed to zero. Thus, all zero values in the figure represent years in which there were no proposals affecting private enforcement. Years in which the bar is greater than zero were those in which the Committee made more proposals favoring plaintiffs than defendants, and the value of the bar represents the margin by which this was so. Years in which the bar is less than zero were those in which the Committee made more proposals favoring defendants than plaintiffs. The period from 1960 to 1971 was one in which the net balance clearly favored plaintiffs. The two decades from 1971 to 1991 saw only three years with proposals affecting private enforcement (leading to the 1980, 1983, 1991 amendments to the Federal Rules), and the net result over that period was roughly an even balance between plaintiff- and defendant-favoring proposals. From 1991 through 2014, the net balance favored defendants in every year in which a proposal was made.

We next estimate a smoothed regression curve of the probability of a pro-plaintiff proposal over time, conditional on the existence of a proposal affecting private enforcement. For this purpose, proposals favoring defendants were coded 0, and proposals favoring plaintiffs were coded 1. For proposals containing both pro-plaintiff and pro-defendant elements – which occurred only four times in the data – we took the mean value. For example, if we treated three changes on the same subject as constituting a single subunit, where one was pro-defendant (0) and two were pro-plaintiff (1) in direction, the value for the unit would be .67. The variable thus ranges between 0 and 1. Figure 3.6 represents the results. After increasing in the early 1960s, the predicted probability that a proposed amendment would favor plaintiffs declined from 87% in the mid-1960s to 19% by the end of the series. Because smoothed regression curves do not allow one to observe key breakpoints in the data, this figure should be interpreted in conjunction with the descriptive representation of the data in Figure 3.5.

In order to assess the statistical significance of this negative time trend, we regressed an annual time trend on the dependent variable that is used to estimate the curve in Figure 3.6. Although we have only 44 observations, the negative time trend is highly statistically significant ($p = .000$), with a coefficient $-.017$, indicating that from 1960 through 2014 the

---

preponderantly pro-plaintiff and thus coded 1, and one was evenly divided in its directionality and thus coded 0.

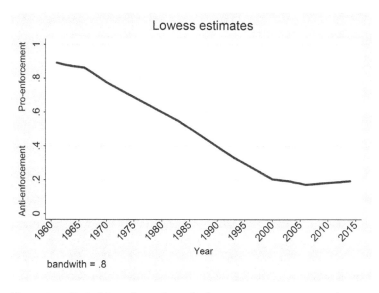

Figure 3.6 Probability of pro-plaintiff Advisory Committee Proposal, 1960–2014

passage of each year was, on average, associated with a reduction of about 1.7% in the probability that a proposal would be pro-plaintiff. Overall, the data show that, conditional on the existence of a proposal affecting private enforcement, the predicted probability that it would favor plaintiffs went from highly likely at the beginning of the series to highly unlikely at the end.

Starting Over, Again

The architects of the 1938 Federal Rules constructed a broad highway for litigation that was free of some imposing roadblocks found in prior systems. The work of a very active committee in the 1960s added lanes and cleared other roadblocks. The "highway effect" was not, however, evident for many years. A small federal judiciary managed to dispose of its caseload without evident strain for more than 20 years after the Federal Rules went into effect. By the mid-to-late 1960s, however, leaders of the federal judiciary were voicing serious concern about increasing caseloads.

For some, including in particular judges, docket growth presented primarily institutional challenges. Among them were federal judges who advocated and lobbied for what became the Multi-District Litigation Act of 1968 (MDLA)[33] (Bradt 2016). The MDLA established authority and a system to transfer civil suits sharing a common question of fact to a single district judge for coordinated or consolidated pre-trial proceedings, with the goal of conserving judicial resources. In testimony before the House, Judge William Becker, stated:

> We feel that there is a litigation explosion occurring in the Federal courts along with the population explosion and the technological revolution, that even with the addition of many new judges, the caseload, the backlog of cases pending, is growing, and that some new tools are needed by the judges in order to process the litigation which results from the matters which I have mentioned, as well as from the extensions of the jurisdiction of the federal courts by acts of Congress, and this is a method which we think will work.[34]

Others, aware of the sources and goals of much of the new litigation, saw different challenges, as well as opportunities. Among them was Lewis Powell. In 1971, two months before he was nominated to the Supreme Court, Powell wrote a confidential memorandum to the Chair of the Education Committee of the Chamber of Commerce. Powell described a "broad attack" on the "American economic system" and the steps that he recommended in response. He observed that "American business and the enterprise system have been affected as much by the courts as by the executive and legislative branches of government," and he argued that "especially with an activist-minded Supreme Court, the judiciary may be the most important instrument for social, economic and political change." Powell contended that "[o]ther organizations and groups, recognizing this, have been far more astute in exploiting judicial action than American business," singling out the American Civil Liberties Union. He noted that "[l]abor unions, civil rights groups and now the public interest law firms are extremely active in the judicial arena" and that "[t]heir success, often at business' expense, has not been inconsequential." He concluded that "[t]his is a vast area of opportunity for the Chamber."[35]

Control of procedure ensures that means are available for courts to frustrate legislative policy favoring private enforcement, whether for ideological reasons or to manage caseloads. The evidence we discuss in

---

[33] Pub. L. No. 90–296, 82 Stat. 109 (1968), codified at 28 U.S.C. § 1407.

[34] Statement of Chief Judge William H. Becker on H.R. 8276, *Hearing before the House Committee on the Judiciary*, 89th Cong. (1966), at 26–7.

[35] Confidential Memorandum from Lewis F. Powell, Jr. to Eugene B. Sydnor, Jr., Chairman, Education Committee., US Chamber of Commerce, Attack on American Free Enterprise System 1, 26–7 (August 23, 1971), available at http://law.wlu.edu/deptimages/Powell%20 Archives/PowellMemorandumTypescript.pdf

the remainder of this chapter suggests that, although the retrenchment effort may have started earlier in the rulemaking enterprise than it did in Congress, the counterrevolution has not been notably more successful in that institutional site notwithstanding appointments designed to favor the views of those who were ideologically pre-disposed to its goals.

A Decade of Frustration

In October 1970, the Standing Committee, having observed that "the terms of service of the members of [the Advisory Committee] expired on October 1, 1970," recommended that "the Chief Justice be requested to appoint a new advisory committee on Civil Rules when he deems it appropriate." The report continued:

> The standing committee recognizes that there is presently a crisis in the administration of justice in the federal courts caused, at least in part, by the inordinate delays resulting from the constantly increasing case loads. The committee believes that the time has come when we must consider all serious proposals for modernizing the procedure and improving the efficiency of the courts, without impairing the just determination of litigation, no matter how drastic or fundamental the proposals may be. We accordingly recommend that a small ad hoc committee be appointed by the Chief Justice to consider and report to the conference a list of those proposals which they think might be helpful in this regard and which they believe merit serious discussion and detailed study by an advisory committee and its reporter.[36]

Chief Justice Burger wasted no time in implementing these recommendations. He appointed a special advisory group on civil litigation, which suggested consideration of a number of reforms with anti-plaintiff potential.[37] In 1971 he appointed a new Advisory Committee on Civil Rules.

---

[36] Committee on Rules of Practice and Procedure, Supplemental Report to the Judicial Conference of the United States, October 19, 1970, at 4–6, available at www.uscourts.gov/rules-policies/archives/committee-reports/reports-judicial-conference-october-1970

[37] *See* Special Advisory Group on Federal Civil Litigation, Suggestions for Improving the Processes of Civil Litigation in the Federal Courts (1971) (available from authors). The advisory group suggested that there be "a serious attempt to vitalize and extend some of the procedural devices that have been developed for achieving an accelerated judgment or a determination of litigation prior to trial but that have not been widely used in the past." Ibid. at 14. *See also* ibid. at 2 (recommending that courts "make more effective use of the pretrial disposition procedures presently available, such as summary judgment"). One of the devices mentioned by the Special Committee was "the offer of judgment (Rule 68)" (ibid.). The advisory group also observed that "Rule 11 . . . should be more frequently invoked." Ibid. at 1. Later in this chapter, we discuss both of these Federal Rules and how

Burger "attended briefly and addressed the Committee" at its first meeting in September 1971. According to the minutes:

> He noted certain expressions of dissatisfaction with a number of specific procedural devices and suggestions for improvement. But he emphasized the need, not simply for the betterment of existing procedures, but for major changes in the way in which litigation is being handled. He advised the Committee that it was unique in that it could make recommendations in any area of civil litigation where it considered change desirable.[38]

This was very different from the advice given 11 years earlier by Chief Justice Warren, and it was given to a committee very differently composed. Notwithstanding Judicial Conference policy calling for "members to consist of broadly representative judges, lawyers and law teachers,"[39] of the new committee's 16 members, 11 (69%) were judges, and 5 (31%) were practitioners. There were no academic members.

The perception that the institutional interests of the judiciary – in particular, the interest in active judicial management of a burgeoning docket – were no longer in sync with the interests of lawyers likely played an important role in prompting Chief Justice Burger to change the balance of power on the key rulemaking committees, including the Advisory Committee, strongly in favor of members who were judges (Burger 1972; Yeazell 1998; Burbank 2004a; Remus 2012). The perception of such a divergence was already evident in the judiciary's campaign for the MDLA in the 1960s, when segments of the defense bar, who regarded consolidated proceedings as contrary to their clients' interests, were the bill's chief opponents (Bradt 2016). Burger probably reasoned that judges would be more likely than lawyers or academics to protect the judiciary's institutional interests.

In addition, Burger's subsequent behavior suggests that he wanted to influence, if not control, the retrenchment agenda, and he may have thought that judges are more susceptible than lawyers or academics to direction from on high. A very bright and independent federal judge, who wrote a book advocating reform of the rulemaking process in the 1970s, observed that "there is now strong psychological pressure on individual

---

the Advisory Committee proposed changes to them in the 1980s, igniting significant controversy. The Advisory Committee considered this report at its first meeting and committed to the Reporter for further study "the suggestions contained in the report for improving the pleading structure and accelerating judgment." Minutes of the Meeting of the Advisory Committee on Civil Rules, September 1971, at 3, available at www.uscourts.gov/uscourts/RulesAndPolicies/rules/Minutes/CV09-1971-min.pdf.

[38] Minutes of Advisory Committee Meeting, September 1971, at 1.
[39] Report of Proceedings, *supra* note 10, at 7.

advisory committee members to modify the rules in light of what they think the Chief Justice would wish" (Weinstein 1977: 111).

Apart from docket concerns, Burger made no secret of his antipathy toward the "litigation explosion" (Dunham 2001: 36). In the 1970s, he "frequently spoke out against what he and many others perceived as excessive litigation" (Tonsing 2004: 22). His critique of litigiousness (Burger 1982) had normative weight, which seemed to increase in the 1980s, after the counterrevolution became a partisan issue in the elected branches. Thus, in his first "State of the Judiciary" address in 1970, Burger observed:

> In a free society such as ours, these social and economic upheavals tend to wind up on the doorstep of the courts. Some of this is because of new laws and decisions and some because of a tendency that is unique to America, to look to the courts to solve all problems (1970: 930).

Fifteen years later, what had been a "tendency" became a "form of mass neurosis":

> A host of new kinds of conflicts have flooded the courts. There are cases with students seeking to litigate a failing mark, professors litigating a denial of academic tenure, and welfare recipients with myriad claims under the Equal Protection Clause. There is some form of mass neurosis that leads many people to think courts were created to solve all the problems of mankind.[40]

It is striking that, with the Chief Justice and the Standing Committee urging major changes, and with judges constituting a majority of the reconstituted Advisory Committee for most of the decade, the Committee accomplished little in the 1970s. "[M]ostly the committee foundered" (D. Marcus 2013b: 616). Although sitting for 17% of the study period (1960–2014), the 1970s Advisory Committee sent to the Standing Committee only 5% of the proposals (at the Rule level). Moreover, we determined that only two proposals for amendments predictably implicated private enforcement, comprising only 7% of all such proposals that we identified for the study period. Neither approached the salience of the 1960s Advisory Committee's work, and both were pro-enforcement. Thus, even though reducing the 1960s' tide of pro-enforcement proposals to a trickle, the Committee temporarily frustrated Burger's hope to use court rule-making as an instrument of litigation retrenchment.

A number of influences contributed to the Advisory Committee's meager output during the decade, starting with their decision to spend more

---

[40] "Chief Justice Urges Greater Use of Arbitration," *N.Y. Times*, August 22, 1985, at A21.

than six years studying class actions.[41] We think it probable that the Chief Justice stimulated this interest in Rule 23 – that it was one of the "specific procedural devices" about which he "noted certain expressions of dissatisfaction" at the Committee's first meeting in 1971. It was not, in any event, one of the subjects that received attention from the Special Advisory Group that he had appointed, the report of which the Advisory Committee considered at that first meeting.

Whether or not the Advisory Committee was following the Chief Justice's lead, the decision to revisit class actions is additional evidence that the revolutionary potential of the 1966 amendments was quickly recognized. It may also signal recognition that those amendments were the product of a flawed process – conceived at a time when the Advisory Committee met in private, distributed proposals for comment to a relatively limited group, did not make written comments available to the public, and did not hold public hearings. From that perspective, the Advisory Committee charged by Burger may have been attempting to supplement the record in areas where knowledge was thin before proposing further action on Rule 23. Thus, although saddled with the same cloistered process, the Advisory Committee sent a survey to federal judges, in response to which "50 percent of 145 district judges indicated that they favored prompt amendment of Rule 23."[42]

An additional reason to proceed cautiously emerged during the course of the Advisory Committee's study of class actions.[43] A core limitation that the Rules Enabling Act imposes is that Federal Rules "shall not abridge, enlarge or modify any substantive right." It was a serious question whether material amendments to Rule 23 would do so. The Enabling Act difficulties implicated in consequential class action reform would likely have become apparent by reason of the contemporaneously unfolding controversy surrounding the proposed Federal Rules of Evidence. In 1973 Congress, for the first time since passage of the Enabling Act in 1934, blocked proposed Federal Rules transmitted by the Supreme Court, treating them as proposals for legislation and, after making numerous changes, enacting them as

---

[41] At its first meeting, in September 1971, the Committee requested the Reporter "to undertake a study of the desirability of effecting changes in" Rule 23 (Class Actions) and Rule 16 (Pre-trial Procedure). Minutes of Advisory Committee, September 1971, at 2.

[42] 124 Cong. Rec. 27,860 (1978).

[43] There is a big gap in the public record of Advisory Committee minutes during this period. As a result, with respect to the period between September 1971 and May 1977, our assessment is based on the reports of the Standing Committee to the Judicial Conference. See, e.g., the September 1973 Report at 6, available www.uscourts.gov/uscourts/RulesAndPolicies/rules/Reports/ST09-1973.pdf

a statute. One reason for doing so was the belief that some of the proposed rules abridged substantive rights (Burbank 2004a).

Enabling Act difficulties became even harder to miss in the spring of 1977 when Justice Department officials briefed the Advisory Committee on legislative proposals to amend Rule 23.[44] Indeed, the Justice Department subsequently noted "serious questions as to whether such revision is appropriately within the scope of the rule-making authority granted by the Rules Enabling Act" when sponsoring legislation to replace Rule 23(b)(3) (Burbank and Wolff 2010: 58–9), which we discussed in Chapter 2. No such legislation was enacted, but after it was introduced class action reform disappeared from the Advisory Committee's agenda for more than a decade.

Not easily thwarted, however, in 1976 Burger stimulated and presided at the Pound Conference, which was a showcase for those seeking retrenchment through rulemaking. Billed as the National Conference on the Causes of Popular Dissatisfaction with the Administration of Justice, the Pound Conference sought to address the problem of growing caseloads through procedural reform (Wallace 1982). In his keynote address, Burger noted "widespread complaints that [pre-trial procedures] are being abused and overused," and that "the cure is in our hands," making clear that he meant a cure by rulemaking under the Enabling Act (Burger 1979: 35). Prominent critics took aim at notice pleading and discovery – the cornerstones of modern, litigation-friendly federal procedure – as well as at the recently amended class action rule (Rifkind 1979; Kirkham 1979; Subrin and Main 2014). Some scholars have "characterized the Burger-organized Pound Conference in 1976 as the most important event in the counteroffensive against notice pleading and broad discovery" (Tonsing 2004: 25).

Following the Pound Conference, although the Advisory Committee established a Subcommittee on Abuse of Discovery, the American Bar Association (ABA) was permitted to set the discovery reform agenda through a Special Committee for the Study of Discovery Abuse of its Section of Litigation.[45] Contrary to the ABA Special Committee's

---

[44] Minutes of Advisory Committee on Civil Rules, Minutes of the Meeting on May 23, 1977, at 2–3., available at www.uscourts.gov/rules-policies/archives/meeting-minutes/advisory-committee-rules-civil-procedure-may-1977

[45] The preliminary draft of proposed amendments that the Advisory Committee circulated for comment in March 1978 "was in major part the response of the Advisory Committee to a study of the discovery rules that had been undertaken by the [ABA Special Committee]." Memorandum from Judge Walter R. Mansfield, Chair of the Advisory Committee on Civil Rules, to Judge Roszel C. Thomsen, Chair of the Standing Committee 2 (June 14, 1979) (available from authors).

recommendation and its own initial inclination, however, the Advisory Committee decided not to propose narrowing the scope of discovery. The ABA Special Committee had recommended reducing the scope of discovery from material "relevant to the subject matter involved in the pending action," to material "relevant to the issues raised by the claims or defenses of any party." The Committee's Chair observed that "we are not satisfied on the present record, including such empirical studies as have been made, that changes suggested so far would be of any substantial benefit." The Advisory Committee also rejected an ABA proposal to limit the number of written interrogatories.[46]

Comments of a number of participants at the Pound Conference suggest an additional reason that it did not lead to retrenchment of the sort Burger sought, and they point to a further possible reason for the Advisory Committee's lack of alacrity in pursuing Burger's agenda. The comments highlight that some important figures tapped to participate in the conference, including people who might have been expected to support Burger's efforts, ultimately did not share his normative characterization of the problem as arising from a litigious society, let alone "mass neurosis." Simon Rifkind, whose remarks at the Pound Conference included criticisms of notice pleading and broad discovery, acknowledged "a fear that this conference is conspiring to promote a counterrevolution" in the area of civil rights, and he was at pains to "disengage [him]self from any such enterprise" (Rifkind 1979: 55). Rifkind, formerly a federal judge, was a litigation partner at Paul, Weiss, Rifkind, Wharton & Garrison LLP, with a nationally renowned corporate defense practice.

The same concern animated the eloquent address of Judge Leon Higginbotham on "The Priority of Human Rights in Court Reform," in which he reminded his audience that Pound himself had argued that "in discouraging litigation we encourage wrongdoing" (1979: 88). Moreover, in their Foreword to the volume that emerged from the Pound Conference, three former presidents of the ABA, having listed other reasons "for the rush to litigation that overburdens our federal and state judicial systems today," observed:

> But perhaps an overriding cause of excessive resort to litigation is that people, and especially the traditionally disadvantaged, do, as Lord Herschell put it, "feel and see that they are getting" a measure of justice in the courts, the kind of respectful attention and thoughtful consideration that they do not think they get anywhere else. (Gossett, Segal, and Smith 1979: 11)

[46] Ibid. at 8, 9.

As in the legislative context discussed in Chapter 2, advocates of retrenching private enforcement through rulemaking had difficulty partitioning their project from retrenchment of substantive rights. This presented obstacles for coalition building.

A final reason that may explain why the 1970s Advisory Committee proceeded carefully with class action reform, which is also suggested by its ultimate rejection of major discovery reform, is that the Committee was not ideally composed to respond favorably to calls for major litigation retrenchment from organized bar groups or to pressure from the Chief Justice. For most of the decade judge-members who had been appointed by Democratic presidents, although in the minority, had substantial representation. A material imbalance arose (through attrition) only in the last two years. Chief Justice Burger appears to have learned his lesson, and his successors have usually followed his lead.

In 1980 Justice Powell, joined by Justices Stewart and Rehnquist, dissented from the promulgation of the proposed discovery amendments that emerged from this process, deriding them as "tinkering changes" that would "delay for years the adoption of genuinely effective reforms."[47] In this, Justice Powell, who had been President of the ABA, was echoing the reasoning of the ABA Special Committee, which had urged the Advisory Committee not to transmit its proposals, "[m]indful that the rules which are ultimately adopted will likely govern discovery proceedings for the next decade."[48] Even though Chief Justice Burger's role in the Enabling Act process probably prevented him from joining Justice Powell's dissenting statement, he cannot have been pleased. Moreover, his disposition cannot have been improved by Powell's use of the term of disparagement – "tinkering" – that Burger himself, channeling Roscoe Pound, had used in his call to action at the 1976 Pound Conference (Burger 1979).

Lessons in Control Strategy: Changes in the Process of Making Procedural Law by Federal Rule

While sitting for 19% of the study period, the 1980s Advisory Committee sent forward 15% of the total proposals (at the Rule level). Four of these proposals predictably implicated private enforcement, comprising 14% of all such proposals. Of these, two sets of proposals (amending Rules 4 and 15) predictably would favor private enforcement, while two sets of

---

[47] 446 U.S. 997, 1000 (1980).
[48] Mansfield Memorandum 1979, at 8.

proposals (amending Rules 11 and 26) predictably would disfavor private enforcement. At the subunit level we use for statistical purposes, the decade yielded a small net disfavoring private enforcement. Qualitative assessment of these proposals leads to a different conclusion, however, one in which the anti-private enforcement potential of the 1983 amendments to Rules 11 (sanctions) and 26 (discovery) swamped the contrary tendencies of the amendments to Rules 4 (service of process) and 15 (amended pleadings).

The 1980s Advisory Committee was a group chiefly distinguishable from their predecessors in the 1970s by reason of the greater representation of judges appointed by Republican presidents, whose presumed ideological preferences made them more likely to favor retrenchment and thus to take their lead from a Chief Justice who was not shy about telling them what he wanted. They were, moreover, operating in a political environment in which, as we demonstrated in Chapter 2, private enforcement retrenchment had emerged as a salient issue championed by the Republican Party in the White House and Congress, and as an issue cleavage between the parties. The attempt to use Federal Rules as the vehicle of retrenchment backfired, however, leading to major changes in the Enabling Act process – with the Advisory Committee laboring in the shadow of impending legislation for most of the decade.

In the early 1980s the Committee advanced proposals to amend Rule 11, and considered proposals to amend Rule 68, whose tenor was predictably anti-private enforcement. The Special Advisory Group that Burger appointed in 1971 had identified these rules as potentially fruitful sources of litigation retrenchment.[49] As promulgated in 1938, Rule 11 required an attorney to sign every pleading, thereby certifying that the attorney had read it, that there was good ground to support it, and that it was not "interposed for delay." Original Rule 11 also empowered the district court to strike a pleading that was not signed or that was signed with an intent to defeat the purpose of the rule, and in the event of a willful violation to initiate "appropriate disciplinary action." The Advisory Committee proposed to broaden the scope of the rule to include motions and other papers in addition to pleadings, to broaden the scope of an attorney's (or unrepresented party's) certification, to broaden the scope of permissible sanctions, and to make sanctions for a violation mandatory rather than discretionary.

The proposed amendments to Rule 11 applied equally to papers signed by counsel for plaintiffs and defendants, but they were prompted by

---

[49] See *supra* note 37.

oft-repeated arguments attributing cost and delay to frivolous lawsuits. On that worldview the sanctions target of choice would be the complaint. Lacking empirical foundation, the proposals were widely regarded as a threat to private enforcement because they would chill the legitimate zeal of plaintiffs' attorneys in representing their clients. This helps to explain why they were controversial and elicited widespread opposition from the bar (Burbank 1989a; Burbank 2004a). Indeed, the opposition to the Rule 11 proposals was so strong that opponents almost succeeded in blocking the 1983 proposed amendments in Congress. Because that requires legislation, opponents of proposed Federal Rules must navigate the separation of powers and checks and balances gauntlet that we discussed in Chapter 2. The House passed a bill to prevent the proposed amendments from taking effect, but, although "a bill to delay their effectiveness was sitting in the well of the Senate on the appropriate morning... no one hauled it out" (Miller 1984: 1).

Following the 1983 amendments, the Committee turned its attention to offers of judgment (settlement) under Rule 68. Rule 68 provides that a prevailing party who has rejected an offer of judgment more favorable to that party than the judgment ultimately obtained must pay the "costs incurred after the offer was made." Imagine that a plaintiff declines an offer of judgment in the amount of $100,000 and subsequently wins a verdict for $60,000. Even though the plaintiff is the prevailing party and thus presumptively entitled to an award of costs (other than attorney's fees) from the defendant under Rule 54(d), by reason of Rule 68 the plaintiff will have to pay the "costs" it incurred in the litigation after the offer was made. The rule seeks to promote settlements through financial incentives keyed to a comparison of a rejected offer and a subsequent judgment. According to the Advisory Committee, a principal reason that it had been ineffective was "that 'costs,' except in rare instances in which they are defined to include attorney's fees . . . are too small a factor to motivate parties to use the rule."[50]

In the 1983 proposal, the Advisory Committee "sought a more effective incentive for parties to settle cases promptly by making the proposed Rule available to all parties, adding reasonable attorney's fees to the costs that are shifted, and providing for an award of interest" (Burbank 1986: 427–8). One of the concerns about the newly amended Rule 11 was that it could be used effectively to reverse the American Rule on fees (each side pays its own). Indeed, as critics of the Committee's proposal had feared, many

---

[50] Proposed Fed. R. Civ. P. 68 advisory committee note, 98 F.R.D. 363–4 (1983).

courts awarded attorney's fees as the sanction for filing a complaint found to violate the rule. The 1983 proposal to amend Rule 68 likewise put the American Rule at risk, but it also threatened to undermine one-way statutory fee-shifting provisions that Congress included in legislation in order to stimulate private enforcement, notably those applicable in civil rights actions (Burbank 1986; Burbank 1989a; Burbank 1989b).

It is suggestive of the Chief Justice's influence on federal court rulemaking in the early 1980s that, notwithstanding the intense controversy that greeted their 1983 Rule 68 proposal, the Advisory Committee elected to forge ahead. The Rule 11 amendments had barely survived an override effort, and the Committee was forcefully and repeatedly alerted to serious opposition to its 1983 proposal to amend Rule 68, including by Robert Kastenmeier, the Democratic chair of the subcommittee of the House Judiciary Committee with jurisdiction over the federal judiciary. In floor remarks in October 1984, Representative Kastenmeier argued that the 1983 proposal "would have crossed the line from procedural to substantive [under the Enabling Act]" and that "Congress conferred a substantive right by enacting the Civil Rights Attorney Fee Award Act."[51]

Encouraged by the Chief Justice (Burger 1985), the Committee substituted a 1984 proposal that sought to defuse opposition by moderating the 1983 proposal somewhat. Opposition persisted, including from Kastenmeier, who ultimately wrote a letter to the new chair of the Advisory Committee giving notice that he was "very seriously concerned" about the proposals (Burbank 1986: 426, 428–30, 440 n. 81). Indeed, as we will discuss shortly, over the course of three hearings in the House from 1983 to 1985, proposals to amend Rule 68 came to occupy center stage in the discussion of changes in the Enabling Act process. Ultimately, the Advisory Committee abandoned the effort.

The controversies over Rule 11 and Rule 68 in the early 1980s arrived on the heels of a decade in which Congress for the first time blocked proposed Federal Rules – the proposed Federal Rules of Evidence – and thereafter blocked a number of other proposed amendments, albeit mostly proposed amendments to rules of criminal procedure. The 1970s was, moreover, a decade in which a number of thoughtful proposals for rulemaking reform appeared in the academic and professional literature, and in which a number of bills designed to implement reforms were introduced in Congress. In addition, the rule-specific controversies of the early 1980s came at about the time (1) the Federal Judicial Center published a study, undertaken at

---

[51] 130 Cong. Rec. H4104 (daily ed. October 1, 1984).

the request of Chief Justice Burger, that comprehensively reviewed the arguments for and against changes in the Enabling Act process, and (2) the ABA approved a policy that advocated substantial changes in that process (Brown 1981; Burbank 1982; Burbank 1983: 998 n. 2).

Both the general debate concerning the Enabling Act process and controversies arising from specific rulemaking proposals led Representative Kastenmeier to convene a series of oversight hearings in the House of Representatives, one each in 1983, 1984, and 1985. The focus of the first hearing was on the general issues, in particular arguments that the Enabling Act process was insufficiently inclusive and transparent. Much of the testimony at subsequent hearings addressed proposed legislation to implement comprehensive reforms that Kastenmeier had introduced. Yet, attention at those subsequent hearings increasingly turned to the question whether the rulemakers had acted, or were proposing to act, beyond the limits of the Enabling Act, abridging substantive rights and thereby subverting congressional preferences. The Advisory Committee's proposals to amend Rule 68 assumed greater prominence during the 1984 and 1985 hearings, as did arguments that those proposals put at risk private enforcement regimes that Congress had carefully constructed to vindicate substantive civil rights law.

Although some of the testimony and discussion at the House hearings lacked obvious ideological or partisan tenor, it is difficult so to describe much of the testimony and discussion concerning Rule 68. A submission by the Alliance for Justice – an umbrella organization representing a wide range of liberal public interest groups – about the 1983 and 1984 proposals specifically linked them to the unsuccessful Republican attempts in Congress to curb pro-plaintiff attorney's fee shifting that we discussed in Chapter 2.[52] There was substantial overlap between the liberal public interest organizations that opposed the Rule 68 proposals and sought to protect statutory private enforcement regimes, and the groups singled out by Powell in his 1971 memorandum as "extremely active in the judicial arena." Burt Neuborne, then the National Legal Director of the ACLU, described the story told by the traditional rhetoric of procedure as "a myth," and he intimated his willingness to acquiesce in "exempt[ing] procedural rules from the traditional democratic process" only because (and

---

[52] See Testimony of the Alliance for Justice on the 1984 Proposal to Amend Rule 68 before the Judicial Conference Advisory Committee on Civil Rules (January 28, 1985), *reprinted in Rules Enabling Act of 1985: Hearing before the Subcommittee on Courts, Civil Liberties and the Administration of Justice of the H. Comm. on the Judiciary*, 99th Cong. 113, 144 (1985) (hereinafter *1985 House Hearings*).

so long as) the rulemakers produced "good rules" from his perspective.[53] Like others testifying at the hearings – most prominently Alan Morrison of Ralph Nader's Public Citizen Litigation Group – Neuborne had in mind specific communities whose views, he argued, tended to be excluded by unrepresentative committees that did not actively seek a broad base of information.[54]

These hearings culminated in amendments to the Enabling Act in the 100th Congress (1987–8), the first in which Democrats controlled both chambers since the emergence of controversy in the early 1980s. Scholars have disagreed about the extent to which the changes in the Enabling Act process that occurred during the 1980s and the changes that were formally prescribed by statute in 1988 should be attributed to the judiciary or to the Congress. The dichotomy is misleading (Burbank 2004a). A dynamic of institutional dialogue in the shadow of possible legislation yielded particular compromises on a range of matters that were important to those seeking reform.

Spurred by the rulemaking debate in the 1970s and by the Chief Justice's apparent willingness to consider reform, the judiciary had experimented with some changes prior to the congressional hearings convened by Representative Kastenmeier.[55] It was not institutionally committed to any of them until, avowedly in response to those hearings, the rulemakers finally made public a set of rulemaking procedures to which they could be held accountable.[56] Moreover, the judiciary sought to maintain as much power and autonomy as possible. Its representative, Judge Gignoux, who was chair of the Standing Committee, continued to resist legislatively prescribed rulemaking procedures, arguing that legislation would lack adequate flexibility and was largely unnecessary given the action taken by the judiciary.[57] He also continued to resist a requirement of open meetings.[58]

The rulemaking changes that were urged upon the federal judiciary, some of which were ultimately statutorily required, were similar to changes that Congress had imposed on executive branch advisory committees and

[53] *Rules Enabling Act: Hearings before the Subcommittee on Courts, Civil Liberties and the Administration of Justice of the H. Comm. on the Judiciary*, 98th Cong. 150 (1985) (hereinafter *1983 and 1984 House Hearings*) (statement of Burt Neuborne).

[54] *See* ibid. at 147–8.

[55] *See 1983 and 1984 House Hearings, supra* note 53, at 4–5, 10 (Statement of Judge Gignoux, Chair of the Standing Committee).

[56] *See* ibid. at 90 (statement of Judge Gignoux).

[57] *See* ibid. at 90, 100, 103 (statement of Judge Gignoux).

[58] *See* ibid. at 11, 18–19 (statement of Judge Gignoux); *1985 House Hearings, supra* note 52, at 239, 249 (statement of Judge Gignoux).

administrative agencies in the 1970s (Schiller 2001; Burbank 2004a). In both domains, concern about abuse of delegated lawmaking power was accompanied by skepticism about either the expertise of those exercising such power or the monopoly that deference to the claim of expertise effectively conferred. In the 1988 legislation, Congress required rulemaking committees to hold open meetings, preceded by "sufficient notice to enable all interested persons to attend," to keep and make available to the public minutes of such meetings, and to provide an explanatory note with any proposed rule, as well as a report "including any minority or separate views." It also lengthened the minimum period before proposed Federal Rules can become effective after being reported to Congress – from three to seven months.[59]

In combination with the judiciary's published procedures, these amendments ensured that interest groups with a perceived stake in the subject of proposed rulemaking could provide pertinent information to the rulemakers and serve as whistleblowers or fire alarms for members of Congress in the event they thought something was seriously wrong. The 1980s reforms also effectively increased the evidentiary burden on the Advisory Committee when seeking to change the status quo and increased the window of time for vetoing attempted rules changes.

The goal was not to control the rulemaking function by taking it over (but see Staszak 2015: ch. 4). On the contrary, numerous participants in the lawmaking process leading to the reforms lauded them on the ground that they would reduce the need for congressional action at the end of the process.[60] Reform was, instead, a control strategy designed, at the least, to free Congress from regular active involvement, easing the legislative costs of monitoring the rulemakers ex post. Such a strategy has no necessary ideological or partisan inspiration. However, the concurrence of attacks by liberal interest groups and Democratic legislators on specific products of a rulemaking process undertaken by a committee appointed by a Republican Chief Justice, and advocacy of changes to that process, suggests a more ambitious ideological or partisan agenda than is evident by considering either element in isolation.

---

[59] Judicial Improvements and Access to Justice Act, Pub. L. No. 100–702, § 401, 102 Stat. 4642, 4649 (1988) (codified as amended at 28 U.S.C. § 2073(c) (2), (d) (2012)).

[60] *See, e.g., 1983 and 1984 House Hearings, supra* note 53, at 33, 48 (statement of Alan Morrison); ibid. at 154–5 (introductory remarks of Hon. Robert W. Kastenmeier); letter from Stephen B. Burbank to Hon. Robert Kastenmeier (January 13, 1984), *reprinted in* ibid. at 204, 213.

A study of the political origins of the Administrative Procedure Act (APA) supports the hypothesis that New Deal Democrats changed their position on the APA in 1946 because they feared losing control of Congress and the presidency, and because they were comfortable giving federal judges, most of whom President Roosevelt had appointed, the power to check the agencies they feared would come under Republican control. The New Deal Democrats' support represented, in part, a strategic use of statutory process to increase the cost and political difficulty for administrative agencies to change the status quo, in particular the laws and regulations enacted by a series of Democratic Congresses in the New Deal period. This legislative strategy deployed formal administrative process in order, among other things, to empower and mobilize interest group monitoring of agency actions, and impose burdens of evidence and justification on agencies seeking to change the status quo, thereby lessening the need for active oversight by Congress (McCubbins and Schwartz 1984; McNollgast 1987; McNollgast 1999).

Aside from making change more difficult, these types of process reforms – widening access, enlarging information flows, heightening evidentiary burdens – can be used to enhance the quality of policymaking, conceived from the enacting coalition's point of view. Particularly in the face of uncertainty about how best to regulate problems that will arise under a statute, procedural machinery geared to generate information needed for effective regulation as problems arise facilitates general delegations. An enacting coalition, cognizant that it may not be in power, or for other reasons may not be able, to solve future problems by new legislation, may see such procedural devices as a more effective way to regulate than resolving policy in greater detail in Congress at the time of enactment (McNollgast 1987).

The changes to the rulemaking process advocated by interest groups and congressional Democrats (including an influential committee chair) in the 1980s served similar goals. ACLU National Legal Director Burt Neuborne's testimony at the 1984 House hearing suggested a goal of using process changes to preserve "good rules" as the civil rights and civil liberties communities would define them. Under the 1980s reforms, the trans-substantive reach of Federal Rules assures monitoring by a broad swath of interest groups, because the effects of any rule change have the potential to radiate widely across substantive fields of federal litigation. Such monitoring should make it more difficult for the rulemakers to exceed their charter, and it provides a credible threat of whistleblowing if the rulemakers proceed with proposals deemed to be ultra vires, unsupported by evidence, or otherwise seriously objectionable.

Unlike the situation under the APA, the courts are not realistically available to preserve the status quo by policing either the consistency of Federal Rules with the terms of the statutory delegation or the process leading to their promulgation. The Enabling Act confers broad power to promulgate rules of "procedure" but specifies that they may not "abridge, enlarge, or modify any substantive right." During the House hearings, some criticized the Court's jurisprudence interpreting the Enabling Act, arguing that it eviscerated the statute's limiting language by equating "substantive rights" with rules of substantive law[61] and establishing as the test of validity whether a rule "really regulates procedure."[62] To be sure, the legislative record of the 1988 amendments contains a renewed commitment on behalf of the rulemakers to abide by the statutory limits on their work. As part of a successful effort to persuade the House not to insist on eliminating the Enabling Act's supersession clause – pursuant to which valid Federal Rules supersede previously enacted statutes with which they are inconsistent – Chief Justice Rehnquist asserted that the rulemakers "have always been keenly aware of the special responsibility they have in the rules process and the duty incumbent upon them not to overreach their charter."[63]

Yet, even if the Court were to invigorate the Enabling Act's limitations through reinterpretation, given the breadth of the delegation, they would not provide much protection against changes in the status quo, let alone bad public policy. Moreover, failure to comply with the statutory rulemaking process put in place in 1988 "does not invalidate" a Federal Rule.[64] Thus, although a goal of the Enabling Act process reforms was to lessen legislative monitoring costs, it was important that a "second bite at the apple" be available to "organized interests that seek to preserve the status quo" (McNollgast 1999: 181) through the provision requiring proposed Federal Rules to lie before Congress for seven months before becoming effective. "In the absence of effective judicial review of court rules, (the potential for) congressional review becomes the only feasible alternative" (Burbank 2004a: 1725).

After 1988, as before, it is difficult to muster the forces needed to pass legislation that blocks a Federal Rule promulgated by the Supreme Court. Moreover, securing such legislation may be especially difficult because,

[61] *See, e.g.*, Burbank letter, *supra* note 60, at 208–11.
[62] *Sibbach* v. *Wilson and Co.*, 312 U.S. 1, 14 (1941). *See also Hanna* v. *Plumer*, 380 U.S. 460 (1965); *Shady Grove Orthopedic Assocs.* v. *Allstate Insurance Co.*, 559 U.S. 393 (2010).
[63] Letter from Hon. William H. Rehnquist to Rep. Peter W. Rodino, Jr. (October 19, 1988), *reprinted in* 134 Cong. Rec. H10,441 (daily ed. October 19, 1988).
[64] 28 U.S.C. § 2073(e) (2012).

due to the transsubstantive scope of Federal Rules, a vote against a proposal may help some constituents or interests while harming others (*see* Landes and Posner 1975: 885). In such circumstances, action may carry more electoral perils than inaction. As a result, it is primarily the 1980s process reforms, combined with other influences promoting institutional self-restraint, that make bold reforms difficult to achieve through court rulemaking (Burbank 2004a: 1736–7).

The New Regime of Open Rulemaking: Process, People, or Politics?

In contrast with its record during the two previous decades, the Advisory Committee was very busy in the 1990s. While sitting for 19% of the study period, it sent forward 24% of the total proposals (at the Rule level). Eight proposals for amendments predictably implicated private enforcement, comprising 28% of such proposals that we identified for the study period, all of them in the proposals that led to the 1993 and 2000 amendments to the Federal Rules. From that perspective the decade was a mixed bag of proposals favoring and disfavoring private enforcement, although in the area that dominated rulemaking activity – discovery – the Advisory Committee's proposals tilted heavily against private enforcement.[65]

The balance of power on the Committee between judges appointed by Republican versus Democratic presidents tilted more sharply in favor of Republican appointees starting in 1991–2. Indeed, the only two judges associated with Democratic appointment authorities for four years were state court judges, and there was only one of them in any year. In addition, members with practices primarily representing corporations/ business had much higher representation than those primarily representing individuals (46% vs. 5% of service years).

A likely reason for the Advisory Committee's mixed record in the 1990s has to do with the qualities and priorities of the leadership of the Committee. "Perhaps the most important task of the chair [of the Advisory Committee] is to set the Committee agenda" (Cooper 2014: 592). The perceived importance of the chair's role in this respect is suggested by the fact that, with one exception, all chairs appointed by a succession of Republican-appointed Chief Justices between 1971 and 2014

---

[65] The 1993 amendments to Rule 4, which liberalized service of process in numerous respects, are primarily responsible for the spike in pro-private enforcement items we see when we map pertinent proposals at the most granular level. See appendix.

were themselves appointed by Republican presidents. As we note earlier in this chapter, the resulting imbalance is vastly greater than the comparable imbalance in appointments to the Committee as a whole, and it resulted in the Committee being chaired by a Republican-appointed judge in 41 of 43 years. Ironically, the one exception – Judge Frank Johnson's two-year term in the mid-1980s – may also illustrate the importance of the chair's role, albeit with quite different inflection.

President Eisenhower appointed Johnson to the District Court in 1955, and, following conspicuously distinguished service during the civil rights era, President Carter appointed him to the Court of Appeals in 1979. Chief Justice Burger appointed him chair of the Advisory Committee in 1985, at the height of the controversy concerning the Rule 68 proposals in the rulemaking process and in Congress. Johnson was the "new chair" to whom Representative Kastenmeier sent the letter detailing his concerns about those proposals that we mention earlier in this chapter. Just as that letter was intended as a signal, so, we believe, was Chief Justice Burger's act in appointing Johnson. Of course, for that purpose, the party of the appointing president was secondary to the judge's reputation as a hero of the civil rights movement.

For three years under Judge Patrick Higginbotham, the 1990s Committee concentrated on outreach to the bar and the academy as a means of healing wounds that had emerged in the 1980s, educating the Committee, and seeking consensus on reform. Judge Higginbotham described the Advisory Committee's renewed consideration of Rule 23 to the Standing Committee as follows:

> Judge Higginbotham explained that after he had become chairman, the advisory committee returned to Rule 23 and decided that it needed to reach out widely and learn as much as it could about class actions. This required not just seeking reactions to a particular proposal for amending the rule, but also a broad effort to deal with basic concepts and to explore the practical operation of all aspects of class actions. Judge Higginbotham pointed out that the advisory committee had invited prominent class action lawyers to attend its meetings and discuss class action issues. It had also convened symposia and meetings on class actions with practitioners and scholars at university settings in Philadelphia, Dallas, New York, and Tuscaloosa. Many people had participated in these gatherings, and they had been encouraged to speak freely and share their differing viewpoints. Judge Higginbotham stated that the lawyers and academics had been generous with their time, and he thanked them for their contributions to the work of the advisory committee.[66]

---

[66] Minutes of Meeting of Committee on Rules of Practice and Procedure, June 19–20, 1996, at 20, available at www.uscourts.gov/rules-policies/archives/meeting-minutes/committee-rules-practice-and-procedure-june-1996

The Chief Justice did not extend Judge Higginbotham's term, replacing him with Judge Paul Niemeyer, who had different priorities and preferences. In stark contrast with the Advisory Committee's care when considering possible amendments to Rule 23 in the 1990s, in the latter part of the decade the Committee eschewed caution when proposing discovery amendments.

The Committee had resisted calls to reduce the scope of discovery for more than 20 years. In the late 1990s, however, it proposed amendments to Rule 26 that would shrink the scope of discovery as of right from material relevant to the subject matter of the action, which would be available only on a showing of good cause, to material relevant to a claim or defense. As we discuss earlier in this chapter, the Advisory Committee had rejected a change to the scope of discovery when fashioning the proposals that became the 1980 discovery amendments, on the ground that there was insufficient empirical evidence to support it. The 1990s proposed amendments also included a cost-shifting provision that in some circumstances would have required the information-requesting party to bear some or all of the costs of the responding party. Such a rule could have been particularly disadvantageous to parties of modest means, including in particular plaintiffs seeking information in the voluminous records of corporate and government defendants.

In explaining the Committee's decision to revisit discovery, Judge Niemeyer invoked persistent pressure for litigation retrenchment from elite elements of the bar and a report from President Bush's Council on Competitiveness issued in 1991. The Council, chaired by Vice President Quayle, advocated a variety of anti-litigation proposals, including damages caps, a loser pays rule, and a moratorium on federal statutory one-way fee-shifting provisions. The Vice President explained that the Council's proposals were "geared toward reducing excessive and unnecessary litigation and decreasing the costs and time associated with resolving disputes" (Quayle 1992: 561). More candidly, the Council's charge concerned reducing costs imposed on business by government regulation (Krent 1993). Some of the Council's litigation reform proposals were subsequently incorporated into the Republicans' 1994 Contract with America, with Newt Gingrich as their public champion (Hixson 2013).

In a remarkable display of candor, Judge Niemeyer, whom President Bush appointed to the bench, acknowledged both the lack of empirical evidence for the position being urged on the Advisory Committee and the influence of repeated calls for limitations on discovery. He explained:

> Indeed, in August 1991, the President's Council on Competitiveness issued a report claiming that "over 80 percent of the time and cost of a typical

lawsuit involves pre-trial examination of facts through discovery." While I am not aware of any empirical data to support this claim, the fact that the claim was made and is often repeated by others, many of whom are users of the discovery rules, raises a question of whether the system pays too high a price for the policy of full disclosure in civil litigation (Niemeyer 1998: 518; see ibid. at 520).

For those favoring retrenchment, the timing was right. The political climate favored the counterrevolution, and, given the post-1994 locus of partisan control of Congress, there was no risk of congressional override.[67] In a memorandum to his colleagues on the American College of Trial Lawyers' Federal Civil Procedure Committee describing a conversation with Judge Niemeyer, Robert Campbell reported that Niemeyer had delivered the "extremely good news" that the Judicial Conference had approved the proposed discovery scope amendment. The College is an organization of primarily defense lawyers, and it is a long-time advocate of litigation retrenchment (D. Marcus 2013b: 615; Galanter and Luban 1993: 1418). Observing that members of the College had spent "thousands of hours" working for the amendment, Campbell also noted that credit was due to a member of the College, Francis Fox, who "played a major role" on the Advisory Committee when it was considering the proposal.[68]

Even so, the Judicial Conference rejected one of the Committee's proposed discovery amendments (on cost-shifting), and the scope amendment passed that body by a vote of 13 to 12 (Stempel 2001: 619, 621). This was an important reminder that the multi-tiered process that was first put in place to exercise the Judicial Conference's responsibilities under the 1958 legislation, and that was subsequently solidified by the 1988 legislation, contributes to the stickiness of the court rulemaking status quo.[69]

[67] For a detailed account of the 2000 amendments, many aspects of which are confirmed by our systematic longitudinal data, see Stempel (2001). As we suggest more generally concerning the 1990s, Stempel observes that the "Committee seems to have been operating under both a preference for scientific inquiry and the gravitational pull of the venerable myth of discovery abuse" (555; see also ibid. at 613–14) ("What has changed, of course, are the pressure points of political power, particularly the Advisory Committee's receptiveness to certain arguments preferred by certain groups. Although the Committee and the other Rulemakers continue to strive for nonpartisan fairness, the composition of the Rulemakers has become distinctly more conservative in both ideology and social background.").

[68] Memorandum from Robert S. Campbell, Jr., Committee Chair, to Members, Federal Civil Procedure Committee, American College of Trial Lawyers (September 16, 1999) (available from authors).

[69] Under the 1988 legislation, the Conference is permitted but not required to authorize the appointment of advisory committees, but without them the statutorily required Standing Committee would have primary responsibility for all rulemaking (i.e., civil, criminal,

But the Committee presumably needed no such reminder, because the Conference had rejected a proposed amendment concerning jury size within the preceding five years (Burbank 2004a).

Although the 2000 discovery scope amendment was a retrenchment victory, its significance was questioned at the time, with many deeming the change unlikely to have much practical, as opposed to symbolic, effect. On that view, the episode illustrates that retrenchment of even modest ambition by rulemaking under the 1980s process reforms will elicit controversy and may have difficulty successfully navigating that process.

We have suggested that one reason for the Committee's mixed record in the 1990s – why it did not attempt more and bolder retrenchment – had to do with the very different qualities and priorities of its leadership over the decade, contrasting the process by which the Advisory Committee considered class action reform with its consideration of discovery reform. The qualities and priorities of the Committee's leadership also help to understand why rulemaking in the first decade of the new millennium was restrained.

While sitting for 19% of the study period, the Advisory Committee sent forward 20% of the total proposals (at the Rule level). Only two of them were salient from the perspective of private enforcement, comprising 7% of such proposals that we identified for the study period, and both were inimical to private enforcement. Judging only from the presumed committee preferences suggested by our data, one might have predicted significantly more retrenchment. Judges appointed by Republican presidents accounted for 77% of the service years of Article III members across the decade. Moreover, by this time unaligned practitioners on the Committee were a thing of the past, and of the 10 lawyer members serving during the decade, those representing primarily defendants and primarily corporations/business dominated with 72% of the years of service.

Yet, on a number of occasions the Advisory Committee prevented anti-private enforcement proposals from going forward. Moreover, prominent rulemakers celebrated these examples of restraint as evidence that the Enabling Act process works (Kravitz et al. 2013). From this perspective, restraint reflected the deeper epistemic foundation that results from an open process and greater commitment to empirical study, as well as the rulemakers' commitment to take seriously the Enabling Act's prohibition against abridging, enlarging, or modifying substantive rights (ibid.;

---

appellate, evidence, and bankruptcy) under the Enabling Act, which would be untenable. *See* 28 U.S.C. § 2073 (2012).

Burbank 2004a). We suggest earlier in this chapter that some proponents of the Enabling Act process reforms of the 1980s sought to increase the stickiness of the rulemaking status quo, in part by increasing the burdens of evidence needed to justify changes, in precisely this way.

As one example, during the 1990s leaders of the federal judiciary became increasingly frustrated by the inability of the federal courts under existing law to deal with the problem of duplicative class actions dispersed between the federal and state courts. In 2001–2, the rulemakers considered informal proposals to enable federal courts that had denied certification or settlement approval to enjoin state courts from certifying substantially similar classes or approving substantially similar settlements. "But after reflection, and after considering potential problems with the Anti-Injunction Act and the scope of rule making authority under the Rules Enabling Act, the Civil Rules Committee withdrew the proposals from consideration by the Standing Committee."[70] Thereafter, the judiciary's leadership sought relief elsewhere, adding the judiciary's support to the legislative effort that eventually yielded the Class Action Fairness Act of 2005 (Burbank 2008).

As another example, starting in 2006 the rulemakers considered whether they should pursue potentially significant changes to Rule 56 on summary judgment. Through a summary judgment motion, after adequate opportunity for discovery, a party (in most cases the defendant) asserts that the opposing party has not adduced sufficient evidence to warrant a trial on one or more material issues of fact, and that the movant is therefore entitled to judgment as a matter of law. A number of changes discussed by the Committee could be regarded as anti-plaintiff (Cooper 2014). Conscious of potential objections that some amendments under consideration would abridge substantive rights in violation of the Enabling Act, and of assured political controversy, the Advisory Committee focused on proposals ostensibly designed to improve the process for ruling on summary judgment motions. At that, they abandoned the most controversial of those proposals when testimony and written comments from numerous witnesses, including trial court judges (Kravitz et al. 2013), and empirical data demonstrated that it might well not yield the benefits sought and could have a significant, adverse effect on plaintiffs in employment

---

[70] Letter from Hon. Anthony J. Scirica to Committee on Rules of Practice and Procedure 1 (May 30, 2002) (available from authors).

discrimination litigation.[71] Although cited by prominent rulemakers as an example of the Enabling Act process working, the experience contributed to a practitioner's description of the rulemakers as having an "instinct for the capillary" (Joseph 2012: 9).

This perspective also helps to understand why, although the rulemakers repeatedly flirted with proposals to tighten up the pleading rules in the years after the Supreme Court's 1957 embrace of notice pleading in *Conley* v. *Gibson*,[72] they always abandoned them. Even after two post-*Conley* Supreme Court decisions that could be viewed as inviting rulemaking on the subject, the second issued in 2002, the Committee concluded that the game was not worth the candle, probably because any such proposal would generate significant controversy with inescapable political overtones (Burbank 1989b; Burbank 2009; R. Marcus 2013).

Finally, the rulemakers continued studying possible class action reforms into the early 2000s, this time supported by the empirical research of the Federal Judicial Center and, following the initial outreach meetings and conferences described by Judge Higginbotham in 1996, a voluminous record of public hearings.[73] At the end of the day, the Committee concluded that significant change to Rule 23 was so freighted with controversy among interest groups, and so problematic under the Enabling Act's requirement that rules not abridge substantive rights, that it should not be attempted by rulemaking. In 2000, the chair of the Advisory Committee's Rule 23 subcommittee, Judge Rosenthal, commented that "[e]arlier committee efforts were incredibly ambitious, addressing head-on some of the most important questions about class-action practice. But the rulemaking process itself will make it difficult to implement whatever answer may be found to some of these questions. The subcommittee has concluded that it is better to focus future efforts on the process of class actions."[74]

---

[71] *See* letter from Stephen B. Burbank to Committee on Rules of Practice and Procedure (January 28, 2009), available at www.uscourts.gov/rules-policies/archives/comments/professor-stephen-b-burbank-08-cv-145

[72] 355 U.S. 41 (1957).

[73] "Proposed Rule 23 amendments were published in August, 1996, for comment. The volume of written comments, statements, and testimony was impressive. All have been collected in a four-volume set of materials." Minutes, Civil Rules Advisory Committee, May 1 and 2, 1997, at 4, available at www.uscourts.gov/rules-policies/archives/meeting-minutes/advisory-committee-rules-civil-procedure-may-1997

[74] Minutes, Civil Rules Advisory Committee, April 10 and 11, 2000, at 30, available at www.uscourts.gov/rules-policies/archives/meeting-minutes/advisory-committee-rules-civil-procedure-april-2000. Similarly, in 1998 Judge Niemeyer observed that "[t]he problems identified by the comments were far-reaching, and often seemed to call for answers that are beyond the reach of the Enabling Act process. The Committee

The changes they recommended instead, which went into effect in 1998 and 2003, were far more restrained than champions of class action retrenchment advocated, and they avoided the core elements of the rule (Kravitz et al. 2013).

Ironically, however, Rule 23 amendments that seemed modest at the time have facilitated major change in class action jurisprudence through court decisions. The most obvious and important example is the 1998 amendment adding Rule 23(f).[75] Facially neutral as between plaintiffs and defendants, this amendment permits courts of appeals in their discretion to entertain immediate appeals from class certification decisions.[76] It has enabled and highlighted another path to retrenchment of private enforcement by substantially expanding the opportunities for conservative federal appellate courts, including the Supreme Court, to control the course of class action jurisprudence. This suggests that, even in the domain of rulemaking, some consequential reforms can fly under the radar screen. In Chapters 4 and 5 we argue that this phenomenon has been an important reason for the Supreme Court's success in furthering the goals of the counterrevolution through decisions on issues salient to private enforcement.

Judges as Legislators?

The 1980s reforms opened the rulemaking process to more and more diverse sources of information, anecdotal and empirical – a development profoundly accelerated by the advent of the Internet. The imposition of these reforms on rulemaking committees that had come to be dominated by judges triggered institutional dynamics that were less likely to operate when committees were dominated by non-judges and when rulemaking was the product of "a relatively cloistered culture" (Higginbotham 2013). Smart people operating as part of a group may be perfectly willing to make decisions on the basis of their pooled reflections. Particularly if they can

---

found so many puzzles that it recommended present adoption only for the interlocutory appeal provision . . . " Minutes, Civil Rules Advisory Committee, November 12 and 13, 1998, at 8, available at www.uscourts.gov/rules-policies/archives/meeting-minutes/advisory-committee-rules-civil-procedure-november-1998

[75] Less obvious are 2003 amendments that, together with the accompanying Advisory Committee Note, courts have been able to leverage in influential decisions that have made class certification more difficult. *See, e.g., In re Hydrogen Peroxide Antitrust Litigation*, 552 F.3d 305 (3d Cir. 2008). The author of the opinion in this case, Judge Scirica, was a major player in rulemaking concerning Rule 23 in the 1990s and 2000s.

[76] A similar mechanism was part of the Carter Administration's proposed statute replacing Rule 23(b)(3). *See* S. 3475, 95th Cong. § 4 (1978); 124 CONG. REC. 27,866 (1978).

claim expertise or are confident about their power, they may also be willing to recommend bold action that they deem normatively desirable without worrying about empirical support, and without any rigorous attempt
to assess costs and benefits.

However, when rulemakers are judges, and when justification for
rule changes must be publicly articulated in light of a public evidentiary
record, in addition to (and potentially contradicting) judicial experience
and common sense, those judges may be reluctant to become involved in
controversies in which their decisions can be tarred with a political label.
This is especially true when the decision-makers' monopoly of expertise is
in question, in part, because the effect of potential procedural choices on
substantive rights is plain for all to see. The possibility that the ostensibly
procedural will be revealed as manifestly substantive is made more likely
by public hearings, a public record, and the virtual certainty that advocates
for those opposing a rulemaking proposal will articulate an impending
injury to substantive rights.

As we discuss earlier in this chapter, the rulemakers are not courts, and
rulemaking under the Enabling Act is not an exercise of judicial power
under Article III. It is essentially a legislative, not a judicial, activity, and
most federal judges are understandably reluctant to be seen as active participants in a political process. The rulemaking controversies of the 1970s
and early 1980s "were a threat to the prestige and influence of the Court
itself" (Burbank 2004a: 1721). Although Chief Justice Burger did not succeed in extricating the Supreme Court from the Enabling Act process in
the 1980s, justices have been at pains to distance the Court from responsibility for the content of Federal Rules (ibid.; Burbank 1993).

Conclusion

The 1980s Enabling Act process reforms contributed to an inclusive and
transparent rulemaking process, and the controversies from which they
arose helped to elicit, at least from some rulemakers, commitments to seek
and take seriously reliable empirical data and to follow a realistic view of
the Enabling Act's limitations. The tendency of such a process to inhibit or
derail major changes to Federal Rules that would affect private enforcement is furthered by such commitments, by the reluctance of most judges
(when acting as rulemakers) to be part of a public controversy perceived as
political, let alone partisan, and by the potential for override of Advisory
Committee proposals within the judiciary and by the Congress: they all
contribute to the stickiness of the rulemaking status quo. Whether this

tendency is counted a benefit depends on one's normative views about the need for, or the desirability of, major changes, and about the appropriate relationship between court rulemaking and legislative policy concerning private enforcement.

Even before the 1980s reforms, the Enabling Act process held the potential for stickiness once drafting responsibility was committed to the Judicial Conference, and the Conference chose to operate through a multi-stage process. However, that potential likely expands or contracts depending on the degree of deference shown to the Advisory Committee, which in turn is in part a function of the degree of control exercised by the Standing Committee. In that regard, however, it is worthwhile recalling that the Chief Justice not only appoints all members of both committees but also presides at the next two stages of review within the judiciary – the Judicial Conference and the Supreme Court (Brown 1981).

An important question as federal court rulemaking entered the current decade was whether the relative restraint evident in the immediately preceding period would continue. Our interpretation of rulemaking's vacillation between restraint and episodic retrenchment efforts is that there are contending perspectives among rulemakers, even those who support retrenchment. For some influential rulemakers, the important lessons of the 1980s concerned the threat that epistemic deficits of proposed reforms, or overreaching the Enabling Act's charter by abridging substantive rights, pose to the perceived legitimacy of the Enabling Act process. Rulemaking's perceived legitimacy serves the judiciary's institutional interest in control of procedure; it helps the judiciary resist legislatively imposed procedure. For others, the key lessons focused attention on what retrenchment could actually be accomplished given the preferences of bodies with veto power, in particular Congress. They recognized that if power is to be exercised effectively, it must be exercised strategically, with attention to potential responses of other institutional actors.

In considering rulemaking's likely future in this respect, the 2010 Conference on Civil Litigation organized by the Advisory Committee (the "Duke Conference") may be a significant inflection point. On the one hand, notwithstanding the evident hope of some organizers and participants that it would function like the 1976 Pound Conference as a catalyst of significant retrenchment efforts,[77] in their joint report to the Chief

---

[77] On the basis of the Duke Conference program, Patricia Moore concludes that "defense speakers on panels at the Duke Conference outnumbered plaintiffs' speakers almost two-to-one" (Moore 2015: 1140).

Justice the Advisory Committee and the Standing Committee provided no encouragement on the issue that, for 40 years, has been the brass ring for those seeking to limit private enforcement – the scope of discovery. They wrote:

> The extent of the actual change effected by [the 2000 scope] amendment continues to be debated. But there was no demand at the Conference for a change to the rule language; there is no clear case for present reform. There is continuing concern that the proportionality provisions of Rule 26(b)(2), added in 1983, have not accomplished what was intended. Again, however, there was no suggestion that this rule language should be changed.[78]

The "proportionality provisions" referred to under Rule 26(b)(2) then required the court to "limit the frequency or extent of discovery otherwise allowed" if it determined that "the burden or expense of the proposed discovery outweighs its likely benefit," taking into account the "needs of the case, the amount in controversy, the parties' resources, the importance of the issues at stake in the action, and the importance of the discovery in resolving the issues."

On the other hand, in 2013 the Advisory Committee adopted recommendations of a subcommittee that was established to translate the knowledge and insights generated for and at the Duke Conference into Federal Rules amendments. Under new leadership – with the approval of the Standing Committee, also under new leadership – the Committee published for comment proposals to amend the discovery rules that in significant respects contradicted the summary previously provided to the Chief Justice and were decidedly anti-private enforcement.[79] The proposals included eliminating the possibility of "subject matter" discovery on a showing of good cause, completing a process begun in 2000 that we discuss earlier in this chapter, and, most controversially, making proportionality part of the definition of the scope of discovery. The concerns expressed about the proportionality proposal included the likelihood that it would increase the transaction costs of discovery by stimulating more objections, that it would have the effect of changing the burden in discovery disputes to the party seeking discovery, and that as a result parties would

---

[78] Report to the Chief Justice of the United States on the 2010 Conference on Civil Litigation, at 8, available at www.uscourts.gov/rules-policies/records-and-archives-rules-committees/special-projects-rules-committees/2010-civil

[79] See Preliminary Draft of Proposed Amendments to the Federal Rules of Civil Procedure 264–6 (2013), available at www.regulations.gov/#!documentDetail;D=USC-RULES-CV-2013-0002-0001

be prevented from securing discovery central to their claims and defenses, imposing costs of a different order.[80]

It appears that, apart from, and prior to, the change of leadership on both committees, the impulse for restraint was overwhelmed by a call to action from the Chief Justice. In 2014 one of the authors asked a member of the Advisory Committee about the inconsistency between the report of the Duke Conference quoted above and the tenor of subsequent deliberations and proposals concerning the scope of discovery. The member responded that the Chief Justice had reacted to the report by strongly encouraging the Chair of the Advisory Committee to make use in rulemaking of the information acquired for and at the Conference.

Moreover, once the subcommittee was at work, retrenchment received support from the Chairman of a subcommittee of the House Judiciary Committee, who had presided at a hearing on the "Costs and Burdens of Civil Discovery." Congressman Trent Franks, a member of the House Tea Party Caucus and the conservative Republican Study Committee,[81] wrote to the Chairs of the Advisory and Standing Committees, expressing the hope that their committees would "recommend enacting rule reforms to address the principal concerns discussed at the hearing" (R. Marcus 2013: 1723). Given the difficulty of enacting legislation on salient issues like discovery, particularly in a period of divided government and at a time of general congressional paralysis, such a communication was not a credible threat of congressional action in the absence of rulemaking. It was, however, confirmation that, given the locus of partisan control, Federal Rules amendments retrenching discovery would not be overridden.

The fact that more than 2,300 comments were submitted on the preliminary draft of the proposed discovery amendments shows that, notwithstanding repeated characterization of the proposals as "modest" or "measured" by some rulemakers and interest groups, they triggered powerful interest group mobilization on both sides. Indeed, the intensity of interest group participation in the comment process and at the Committee's hearings was akin to that which, as we discuss in Chapter 2, makes legislation retrenching private enforcement of federal rights very difficult to enact. Perhaps that is because opponents feared, and proponents expected, a large transformation in discovery resulting from a succession of Federal Rules amendments. Alternatively, some individuals on

---

[80] *See, e.g.,* letter from Stephen B. Burbank to Committee on Rules of Practice and Procedure 12 (February 10, 2014) (available from authors).
[81] Sean Sullivan, "Who Is Trent Franks," *The Washington Post*, June 12, 2013.

both sides may have regarded the characterizations as sheep's clothing for a wolf.

Although modified in some respects thereafter, the proposed discovery amendments retained the core of their most controversial provision – changing the scope of discovery to include a proportionality requirement – when they went into effect on December 1, 2015. Long before that point, an effort was underway to ensure that, once effective, the amendments would not be ignored, and to influence their interpretation. Organized by the privately funded Duke Center for Judicial Studies, the effort involved the development of guidelines and practices (for amendments not yet effective) through a consensus-forcing process that was neither inclusive nor transparent and that operated primarily after a draft had already been produced. That process quickly became controversial, especially when it became known that some 60 magistrate judges had already been introduced to the guidelines and practices in their initial draft.

The controversy became public when it was announced that training sessions using the resulting guidelines and practices[82] would continue in courthouses throughout the country under the auspices of the ABA Section of Litigation (which had championed narrowing the scope of discovery since the Pound Conference) and the Duke Center.[83] The Advisory Committee disclaimed any responsibility, which may help to explain why a number of members and former members of that committee and the Standing Committee disappeared from the Duke Center Advisory Board and Advisory Council.

Whatever doubt there may be about the extent of legal change augured by the 2015 discovery amendments, the Chief Justice has made his hopes clear. Having prodded the Advisory Committee to do more than the joint report from the Duke Conference suggested, after the amendments went into effect Chief Justice Roberts added his voice to the effort to ensure that they would not be ignored and to influence their interpretation. Devoting his entire year-end report for 2015 to the amendments, Roberts emphasized their potential importance. Thus, he observed, although "[m]any

---

[82] See "Guidelines and Practices for Implementing the 2015 Discovery Amendments to Achieve Proportionality," *Judicature* 99 (2015): 47.

[83] See, e.g., Suja A. Thomas, "Via Duke, Companies Are Shaping Discovery," Law360 (November 4, 2015), available at www.law360.com/articles/723092/opinion-via-duke-companies-are-shaping-discovery; Patricia W. Moore, "Law Professor Challenges the Seeming Federal Endorsement of Duke Nonbinding 'Guidelines' on Proportionality Amendments," Civil Procedure & Federal Courts Blog (November 17, 2015), available at http://lawprofessors.typepad.com/civpro/2015/11/law-professor-challenges-the-seeming-federal-endorsement-of-duke-nonbinding-guidelines-on-proportion.html

rules amendments are modest and technical, even persnickety . . . the 2015 amendments to the Federal Rules of Civil Procedure are different." That is because "[t]hey mark significant change, for both lawyers and judges, in the future conduct of civil trials," with the result that, although they "may not look like a big deal at first glance . . . they are."[84]

Having emphasized the importance of training for both judges and lawyers, the Chief Justice noted that the "success of the 2015 civil rules amendments will require more than organized educational efforts. It will also require a genuine commitment, by judges and lawyers alike, to ensure that our legal culture reflects the values we all ultimately share."[85] If the data on decisions interpreting Federal Rules that we present in Chapter 4 tell us anything, it is that, when those rules have obvious implications for private enforcement, shared values have become increasingly hard to find.

---

[84] 2015 Year-End Report on the Federal Judiciary, at 4, 5, available at www.supremecourt. gov/publicinfo/year-end/2015year-endreport.pdf. It is unclear whether, as Adam Steinman (2016) argues, the Chief Justice's take on the 2015 amendments is spin designed to persuade lower court judges that they mean something they do not, or vindication of those who regarded claims that the amendments are "modest" and "measured" as a smokescreen.

[85] Ibid. at 10.

APPENDIX

Coding Practitioner Practice Types

For every practitioner, coders conducted separate searches in Westlaw and Lexis. We used both databases because we found that they sometimes contained different sets of cases, and we did not want our coding to be affected by the decision to rely on one database. We identified cases in which the practitioner appeared as counsel going back in time from their date of appointment and stopping when we reached 25 cases. If we did not obtain 25, we extended forward through the duration of their service on the Committee. In only a handful of instances did this protocol yield fewer than 25 cases. Criminal cases were not counted toward our ceiling of 25.

Practitioners were classified in each case according to whether they represented a corporate/business defendant; corporate/business plaintiff; individual person civil defendant; individual person civil plaintiff; union defendant; union plaintiff; government defendant; government plaintiff; or other type of party. From this information we calculated whether each practitioner represented 75% or more (1) defendants, (2) plaintiffs, (3) corporations/businesses, or (4) individuals. Infrequently, the cases obtained in Lexis and Westlaw would produce different classifications. In these instances, we consolidated the two sets of cases, eliminated duplicates, and assigned codes based on the combined cases.

We also collected information on attorney biographies, firm affiliations, firm profiles, and news coverage of practitioners that discussed their practice, such as in obituaries. In no instance did we find that this additional information contradicted the code assigned based on our review of cases. In rare instances, our search in Lexis and Westlaw yielded no cases or only a few, in which case we relied heavily on these additional historical sources. In nearly all of those cases, the practitioner was a partner in a corporate firm. When we had only that information, we coded the practitioner as corporate/business on the individual versus corporate/business scale, and coded them as having a mixed practice on the plaintiff versus defendant scale.

Model of Federal Judicial Appointments
to the Advisory Committee

Using Federal Judicial Center data, we constructed the dataset analyzed in Tables 3.1 and 3.2 as follows. Initially, for *each year* in the data, each federal District Court and Court of Appeals judge, both active and senior, is included. This produced 42,685 judge-year observations. A committee service variable was created and coded 1 for each year in which a judge served on the Advisory Committee, and coded 0 otherwise. There are a total of 277 years of committee service by Article III judges in this period. An appointment variable was also created and coded 1 in years that a decision was made by the Chief Justice to appoint or reappoint a judge to the Advisory Committee, and was coded 0 otherwise. There were 103 appointments or reappointments in this period: 50 initial appointments, 38 reappointments to all or part of a second term, 11 to a third, and 4 to a fourth. These committee service and appointment variables are dependent variables in our statistical models. Judges are dropped from the data when they are no longer eligible for service on the Committee – we assume that they are not eligible for appointment (to the Civil Rules Advisory Committee) after they have terminated service on the Committee.

Finally, for models of initial appointments, because of the small number of events, we examined an alternative specification using a Firth model, which is designed for "rare events" logit (Firth 1993). The party variable remained statistically significant.

The Unit of Analysis in Proposed Amendments
by the Advisory Committee

We examined two approaches to counting Advisory Committee proposals as alternatives to the approach discussed in the text, in order to confirm that the results we observe are not an artifact of the counting strategy used. In the first, we simply use the Rule-level count, avoiding the need to make judgments necessary to disaggregate a Rule-level proposal into smaller subunits. There were 33 proposals salient to private enforcement at the Rule level from 1960 to 2014. In the second, we took a more granular approach than that presented in the text. We counted every discrete proposed change to a Rule, but, unlike the approach taken in the text, we did not aggregate them into subject matter categories.

For example, the 1983 proposal to amend Rule 11 (1) expanded coverage to include not just pleadings but also any motion or paper, (2) added parties to attorneys as making certain certifications by signing a paper, and (3) strengthened the substance of the certification from the "good ground" standard to something more demanding; (4) introduced mandatory sanctions; and (5) identified costs and fees as potential sanctions. At the Rule level, this contributes one unit to the count. In the approach taken in the text, we count this as contributing two units to the count of proposed changes: one widening the scope of the Rule's application (items 1 to 3); and one strengthening sanctions (items 4 and 5). In the more granular approach, we count five proposed changes – one for each enumerated item. The last approach to counting renders a total of 70 proposed changes over the 33 Rule-level proposals from 1960 to 2014.

We estimated regression models of the probability of pro-plaintiff proposals over time using both of these alternative dependent variables. Figure A.3.1 displays the results. The Rule-level results look nearly identical to the intermediate-level estimates presented in Figure 3.6. The regression estimates generated by the Rule-level dependent variable are correlated with the intermediate-level ones at .99. The count at the more granular level follows the same long-run trajectory of decline, but with greater variation around the trend line. The estimates generated by the more granular dependent variable are correlated with the intermediate-level ones at .95.

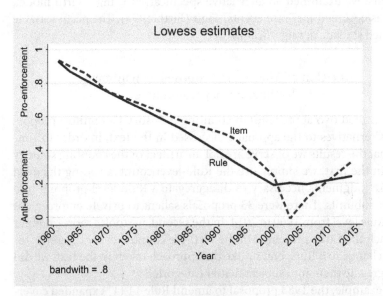

Figure A.3.1   Probability of pro-plaintiff Advisory Committee proposal, item level and rule level, 1960–2014

Finally, we regressed the alternative dependent variables on an annual time trend using ordinary least squares regression. As with the intermediate-level dependent variable discussed in the text, the results reveal that the negative time trend in the probability of pro-plaintiff proposals is statistically significant at better than .01 in both models. The coefficient on the year variable was −.015 in the Rule-level model, and −.013 in the more granular model. Overall, then, we conclude that the long and steep decline in the probability of pro-plaintiff proposals, conditional on the existence of a proposal affecting private enforcement, is a durable and robust feature of the data. It is not an artifact of any particular approach to constructing the unit of analysis.

4

Counterrevolution in the Supreme Court:
Succeeding through Interpretation

Introduction

In this chapter we deploy qualitative and quantitative evidence to document the course of the counterrevolution in the Supreme Court of the United States. One result emerges with striking clarity from both case studies and statistical analysis of an original dataset comprising all of the Court's private enforcement decisions in six critical areas spanning the years 1960 to 2014. When acting under Article III rather than as a delegated lawmaker under the Rules Enabling Act, the Court has been far more successful than either Congress or the rulemakers in changing the law that governs private enforcement. We argue that, increasingly during the study period, conservative Court majorities on private enforcement issues were composed of justices who were themselves increasingly influenced by ideology on those issues, which we believe contributed to the escalating levels of polarization our data reveal. Equally clear, although likely surprising to many, is the fact that both trends – toward voting influenced by ideology and polarization – have in recent years been most pronounced in cases with private enforcement issues governed by the Federal Rules of Civil Procedure. Finally, having charted the mix of our cases that involve government as opposed to business defendants, we show that the latter have come to dominate the Court's private enforcement docket in recent years and that, particularly in Federal Rules cases, business defendants are prevailing at an extraordinary rate.

The Supreme Court's jurisprudence affecting private litigation has been a frequent topic of attention by scholars, particularly over the last decade. Although some of the literature has focused on civil rights and other areas in which Congress has sought to promote private enforcement of federal law (Karlan 2003; Dodd 2015), other articles have broadened the field of inquiry to include court access more generally (Siegel 2006; Chemerinsky 2012; Staszak 2015). This literature has usually focused on the recent past, particularly the Rehnquist Court. Much of it asserts or assumes that the phenomenon in question is a manifestation of the ideological preferences of an increasingly conservative Supreme Court (see, e.g., Chemerinsky 2003: 540, 556).[1] With a few notable exceptions, there has been little attention to other possible influences on the results.[2] None of the work of which we are aware deploys statistical analysis of systematic data.[3]

Perhaps the most comprehensive contribution to this literature is Andrew Siegel's interesting article (2006) arguing that hostility to litigation best explains the jurisprudence of the Rehnquist Court – that it is the one unifying theme in the Court's jurisprudence in the Rehnquist years (1115–16), a theme that helps to explain some otherwise inconsistent results (1153).

We are particularly interested in the author's empirical claims about the role that liberal justices have played in the phenomenon he describes. Siegel adduces the "frequent participation – and occasional leadership – of the Court's more liberal members in shaping a Court fundamentally hostile to litigation" as evidence of the need for a "more nuanced explanation," arguing that any "prior ideological commitments" underlying the Court's hostility to litigation "are just as likely to stem from the Justices' class position or professional and educational experience as from their partisan political allegiances" (1116–17). Staszak (2015) and Bagenstos (2016), in the same vein, argue that liberals have contributed materially to erosion of access to courts to enforce rights. As Bagenstos (2016: 903) puts it, "even in the present day many liberal Justices have signed on to the key decisions that have severely restricted civil-rights litigation."

We agree that the justices' ideological preferences need not stem from "partisan political allegiances," although they may do so.[4] But such a strong claim about liberal justices' role "in shaping" a hostile Court calls for

---

[1] In their study of business cases in the Supreme Court, Lee Epstein, William Landes and Richard Posner conclude that "there is no uniform conservative or uniform liberal ideology. Instead there are multiple imperfectly overlapping ideologies." They also observe, however, that "it should be possible to . . . distinguish between business-liberal and business-conservative Justices" (2013a: 1433).

[2] Margaret Lemos (2011) explores a phenomenon she calls "judicial backlash," arguing that judicial concerns about overcrowded dockets and inadequate resources may cause the judiciary to seek to thwart congressional private enforcement regimes through statutory interpretation and judicial control of procedure, particularly if the claims involved are otherwise disfavored. Staszak (2015) also also emphasizes non-ideological explanations.

[3] *But cf.* Epstein, Landes, and Posner (2013a), reporting the authors' analysis of data to test various claims about the business friendliness of the Roberts Court.

[4] Stephen Yeazell notes that "[t]he recently concluded 2012 presidential campaign was the first in decades in which the topic of civil litigation appeared neither in party platforms nor in the candidates' stump speeches" (2013: 1788).

systematic evidence. In that regard, we note Siegel's conclusion that "the political valence of the Court's decisions seems sufficiently correlated to the results of the case to demand careful historical consideration" (2006: 1200).

There has been no systematic attempt to analyze the Supreme Court's private enforcement decisions, let alone to do so over time. That is our goal in this chapter. We pursue it by first focusing on qualitative analysis of selected Supreme Court decisions and then presenting and analyzing comprehensive data on decisions from 1960 through 2014. Given abundant existing commentary on the cases we highlight, the qualitative material in this chapter might not be necessary if it simply exemplified findings based on systematic data. Our goal, however, is to show how the decisions in question can be illuminated by an institutional perspective that draws on our discussion in earlier chapters of attempts to retrench private enforcement through legislation and court rulemaking on the same issue-terrain. The cases we use to illustrate these dynamics focus on Federal Rules issues because they have the important advantage of traversing legislation, rulemaking, and judicial interpretation.

Decisions in Institutional Context

Offers of Judgment

In Chapter 2, we refer to a number of bills from the early 1980s, put forward by the Reagan Administration or originating in Congress, which sought to reduce the incentives for private enforcement through changes to the law governing attorney's fees. The bills in question targeted suits against federal, state, or local government. Although different in their particulars, all of them included provisions that, without reference to Federal Rule 68, would have denied recovery of statutory attorney's fees incurred after an offer of judgment (an offer to settle the case) that was rejected by a prevailing party and that was more favorable to that party than the judgment ultimately entered in the case. Recall from Chapter 3 that under Federal Rule 68 a plaintiff in that situation must pay the "costs incurred after the offer was made." The early 1980s bills would have increased the penalty on a plaintiff who declined to accept a settlement and then failed to do better at trial. None of the bills was enacted.

Contemporaneously with much of this legislative activity, as we showed in Chapter 3, the Advisory Committee advanced proposals to amend Rule 68 that would have measurably increased the risks of declining an offer of judgment. The 1983 and 1984 proposals were lightning rods that galvanized support by liberal interest groups for changes in the process that governs how proposals are considered under the Rules Enabling Act, including greater opportunities for public participation. The controversy became a focal point of hearings that an influential member of Congress – who chaired a House Committee with jurisdiction over the federal judiciary – convened to consider such changes. Some of the advocacy in favor of changing the rulemaking process linked the Rule 68 proposals to the partisan effort to enact attorney's fees legislation in Congress that we discussed in Chapter 2. Chapter 3 also highlights the fact that Chief Justice Burger was persistently outspoken in his support for the rulemaking effort, even after it was a source of controversy both in that domain and in congressional hearings.

At the same time that attorney's fees in the context of offers of judgment were the subject of congressional bills and rulemaking proposals – and a source of controversy in congressional hearings on the Enabling Act process – a case was wending its way through the federal courts that posed that issue under the existing Federal Rule. In *Marek* v. *Chesny*,[5] the Supreme Court held that, although the plaintiff in a Section 1983 civil rights action brought against three police officers had secured a jury verdict for $60,000, he was not entitled to the portion of his costs, including attorney's fees, that was incurred after rejecting the defendant's Rule 68 offer of judgment in the amount of $100,000. The settlement offer stipulated that it was inclusive of "costs now accrued and attorney's fees." Eighty-one percent of the total costs, including attorney's fees, sought by the plaintiff was incurred after declining the offer of judgment.

In an opinion for a six-justice majority, Chief Justice Burger held that "costs" for purposes of Rule 68 takes its meaning from the governing fee-shifting statute. In *Marek* that statute, the Civil Rights Attorney's Fees Awards Act of 1976 (42 U.S.C. § 1988), defined attorney's fees as part of the taxable costs that can be awarded to a prevailing party. The Court thus reversed a panel of the Seventh Circuit, which, in an opinion by Judge Posner, had rejected the "rather mechanical linking up of Rule 68 and section 1988" because such a reading would put "Rule 68 into conflict with the policy behind section 1988," which is "intended to encourage the bringing of meritorious civil rights actions," and "designed ... to achieve a substantive objective – compliance with the civil rights laws." Posner had concluded that reading Rule 68 to cut off post-offer fees under the statute would violate the Rules Enabling Act's command that a Federal Rule "shall

---

[5] 473 U.S. 1 (1985).

not abridge, enlarge or modify any substantive right."[6] Justice Brennan, joined by Justices Marshall and Blackmun, dissented.

The Court's opinion in *Marek* is notable for two, arguably related, reasons. First, the majority's reasoning, particularly concerning the implications of the holding for the institutional balance of power among the Court, Congress, and rulemaking, is thin. Indeed, the Court says not a word about the Enabling Act issue that was clearly presented as a result of Judge Posner's opinion, the parties' briefs (and most amicus briefs as well), and Justice Brennan's dissent (Burbank 1986: 437–8). Second, in order to forge a majority, it was necessary for two justices to abandon positions they had taken only a few years before in another case involving Rule 68. One of them was Chief Justice Burger, who had joined Justice Rehnquist's dissenting opinion in *Delta Air Lines* v. *August*.[7] As one of the arguments in support of his position that "costs" in Rule 68 do *not* include attorney's fees, Rehnquist had observed that including them would "seriously undermine the purposes behind the attorney's fees provision of the Civil Rights Act."[8]

In *Marek* Rehnquist wrote a two-sentence concurrence disavowing this view as to the meaning of "costs" on the ground that "further examination of the question convinced [him] that this view was wrong."[9] Chief Justice Burger offered no explanation for his change of position, but an explanation is at hand. By the time *Marek* was decided (in late June 1985), Burger must have realized that neither legislation nor rulemaking was likely to succeed as a vehicle for invigorating the offer of judgment mechanism, a goal that he had vigorously and tenaciously championed. *Marek* provided an opportunity to have part of a loaf – in those cases where the fee-shifting provision, like Section 1988, defines attorney's fees as part of costs.

This was not the only occasion on which the Burger Court accomplished by interpretation of a Federal Rule a result similar to one that the Chief Justice had publicly advocated but that he knew probably could not be secured through rulemaking or legislation.[10] As the following discussion

---

[6] *Chesny* v. *J. Marek*, 720 F.2d 474, 478–80 (7th Cir. 1983).
[7] 450 U.S. 346 (1981).
[8] Ibid. at 378 (Rehnquist, J., dissenting). Justice Rehnquist was assuming, however, that the penalty under Rule 68 could include not just the plaintiff's own post-offer attorney's fees, but the defendant's as well.
[9] *Marek*, 473 U.S. at 13 (Rehnquist, J., concurring).
[10] One of Chief Justice Burger's enthusiasms was to reduce the role of the civil jury. Conscious of a growing movement toward smaller civil juries by local district court rule, he also favored national law to that effect. However, the first act of the Advisory Committee he reconstituted in 1971, in response to a request for advice on the subject from the Judicial Conference, was adopting a resolution that "the better method of effectuating the

of decisions on pleading and class actions demonstrates, it is a technique that has also recently found favor with justices when their retrenchment goals cannot be achieved through lawmaking in more democratic sites.

Pleading

Examples from the domain of pleading provide the most vivid demonstration of both the power of the Supreme Court to retrench private enforcement by effectively amending the Federal Rules, and the importance of historical, institutional, and political perspectives on litigation retrenchment. In Chapter 3 we note that those who drafted the 1938 Federal Rules chose "notice pleading," under which a plaintiff is required to state a claim that is legally tenable on some set of facts that might be established, and only in sufficient detail to give the defendant fair notice of what that claim is. Thus, Federal Rule 8 requires that a complaint include only "a short and plain statement of the claim showing that the pleader is entitled to relief." The drafters' goal was to foster adjudication on the merits after opportunity for both parties to gather evidence in discovery, rather than deciding cases based on the face of the parties' pleadings.

The Court embraced this approach in dictum in *Hickman* v. *Taylor*,[11] and embraced it squarely in *Conley* v. *Gibson*[12] in 1957. Decided shortly after some federal judges urged an amendment to Rule 8 in order to reintroduce fact pleading, and soundly rejecting that approach, *Conley* was repeatedly cited with favor by the Supreme Court and lower federal courts (in fact, thousands of times).[13]

---

proposals would be by statute." Minutes of the Meeting of the Advisory Committee on Civil Rules 2 (September 21, 1971), available at www.uscourts.gov/rules-policies/archives/meeting-minutes/advisory-committee-rules-civil-procedure-september-1971

According to Judge Weinstein, it was "doubtful that Congress would have readily approved such changes by statute" (1977: 131). Indeed, "the idea of the six-person jury had been presented to Congress in 1971 and again in 1973 and 1977, but Congress took no positive action" (Carrington 2010: 622). The Court solved the problem in *Colgrove* v. *Battin*, 413 U.S. 149 (1973), holding that a local district court rule which provided for six-person civil juries did not violate the Seventh Amendment or the Enabling Act, and that it was consistent with Rule 48. At the time, Rule 48 provided in pertinent part that "the parties may stipulate that the jury shall consist of any number less than twelve." "[Colgrove] validated local rules that were not consistent with the text of Rule 48" (Carrington 2010: 621).

[11] 329 U.S. 495, 501 (1947).
[12] 355 U.S. 41 (1957).
[13] *See Has the Supreme Court Limited Americans' Access to Courts? Hearing before the S. Committee on the Judiciary*, 111th Cong. 90 (2009) (statement of Stephen B. Burbank).

Moreover, in two cases decided over the 10-year period from 1993 to 2002, the Court twice reversed lower court decisions that imposed heightened pleading requirements in particular substantive contexts, reasserting the traditional interpretation of the pleading rules articulated in *Conley*. Importantly, the Court in those cases observed that a change to a heightened pleading requirement must come from the rulemaking process or from Congress, rather than from the Court's re-interpretation of the Federal Rules.

> The phenomenon of litigation against municipal corporations based on claimed constitutional violations by their employees dates from our decision in Monell . . . where we for the first time construed § 1983 to allow such municipal liability. Perhaps if Rules 8 and 9 were rewritten today, claims against municipalities under § 1983 might be subjected to the added specificity requirement of Rule 9(b). But that is a result which must be obtained by the process of amending the Federal Rules, and not by judicial interpretation.[14]

It is possible to interpret these observations – which were written by Justice Rehnquist in *Leatherman*, and followed by Justice Thomas in *Swierkiewicz* – as invitations to the Advisory Committee and/or Congress. The outcome of both cases is, however, consistent with the Court's stated interpretive criterion for distinguishing permissible judicial interpretation of Federal Rules from impermissible judicial amendment of them outside the legislatively mandated Enabling Act process.

In order to protect that process, the statute's limitations on rulemaking, and the power it accords Congress to review and, if it so desires, to block prospective procedural policy choices, the Court has disclaimed the freedom to treat as mere interpretation (or reinterpretation) giving meaning to a Federal Rule that is different from the meaning the Court understood "upon its adoption."[15]

Yet, as we have also seen, the status quo is difficult to change through legislation and, with respect to important procedural issues since the reforms of the 1980s that culminated in the 1988 amendments to the Enabling Act, the rulemaking process.[16] Indeed, in Chapter 3 we characterize inaction by

---

[14] *Leatherman v. Tarrant County Narcotics Intelligence and Coordination Unit*, 507 U.S. 163, 168 (1993). *See also Swierkiewicz v. Sorema N.A.*, 534 U.S. 506, 515 (2002); *Crawford-El v. Britton*, 523 U.S. 574, 595 (1998).

[15] *Ortiz v. Fibreboard Corp.*, 527 U.S. 815, 861 (1999). *See also Amchem Products, Inc. v. Windsor*, 521 U.S. 591, 620 (1997).

[16] Because of the difficulty of devising search terms that would enable us with confidence to identify congressional bills seeking to retrench through pleading reform, our bill data

the rulemakers in the face of resurgent calls to move to heightened plead-ing as an example of both the stickiness of the status quo in contemporary federal court rulemaking and the restraint that some leaders of the key com-mittees have shown in recent decades. The Chief Justice not only appoints all members of the rulemaking committees but also meets regularly with the chairs of the key rulemaking committees. It is thus inconceivable that Chief Justice Roberts was unaware of the Advisory Committee's decision not to pursue pleading reform. Moreover, as we show in Chapter 2, Roberts participated in the unsuccessful campaign for a broad fee-retrenchment bill as a member of the Reagan Justice Department, and he initiated con-sideration within the Department of reforms intended to reduce opportu-nities and incentives for civil rights actions under Section 1983, among the most significant American civil rights statutes. It is thus highly unlikely that he was unaware of the reality that broad-scale retrenchment through changes to the pleading rules, if it were to occur, would have to come from the Court acting as such.

In two decisions, one from 2007 (*Twombly*)[17] and the other from 2009 (*Iqbal*),[18] the Court effectively overruled *Conley* and rewrote the Federal Rules' pleading provisions. The decisions shifted away from the notice pleading approach that the drafters of Rule 8 intended and that had been endorsed by the Court in *Conley*, a landmark that had governed federal practice for a half-century. Under the new pleading regime, in order to withstand a motion to dismiss, a complaint must state facts – not conclusions[19] – that give rise to a claim that is "plausible" according to

---

do not include bills targeted at that issue. One of the provisions of the Private Securities Law Reform Act of 1995 did tighten pleading, but it did so in one substantive law context. Moreover, as we note in Chapters 2 and 3, that legislation took years to enact and required the override of a presidential veto. Congress very rarely enacts legislation prescribing procedure on a transsubstantive basis in an area covered by the Federal Rules, and the failure to mark the distinction (*see* Staszak 2015) can lead to institutional misunderstand-ing. Certainly, any serious attempt to retrench through a transsubstantive pleading bill would lead to massive interest group mobilization (Burbank 2009: 8–9) and encounter all the other difficulties of retrenching rights by legislation.

[17] *Bell Atlantic Corp. v. Twombly*, 550 U.S. 544 (2007).

[18] *Ashcroft v. Iqbal*, 556 U.S. 662 (2009).

[19] Compare the explanation given by a member of the original Advisory Committee at a program explaining the new rules: "That the statement or averment includes a conclusion of law is no ground for a motion to strike or for a motion to make definite, merely because the statement or averment embodies a conclusion which might be elaborated by a more particularized detailing of the facts." American Bar Association, Federal Rules of Civil Procedure: Proceedings of the Institute at Washington, D.C. and of Symposium at New York City 308 (1938) (George Donworth).

"judicial experience and common sense."[20] In *Twombly* and *Iqbal*, the Court did what it declined to do in *Leatherman* and *Swierkiewicz*, using judicial power under Article III to institute the legal change desired.

The Court's recent pleading decisions represented a bold and unambiguous shift in the legal status quo. They were followed by legislative override efforts in a Congress (fleetingly) controlled by Democrats, but those efforts gained little traction.[21] This fact starkly demonstrates the importance of institutional dynamics to litigation retrenchment. The stickiness of the legislative status quo is such that, although legislation that incorporated the substance of *Twombly* and *Iqbal* could not have been enacted (without even considering a presidential veto), neither could Congress override the Court's decisions. On the basis of information provided in just two cases, the more important of which (*Iqbal*) was decided by a one-judge majority, the Supreme Court – whose members are unelected, serve for life, and are insulated from individual if not institutional reprisal – changed (nonconstitutional) rules that can dramatically affect private enforcement, portending retrenchment that would be (or has been) impossible to secure from the legislature or its delegated procedural lawmaking bodies.

Such decisions are examples of the "use of case-by-case adjudication to circumvent or preempt court rulemaking obstacles posed by the Enabling Act process" (Burbank 1997: 245). They reflect what Jeb Barnes calls a strategy of conversion (Barnes 2008: 636), adapting the Federal Rules "without . . . 'authoritative change' under the Enabling Act because of the high barriers to such change, whereas the 'obstacles to internal adaptation [through reinterpretation] [were] low'" (Burbank 2009: 10, quoting Barnes 2008: 638).[22]

Class Actions

In Chapter 2 we show that there was a prompt legislative response to experience under the 1966 amendments to Rule 23's class action provisions, with Democrats taking the lead. A number of bills focused on overenforcement of the Truth in Lending Act, motivated by the experience of Rule 23 being used to aggregate a massive number of people asserting the same small, even technical, violations of that statute in lawsuits that

---

[20] *Iqbal*, 556 U.S. at 679.
[21] *See Has the Supreme Court Limited Americans' Access to Courts? supra* note 13.
[22] Sarah Staszak agrees (2015: 116). As previously noted in Chapter 3, however, the primary source of these obstacles is the stickiness of the *rulemaking* status quo effectuated through the reforms we have traced.

threatened devastating liability disproportionate to the offenses committed or harm suffered. There was also concern about small claims in general, culminating in an ambitious bill sponsored by the Carter Administration that would have completely rewritten Rule 23(b)(3), which governs class actions brought primarily for money damages. The common thrust of these proposed legislative reforms to Rule 23 was to restrict or regulate privately prosecuted class actions involving small claims. None of these bills to amend Rule 23 was enacted.

More generally, in an examination of only the class action bills in our dataset (not reported in Chapter 2), we observe that in the late 1970s and early 1980s there was a modest volume of bill activity seeking to limit class actions. Support for the bills was not very partisan, with the balance of support moderately higher among Democrats. Beginning in the 103rd Congress (1993–4), the balance of support for bills limiting class actions shifted decisively to the Republican side, where it remained material until the 109th Congress (2005–6), after which the issue receded from the legislative agenda.

Much of the legislative activity concerning class actions from the 103rd Congress (1993–4) through the 109th Congress (2005–6) was due to Republican-sponsored bills that ultimately led to enacted statutes: The Private Securities Litigation Reform Act of 1995 (PSLRA), and the Class Action Fairness Act (CAFA) of 2005, only the first of which directly affected federal rights, with the second governing class actions brought under state law. As we have previously observed, however, among the bills captured in our data, these statutes (together with the Prison Litigation Reform Act of 1996), were among only a handful of consequential successes in the long-running and much wider legislative campaign for retrenchment of private enforcement of federal rights. Moreover, they were enacted after years of effort, attracting filibusters and presidential vetoes.

The limits on class actions that emerged from this legislative gauntlet in the PSLRA, we believe, are more fairly characterized as modest than as challenges to the core role of class actions in securities litigation, and they addressed class actions in only that one substantive context.[23] Ironically,

---

[23] As John Coffee characterizes the changes affected by the law: "Essentially, it immunized 'forward-looking statements,' gave presumptive control of the class action to a 'lead plaintiff' who had suffered the largest loss (which effectively meant that control went to the largest institutional investor to volunteer for the role), and imposed stricter pleading rules." Coffee concludes that "[d]espite predictions that the PSLRA would be the death knell for securities class actions, not that much has actually changed" (2015: 125–6). For a discussion of the 1998 Securities Litigation Uniform Standards Act (SLUSA), *see* ibid. at 126.

because of congressional compromises on such matters as the fraud-on-the-market theory that were necessary to enact the legislation, the PSLRA reduced the scope for the Supreme Court to raise other enforcement barriers in that context. When legislation is passed on contentious issues in the fragmented American legislative process, the prevailing side and the interest groups that support them rarely get everything they want, leaving a legislative historical record that documents which of their efforts failed to achieve sufficient support for passage and limits their prospects for subsequently prevailing on those issues in court. Indeed, we believe that this may be a major reason why class actions subject to the PSLRA have fared better than other class actions in the Supreme Court's recent jurisprudence. "Because Congress has homed in on the precise policy concerns raised in Amgen's brief, '[we] do not think it appropriate for the judiciary to make its own further adjustments by reinterpreting Rule 23 to make likely success on the merits essential to class certification in securities-fraud suits.'"[24]

The last observation helps to understand the strategy of those proponents of CAFA whose actual agenda, in vastly expanding the jurisdiction of federal courts to hear state law claims brought as class actions, was to ensure that the cases were not certified and went away (Burbank 2006a; Burbank 2008). In contrast with the PSLRA, where class action retrenchment required legislative compromise that limited its reach in later court decisions, CAFA channeled class action retrenchment into the federal courts, an institutional environment in which more aggressive retrenchment was possible under a transsubstantive Federal Rule. The move from state to federal court meant that class certification decisions would be governed not by autonomous and potentially liberal state class action doctrine, but by an ever-more-conservative federal class action jurisprudence. Moreover, the growing volume of state law class actions in federal court provided more and more varied opportunities for federal courts to develop that jurisprudence. Finally, because Federal Rules apply across substantive claims, increasingly anti-class-action doctrine developed in state law cases also governs enforcement of federal rights.

CAFA showed how useful "procedural" legislation could be to furthering the strategy, traceable to the Reagan Administration, of laying the

---

[24] *Amgen Inc.* v. *Connecticut Retirement Plans and Trust Funds*, 133 S. Ct. 1184, 1201 (2013). John Coffee notes that "several recent Supreme Court decisions have declined the opportunity to cut back drastically on the class action" (2015: 132), but, although two of the three decisions he mentions in support of that proposition were securities class actions (ibid. at 268 n. 22), he does not suggest this connection.

foundation to retrench private enforcement by empowering federal judges to accomplish what could not be effectuated in other, more democratic, institutional sites (Graber 1993). No wonder that episodes of legislators' support for class action bills declined from 136 in the 109th Congress (2005–6) to 19 in the 110th Congress (2007–8), to 8 in the 111th (2009–10), to 1 per Congress in the last two Congresses. The counterrevolution had been put in the hands of those best equipped institutionally to achieve its goals.

We observe a similar story in the domain of rulemaking. Although, as Chapter 3 makes clear, court rulemaking was not a source of major class action retrenchment, one of its products has proved key to this strategy. A 1998 amendment to Rule 23 permits courts of appeals in their discretion to entertain immediate appeals from class certification decisions. Previously, such decisions generally could only be appealed by a party after a final order was entered against it in the trial court – so, for example, if the case settled in the trial court (as most do), there would be no appeal and no opportunity for appellate lawmaking.[25] Thus, the 1998 amendments to Rule 23 substantially expanded the opportunities for federal appellate courts, including the Supreme Court, to control the course of class action jurisprudence. And control it they have, making certification more difficult and expensive. Most of this jurisprudence was first developed by the courts of appeals (Burbank 2008: 1495–6), but in recent years the Supreme Court has focused on class actions (Klonoff 2013; Coffee 2015). Conservative majorities of the Court have appeared to bless court of appeals decisions that have assimilated the class certification process to the trial process through enhanced examination of the merits, discovery, and the imposition of evidentiary requirements and burdens. The new class action jurisprudence has increased the challenges and costs of achieving certification.[26]

In itself seizing more opportunities to make class action doctrine, the Court's conservative majority has imposed transsubstantive limits on class actions that were not and probably could not have been imposed through rulemaking or legislation. Indeed, in a 2013 case involving the validity of a provision in an arbitration clause waiving any right to aggregate parties (including but not limited to class aggregation), the perception that the

[25] Interlocutory appeal under 28 U.S.C. § 1292(b) requires written findings about stated criteria by the district court and permission to appeal from the court of appeals. The extraordinary writ of mandamus was occasionally used, but at considerable cost to the notion of what is "extraordinary."
[26] *See, e.g., In re Hydrogen Peroxide Antitrust Litigation*, 552 F.3d 305, 321 (3d Cir. 2008).

majority sought systematically to refashion and narrow Rule 23 through its interpretive powers prompted Justice Kagan to observe: "To a hammer, everything looks like a nail. And to a Court bent on diminishing the usefulness of Rule 23, everything looks like a class action, ready to be dismantled."[27] *Wal-Mart Stores, Inc. v. Dukes*[28] provides perhaps the clearest example of the Court amending Rule 23 through interpretation.

In *Wal-Mart*, the Court was unanimous in holding that the lower courts had erred in certifying a nationwide Title VII class action under Rule 23(b)(2) because the remedies sought included back pay the award of which would require non-ministerial determinations for each member of the class. Having directed the parties also to brief the question whether certification was proper under Rule 23(a), the Court, with four Justices dissenting, reached out to determine that certification was improper under Rule 23(a)(2). The provision requires that "there [be] questions of law or fact common to the class." The Court's decision, holding that such a question must be capable of generating a common answer,[29] marked a decisive change in the meaning of Rule 23. According to a prominent class action scholar and current member of the Advisory Committee on Civil Rules:

> Prior to the Supreme Court's 2011 opinion in Dukes, commonality, like numerosity, was rarely an impediment in class certification. Courts were very liberal in finding a question of law or fact that qualified.
>
> The majority decision in Dukes cannot be squared with the text, structure, or history of Rule 23(a)(2). Nothing in the text of rule 23 (a)(2), or in the Advisory Committee Notes thereto, requires that the common question be central to the outcome. Instead of looking at the traditional methods of interpreting Rule 23 (a)(2), the majority relied heavily on a law review article by Professor Nagareda.
>
> It is ironic that Justice Scalia, who usually rejects sources other than the plain language in interpreting statutes and rules – and who has also criticized his colleagues for relying on law review articles – would author an opinion basing an interpretation of Rule 23 (a)(2) on a commentator's general discussion of "what matters to class certification." Indeed, later in the opinion,

---

[27] *American Express Co. v. Italian Colors Restaurant*, 133 S. Ct. 2304, 2320 (2013).

[28] 564 U.S. 338 (2011).

[29] "Their claims must depend upon a common contention – for example, the assertion of discriminatory bias on the part of the same supervisor. That common contention, moreover, must be of such a nature that it is capable of classwide resolution – which means that determination of its truth or falsity will resolve an issue that is central to the validity of each one of the claims in one stroke." Ibid. at 350.

Justice Scalia refused to give any weight to the Advisory Committee Notes in construing Rule 23 (b)(2).

In sum, the majority turned a minimal requirement into one that could significantly impact class certification, especially in the (b)(2) context. It did so almost entirely on a misreading of a law review article.

(Klonoff 2013: 773–80)

John Coffee agrees, arguing that the Court "employed an entirely new theory" in *Wal-Mart*, and that it "rewrote [the commonality] standard fundamentally" (2015: 127–8).

Marek, Twombly and *Iqbal*, and *Wal-Mart* are a few examples of the Court using its Article III judicial power to achieve results that either would have been, or had already proved to be, impossible to achieve through legislation or the exercise of delegated legislative power (rulemaking) under the Enabling Act. All of them involved interpretations that are inimical to private enforcement, and in most there was a clear divide in the votes of justices generally thought to be conservative and those generally thought to be liberal.[30] Of course, we cannot make general inferences about the role of ideology in the justices' votes on private enforcement issues from the discussion of a handful of cases. We therefore turn to statistical analysis of comprehensive data.

Private Enforcement Case Dataset

We endeavored to collect systematic data with which to evaluate issue outcomes and the voting behavior of justices concerning private enforcement. We identified issues that legislators, judges, and scholars (in the literature discussed above) have commonly associated with private enforcement. For the period from 1960 to 2014, we identified all Supreme Court decisions requiring justices to vote on (1) the existence or scope of a private right of action, either express or implied; (2) whether a party has standing to sue under either Article III or prudential analysis; (3) the availability of attorney's fees to a prevailing plaintiff; (4) the availability of damages to a prevailing plaintiff; (5) whether an arbitration agreement forecloses access to court to enforce a federal right; and (6) an interpretation of a Federal Rule of Civil Procedure that bore on opportunities or incentives for private

---

[30] Although Justices Souter and Breyer voted with the majority in *Twombly* (Souter wrote the opinion), they were naïve in doing so (Burbank 2009), and the implications of that decision in the hands of their conservative colleagues having been made apparent in *Iqbal*, they dissented.

enforcement. Because we are particularly interested in class actions, we additionally included in our Federal Rules cases those that turned on an issue explicitly linked to policies underpinning Rule 23, such as tolling a statute of limitations and claim preclusion in the class action context.

We coded the outcome of each private enforcement issue as pro-private enforcement (=1), anti-private enforcement (=0), or as unclassifiable. We discarded unclassifiable cases. We treated outcomes as pro-private enforcement if they:

- favored recognition of an express or implied private right of action;
- found that standing requirements were satisfied;
- took an approach favorable to plaintiffs' fee awards relative to other options presented by the case;
- took an approach favorable to more expansive availability of damages relative to other options presented by the case;
- concluded that a plaintiff should have access to enforce federal rights in court rather than being restricted to arbitration; and
- construed a Federal Rule of Civil Procedure so as to enlarge opportunities or incentives for private enforcement relative to other options presented by the case.

We treated votes in the opposite direction as anti-private enforcement. At least one of the authors read each majority, concurring, and dissenting opinion in order to assign codes to justices' votes.[31]

Our search yielded 365 cases from 1961 to 2014 (there was none in 1960). Some cases contained multiple discrete private enforcement issues across and within the six private enforcement issue areas. For example, a case might contain two discrete attorney's fee issues or both a private right of action issue and a standing issue. The 365 cases captured by our searches contained 404 issues.

Table 4.1 displays the types of issues and their proportions within the data as a whole. Table 4.2 displays the proportion of private enforcement issues (comprising at least 2% of total issues in the data) by policy area.

---

[31] In coding justices as voting for or against private enforcement, we coded based on the substance of opinions rather than whether those opinions were styled a majority, concurrence, or dissent. For example, if a concurrence repudiated the majority's pro-private enforcement position on an issue, it was coded as an anti-private enforcement vote. If a dissent fully agreed with the majority's reasoning on a private enforcement issue, but dissented on different grounds, it was coded as a pro-private enforcement vote. When we refer to dissent rates in private enforcement issues below, we count as dissents votes against the majority position on a private enforcement issue.

Table 4.1. *Types of private enforcement issues*

Private enforcement issues	Percentage of total issues in data
Standing	29
Private rights of action	24
Federal Rules of Civil Procedure	18
Attorney's fees	16
Damages	9
Arbitration	4

Table 4.2. *Policy distribution of private enforcement issues*

Policy area	Percentage of cases	
Civil rights		36
Employment discrimination	(11)	
Education discrimination	(4)	
Other discrimination	(8)	
Policing	(4)	
Prisoner	(3)	
Voting and elections	(3)	
Other civil rights	(3)	
Civil liberties		9
Freedom of expression	(4)	
Establishment/free exercise clause	(3)	
Abortion and contraception	(2)	
Securities		11
Labor and Employment		10
Social welfare benefits and programs		8
Antitrust		6
Environmental		6
Torts*		2
Governance**		2
Other economic policy		6
Other social policy		4

*Torts enter the data as causes of action in FRCP cases.

**Governance concerns issues bearing on the operation of American government not captured by more specific policy classifications, such as the legislative veto or the line item veto.

Table 4.3. *Party types in private enforcement issues*

Type of party	Percentage of issues
Plaintiffs	
Individual	55
Classes of individuals	19
Business	18
NGO/non-profit	9
Union	2
Other	7
Defendants	
Business	46
State/local government	33
Federal government	17
Individual	4
Union	3
Other	3

*The numbers under both the plaintiff and defendant headings sum to more than 100 because some cases contain multiple party types.

The table makes clear that, assuming our data are representative, the Court's private enforcement decisions range widely across federal regulation. Among the most prominent are anti-discrimination law and other areas of civil rights and civil liberties, labor and employment, securities, social welfare, antitrust, and environmental policy.

Table 4.3 displays the percentage of our private enforcement issues in cases in which various types of plaintiffs and defendants appear, listing party types that appeared in at least 2% of the issues in our data. Plaintiff types, in descending order, are individuals (55%), classes of individuals (19%), businesses (18%), and non-profits, which include NGOs (9%) and unions (2%). Defendant types, in descending order, are businesses (46%), state and local government (33%), federal government (17%), individuals (4%), and unions (3%). Examination of the data shows that in the cases that contain 81% of our private enforcement issues, there is an individual, class of individuals, non-profit, or union plaintiff. If one looks only at individuals and classes of individuals, the figure is 74%. In the cases that contain 94% of our private enforcement issues, there is a business or government defendant. Thus, in the vast bulk of the Supreme Court's private enforcement cases in our data, individuals, classes of them, and non-profits are seeking to enforce regulatory policy against business and government.

We also coded the ideological direction of the underlying claim for each suit. For example, if an issue concerned whether to imply a cause of action for a claim by an environmental group against a business for alleged water pollution, we assigned a liberal ideological direction to the underlying environmental claim. In assigning codes, we followed the definition of liberalism used in the Spaeth Supreme Court Database, which is the most widely used source of data in empirical studies of Supreme Court behavior. As Lee Epstein and Andrew Martin (2010: 272) observe:

> The database's classifications generally comport with conventional understandings. "Liberal" decisions are those in favor . . . of women and minorities in civil rights cases; of individuals against the government in First Amendment, privacy, and due process cases; of unions over individuals and individuals over businesses in labor cases; and of the government over businesses in cases involving economic regulation. "Conservative" decisions are the reverse.

We applied the protocol ourselves,[32] with one of the authors reading each case to assign the codes. Eighty-five percent of our private enforcement issues had liberal underlying claims; only 7% concerned conservative underlying claims. The remaining 8% could not be assigned an ideological direction. Thus, the vast majority of private enforcement issues in our data were presented in cases asserting liberal underlying claims.

In sum, we can characterize the body of our private enforcement issues decided by the Supreme Court over the past half-century as: (1) ranging broadly across federal social and economic regulation, with civil rights being especially prominent; (2) overwhelmingly prosecuted by individuals, classes of them, and non-profit organizations; (3) almost entirely against business and governmental defendants; and (4) asserting rights of a generally liberal nature.

Figure 4.1 reflects the estimated number of private enforcement issues in our data that were decided each year. The estimated number of such issues on the Court's docket grew in the 1970s, and the growth continued until the mid-1980s, peaking at an estimated value of about 11, after

---

[32] For further details on the Spaeth rules for defining liberal versus conservative, *see generally Online Code Book, The Supreme Court Database*, available at http://scdb.wustl.edu/documentation.php?var=decisionDirection (last visited January 31, 2016).

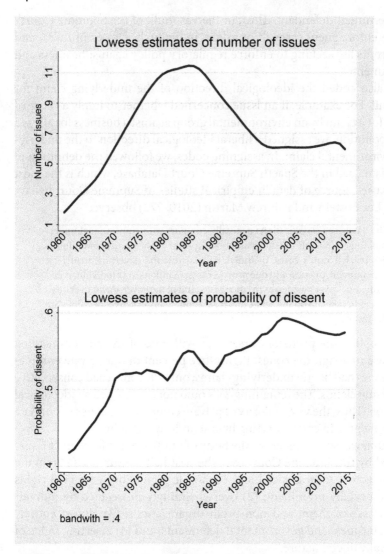

Figure 4.1   Number of private enforcement issues per term, and probability of dissent, 1960–2014

which it declined to an estimated value of about 6 by the late 1990s, when it plateaued to the end of the series. The probability of a dissent on private enforcement issues rose from 42% in 1961, to about 52% through the 1970s, to 59% by the early 2000s, after which it levelled off.

Justice Votes and Case Outcomes over Time

Having identified this set of issues, we coded the votes of each justice as pro-private enforcement (=1), anti-private enforcement (=0), or missing if the justice did not address the private enforcement issue. We coded *votes* as pro versus anti-enforcement according to the same rules described above for pro versus anti-enforcement *outcomes*. Each justice's vote on each private enforcement issue in our data was assigned on the basis of at least one of the authors reading each majority, concurring, and dissenting opinion. This rendered a total of 3,495 justice votes on private enforcement issues.

Our primary interest is to model the relationship between justices' ideological preferences and their votes on private enforcement issues. For our measure of justice ideology, we rely on Martin-Quinn scores. These "ideal point" scores for the justices are based on the voting behavior and alignments of justices in non-unanimous decisions (Martin and Quinn 2002). They are fluid, changing from one term to the next with changes in justices' voting behavior over time. Higher values are associated with more conservative justices. Use of these scores allows us to assess empirically whether private enforcement belongs in the family of issues associated with the left–right divide, such as civil rights and economic regulation. In a secondary analysis we obtain very similar results when substituting Segal-Cover scores for Martin-Quinn scores. Segal-Cover ideology scores are based on pre-confirmation newspaper editorials on the nominations, and thus are independent of justices' voting behavior (Segal and Cover 1989). We present the parallel regressions with Segal-Cover scores as the justice ideology measure in the appendix to this chapter, where we also further discuss differences in the scores and why it is important to assess the robustness of our results using these alternative measures of ideology.

We pay particular attention to the set of issues with dissents (218 or 54% of our 404 issues). We do so because we believe that the presence of one or more dissents suggests the possible influence of ideology on the justices' views about the meaning of law and how it should develop. Thus, many scholars studying the role of ideology in the Supreme Court's decisions have paid particular attention to non-unanimous decisions (Segal and Spaeth 2002; Ho and Quinn 2010; Epstein, Landes, and Posner 2013b), and we too regard them as especially informative.

To attribute the Court's decisions exclusively to the ideological preferences of the justices, however, would neglect "the messiness of lived experience" (Burbank 2011: 53), which teaches that judges – even judges on a court that has the final word (at least within the judiciary) on issues of constitutional law – make decisions based on a number of considerations, including the law as they understand it. The many unanimous decisions that the Court issues every year (46% of our issues) likely reflect the influence of law, including precedent (Cross 2011: 92, 100), and the justices' belief in rule of law values, including stability and predictability (Kritzer and Richards 2005: 33, 35; Burbank 2011: 56).

In cases implicating the volume and mix of litigation, institutional self-interest is another consideration or influence that may affect a justice's vote. Supreme Court justices are surely aware of the supposed workload of the lower federal courts, some determinants of which are canvassed each year in the Chief Justice's Year-End Report.[33] Finding a suitable proxy for the workload of the lower federal courts, however, is difficult.[34] This helps to explain our preference for statistical models (discussed below) that allow us to control for all variables that take the same value for each justice in the case (such as caseload in the federal courts).

Table 4.4 lists the raw percentage of pro-private enforcement votes, relative to total votes, for all justices on the 218 issues (containing 1,903 votes) where at least one justice dissented. Two things stand out: First, the distribution from lowest to highest pro-private enforcement votes appears straightforwardly to track the conservative-liberal dimension. The five most pro-private enforcement scores, in order, are those of Douglas, Sotomayor, Ginsburg, Stevens, and Brennan. The five most anti-private enforcement scores, in order, are those of Scalia, Roberts, Thomas, Alito, and Rehnquist. Moreover, the two most anti-private enforcement justices out of the 29 listed (Roberts and Scalia) were advocates of the unsuccessful Reagan legislative litigation retrenchment efforts that we discussed in Chapter 2. Roberts and Scalia voted against private enforcement at 88% and 89%, respectively. We note that, in relative terms, Roberts is more anti-private enforcement (ranking second behind Scalia) than he is conservative across-the-board (ranking seventh most conservative in Martin-Quinn score). It appears that private enforcement issues have remained particularly salient for him since his formative years in the Reagan Justice Department.

---

[33] There is a summary of annual case filing statistics in all such reports for the years 2000 through 2013, which is available online at www.supremecourt.gov/publicinfo/year-end/year-endreports.aspx

[34] For the complexities of determining federal judicial workload, particularly given the institutional judiciary's goal of attracting more resources from Congress, see Burbank, Plager, and Ablavsky 2012: 23–31.

Table 4.4. *Percentage of pro-private enforcement votes in private enforcement cases with dissenting votes*

Justice	Percentage of pro-private enforcement	Number of votes	Conservative	Average Martin-Quinn score
Scalia	11	108	1	2.45
Roberts	12	32	1	1.30
Thomas	14	79	1	3.47
Alito	16	31	1	1.88
Rehnquist	17	163	1	2.84
Harlan	18	17	1	1.74
Powell	20	86	1	.93
O'Connor	23	111	1	.88
Burger	23	91	1	1.85
Kennedy	24	101	1	.68
Stewart	36	73	1	.54
White	41	135	1	.44
Clark	45	11	0	.23
Warren	53	17	0	−1.26
Fortas	57	7	0	−1.11
Souter	60	68	0	−.93
Blackmun	69	127	0	−.11
Black	72	18	0	−.79
Breyer	75	72	0	−1.27
Kagan	79	14	0	−1.66
Marshall	79	122	0	−2.83
Brenan	81	131	0	−2.10
Stevens	82	157	0	−1.72
Ginsburg	83	75	0	−1.60
Sotomayor	88	16	0	−1.92
Douglas	93	43	0	−6.04
Less than five votes				
Goldberg	0	1	0	−.61
Whittaker	0	2	1	1.24
Frankfurter	0	3	1	1.86

Indeed, the justices with the four most anti-private enforcement voting scores in the past half-century, who together voted against private enforcement 87% of the time in cases with at least one dissent, until recently served on the Court at the same time. In characterizing the conservative majority in recent years as distinctively anti-private enforcement by historical stand-ards, we are mindful of the possibility that change over time in case charac-teristics may confound comparisons of justices across time. To address this, we examined a logistic regression model with justice vote as the dependent variable, case fixed effects (discussed at the beginning of the next section) to control for case facts, and a dummy variable for each justice, with standard errors clustered on justice. This allows evaluating justices' relative degree of anti-enforcement voting while controlling for all case-level covariates. The model results (not displayed), like Table 4.4, rank Justices Scalia, Roberts, Thomas, and Alito as the four most anti-enforcement justices to serve since 1960, with Rehnquist ranked fifth, and Kennedy ranked sixth. Using this approach, then, the recent conservative majority of five were among the six most anti-private enforcement justices to serve since 1960.

Table 4.4 also indicates whether a justice is "conservative" (=1) or "lib-eral" (=0), dividing them according to whether they are above or below the median of the average annual Martin-Quinn scores for justices in our data. The conservative-liberal divide that this yields is fairly consist-ent with conventional understandings. This simple division of the jus-tices above and below the Martin-Quinn median maps to Republican and Democratic appointments, with the exception of justices widely regarded as having departed from expectations: White and Frankfurter are classi-fied as conservatives in this division, and Brennan, Souter, Blackmun, and Stevens are classified as liberals.

Any dichotomous ideology variable is surely a blunt instrument, and we use more granular measures in our statistical models. However, looking at a simple and plausible dichotomous ideology measure is a good first real-ity check on both the underlying continuous measure and on our data. The Martin-Quinn median does a very good job of dividing the justices into two categories. Further, these two categories do an excellent job of predict-ing whether a justice is above or below the median of the percentage of pro-private enforcement votes for justices who voted in at least five cases. When all cases are pooled, the conservative-liberal dichotomy yielded by the Martin-Quinn scores perfectly divides our percentage of pro-private enforcement votes in the following sense: every "conservative" has a lower pro-private enforcement voting rate than every "liberal." A second notable feature of the table is the large disparity between conservative and liberal justices' voting ratios. The scale ranges from Scalia voting in favor of pri-vate enforcement 11% of the time to Douglas at 93%.

Figure 4.2 plots a regression line estimating the probability of an out-come in favor of private enforcement, and the separate probabilities of

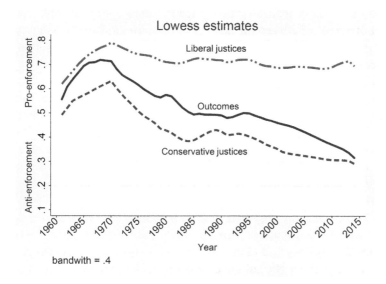

Figure 4.2   Probability of pro-private enforcement outcomes and justice votes in private enforcement issues, 1960–2014

conservative and liberal justices' votes in favor of private enforcement, for all of our private enforcement issues (including unanimous cases). The figure reflects that the estimated probability of a pro-private enforcement vote was increasing in the 1960s. It then turned down at the start of the 1970s, undergoing a long decline from 71% in 1970 to 31% in 2014.

This decline has been substantially driven by the votes of conservative justices, whose estimated probability of a pro-private enforcement vote declined from 63% to 29% over this period. The probability of a pro-private enforcement vote declined for liberal justices by a much smaller degree, falling from an estimated 79% in 1970 to 70% in 2014. Conservative justices achieved a five-justice majority in 1972 and have held it since, with the exception of a six-justice majority from 1991 to 1993. Thus, by 2014, the Court's private enforcement outcomes converge with the votes of conservative justices.

Further, the ideological distance between liberal and conservative justices' voting in private enforcement cases grew materially over the period we examine. This is reflected in the distance between the liberal and conservative justice vote lines. The distance widened from 16% in 1970 to 32% in the early 1980s. That difference remained roughly stable until about 2000, after which it began growing again, reaching 40% by 2014. The growing polarization between the justices on private enforcement issues is driven by the increasingly anti-private enforcement votes of the conservative justices.

Scholars have made similar findings concerning the Court's business decisions, and a similar phenomenon may explain both these trends: "the increasing conservatism of the Court resulted in the Court's taking cases in which the conservative position was weaker than previously, leading to more opposition by liberal Justices," and thus growing distance between liberals and conservatives (Epstein, Landes, and Posner 2013a: 1470).[35] It takes only four justices to grant review, and thus a determined majority of five has the power to pursue an issue when they know they will only narrowly prevail in achieving their desired outcome. This explanation is consistent with our sense, after reading every decision in the database, that the growing distance we find in quantitative analysis reflects increasingly assertive efforts to move the law governing private enforcement in a conservative direction.

Figure 4.3 replicates the regressions in Figure 4.2, restricting the analysis to cases with at least one dissent. The basic structure of the results is very similar to what we found when we analyzed all cases, with a few notable differences. In these cases most likely to have presented substantial legal issues, the early 1980s was an important turning point on the Court in an anti-private enforcement direction. Further, the estimated probability of a pro-private enforcement vote declined to materially lower levels, from 54% in about 1970 to 14% at the end of the series, at which time conservative justices were voting in the private enforcement direction only 10% of the time. Thus, by 2014, when the issue in question elicits any disagreement at all, the pro-private enforcement side is losing an estimated 86% of the time, with conservative justices voting against private enforcement 90% of the time. Over the same period, the probability of a pro-private enforcement vote by liberal justices actually increased from 67% to 78%. The distance between liberals and conservatives grows from 30% in 1970 to 68% in 2014, and again the growing polarization between the justices on private enforcement issues is driven by the increasingly anti-private enforcement votes of the conservative justices.

---

[35] In the domain of procedure, an alternative explanation is that it took time for some of the Court's liberals to realize what was going on (Burbank 2009: 114) (describing failure of Justices Souter and Breyer to realize that *Twombly* could "fundamentally alter the role of litigation in American society" as "understandable but, at least in retrospect, naïve").

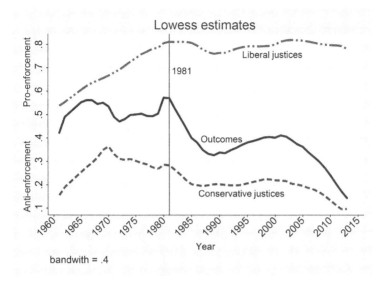

Figure 4.3 Probability of pro-private enforcement outcomes and justice votes in private enforcement issues with dissents, 1960–2014

Returning to the issue, noted at the start of this chapter, of liberal justices contributing materially to the anti-private enforcement project (as some scholars have suggested), we do not find support for this claim at the aggregate level in the issues we study. This is not to deny that liberals have sometimes voted in an anti-private enforcement direction (just as conservatives have sometimes voted in a pro-private enforcement direction). Nevertheless, Figures 4.2 and 4.3 make abundantly clear that the long decline in pro-private enforcement outcomes has been driven by the votes of conservative justices. Since the counterrevolution was undertaken in earnest at the start of the first Reagan administration, liberal justices have voted in a pro-private enforcement direction at fairly high rates, and have done so quite consistently, as they watched pro-private enforcement outcomes decline year after year, ultimately converging with the votes of conservative justices. Indeed, as we discuss below, liberal justices actually voted in an increasingly pro-private enforcement direction over the course of the counterrevolution in cases with business defendants and in Federal Rules cases.

Figure 4.4, still focusing on cases with at least one dissenting vote, splits the data into cases with government defendants and those with

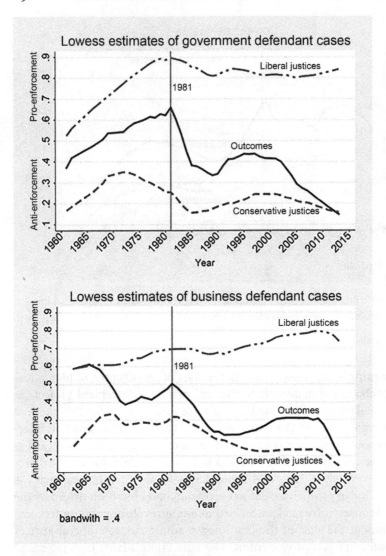

Figure 4.4   Probability of pro-private enforcement outcomes and justice votes in issues with dissents, separately for government and business defendants, 1960–2014

business defendants, each representing about half the data. There were business defendants in 47% of our cases, and government defendants in 49%. The data are sparse in the 1960s, and thus the figure does not convey very meaningful information for this period. Accordingly, we focus on the figure beginning in the 1970s, when the volume of data

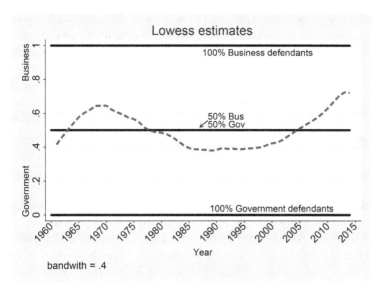

Figure 4.5   Balance between government and business defendants in Court's private enforcement issues, 1960–2014

increases.[36] In the 1970s, the probability of a pro-private enforcement outcome increased somewhat in both government and business defendant cases. Beginning in the 1980s, however, the estimated probability of a pro-private enforcement outcome turns down in both government defendant and business defendant cases, and the two lines move in relative tandem to the end of the series, at which time the estimated probability of a pro-private enforcement outcome is 10% in business defendant cases, and 15% in government defendant cases.

Using all issues with a business or government defendant (94% of our data), Figure 4.5 depicts the probability of a business (=1) versus a government (=0) defendant. The line represents the estimated balance between business and government defendants on the Court's private enforcement docket. The horizontal line at the bottom of the figure represents 100% government defendants, the horizontal line at the top of the figure represents 100% business defendants, and the horizontal line in the middle of

[36] Beginning in the 1970s, there is a sufficient number of each type of case to gauge long-run trends: 1970s (23 business, 17 government); 1980s (24 business, 41 government); 1990s (14 business, 24 government); 2000–14 (27 business, 21 government).

the figure (at the value of .5) represents a 50–50 split. The estimated values reflect that, although the balance has vacillated over time, since the mid-1990s the business defendant share of the Court's private enforcement cases has grown continuously from 39% in the mid-1990s to 72% in 2014. We demonstrate below that this growth maps closely to a sharp increase in attention to, and advocacy for, private litigation retrenchment by the United States Chamber of Commerce. Thus, the growing polarization between liberal and conservative justices on private enforcement issues over the past 15 to 20 years corresponds to an increasing focus on business regulation in the Court's private enforcement docket.

A natural question is how the patterns we describe – the substantial long-run decline in the probability of a pro-private enforcement vote, driven by the votes of conservative justices, and the growing polarization in voting between liberal and conservative justices – compare to the Court's federal rights decisions more broadly. Do the patterns we have observed simply reflect the Court's treatment of federal rights, or is something distinctive going on in the domain of private enforcement? We focus the comparison on cases with dissents. It is informative to contrast the patterns displayed in Figure 4.3 (private enforcement cases with dissents) with the same patterns occurring in the full body of the Court's civil actions asserting federal rights with at least one dissenting vote. To do so, we draw on the Spaeth Supreme Court Database to identify all such cases from 1960 to 2014.[37]

Figure 4.6 depicts the estimated probability of a liberal case outcome in those cases, as well as the estimated probability of a liberal vote separately for liberal and conservative justices. From 1970 to 2014, the probability of a liberal outcome was fairly stable, averaging 48%. We observe nothing resembling the sharp decline that we see in the probability of a pro-private enforcement outcome – from 54% in 1970 to 14% at the end of the series (Figure 4.3). Similarly, at the end of the series, in cases with dissents, the estimated probabilities of a pro-private enforcement outcome (14%), and of a pro-private enforcement vote by conservative justices (10%), are notably lower than the probability of a liberal outcome (48%), and of a liberal vote by conservative justices (35%), in the federal rights cases.

In all federal rights cases with dissents, the distance between liberal and conservative justices' voting was materially more stable than it was on the private enforcement issues. It did not have a clear trajectory of growth over

---

[37] In the Spaeth issue-level data, available at http://scdb.wustl.edu/, we used cases with the "law type" variable coded as federal statutory or constitutional (lawType = 1, 2, or 3), and excluded cases with the "issue area" variable coded criminal procedure (issueArea = 1).

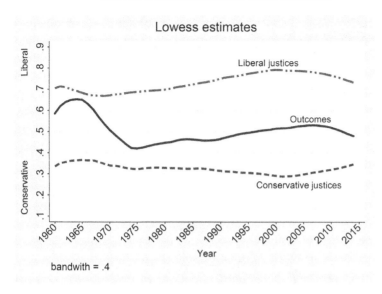

Figure 4.6 Probability of pro-private enforcement outcomes and justice votes in all federal statutory and constitutional rights issues with dissents, 1960–2014

the period we study; and at the end of the period it was much smaller in absolute terms. From 1970 to 2014, there was a net increase of 6 percentage points in distance from liberals to conservatives, from 33 to 39 percentage points. Thus, when all federal rights cases are pooled, we observe nothing like the net increase of 38 percentage points, from 1970 to 2014, in the distance between liberals and conservatives in private enforcement issues, moving from 30 to 68 percentage points (Figure 4.3). The Court has become much more polarized on private enforcement issues than on federal rights in general.

We recognize the possibility that our private enforcement cases arise in a distinctive set of policy fields and that their outcome and voting patterns may differ from those characteristic of federal rights cases in general. That is, if we focused only on Spaeth cases in the same policy fields as our private enforcement cases, perhaps we would observe similar patterns. In addition, we are interested in comparing votes on private enforcement issues to merits votes on underlying causes of action, and although Spaeth's federal rights cases include such votes, they are not limited to them. To address these two issues, drawing on the Spaeth data, we constructed a parallel sample of cases that match the policy distribution of our private enforcement cases and contain only votes on substantive merits issues. This allows a more focused comparison of votes on private enforcement with merits votes on substantive liability issues in the same policy areas as our private enforcement cases. That exercise yielded voting patterns substantially the same as those just discussed for all federal rights cases. This empirical analysis is presented in the appendix. Thus, the precipitous decline in pro-private enforcement outcomes and the polarization we observe on these issues in recent years do not track votes in civil litigation of federal rights generally, nor do they track merits votes in the policy fields that underlie our private enforcement issues. These effects are distinctive in private enforcement cases.

Finally, in observing the sharp decline in the probability of a pro-private enforcement outcome, we considered whether the salience of private enforcement issues on the Court's docket has changed over time. For example, if the Court decided many more major private enforcement issues earlier in the period we study, perhaps by the end of the period the private enforcement issues decided were of less significance. If so, the very low probability of a pro-enforcement outcome at the end of the period may overstate how badly plaintiffs are faring, since, although they lose more and more over time, they are losing on issues that are less and less consequential.

To gauge this, we rely on amicus filings as a measure of salience. When doing this with respect to private enforcement cases, the measure must be viewed relative to amicus filings in general, since it is well-known that amicus filings over the period we study have grown significantly (Collins 2012). Figure 4.7 reflects regression estimates of the average annual number of amicus briefs filed per case in our private enforcement cases that did not present merits issues, and in all cases decided by the Court, from 1960 to 2013.[38] Both grew quite dramatically over the period we study. Interestingly, throughout the period, the number of briefs was very similar for private enforcement and all cases, and they moved in tandem, suggesting that legal elites filing amicus briefs believe that private enforcement issues are as salient as the rest of the Supreme Court's docket, on average. More significantly for present purposes, relative to the benchmark of all amicus filings, the salience level of our private enforcement issues has

[38] In order to isolate amicus briefs on private enforcement issues, we here include from our data only cases in which private enforcement issues were the only ones before the Court (279 cases). If we did not restrict the data in this way, it would not be possible to know whether the amicus briefs actually addressed the private enforcement issues. The amicus data for all cases from 1960 to 2007 come from Collins (2012), which we supplemented through 2013.

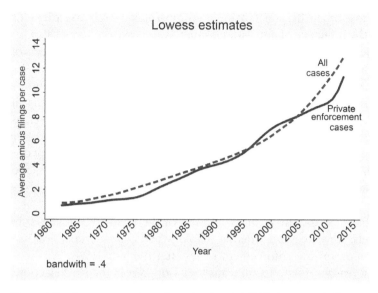

Figure 4.7   Average annual number of amicus briefs filed per case in Supreme Court's private enforcement cases, and in all cases, 1960–2014

been stable over the full period (essentially equal to all amicus filings). By this measure, we conclude that as the probability of pro-private enforcement outcomes has plunged since the early 1970s, plaintiffs have been losing in comparably salient cases over time.

Models of Private Enforcement

We next construct a model using the votes of justices on private enforcement issues as our dependent variable and the justices' ideology scores as our key independent variable. In Chapter 5, we examine models that evaluate the relationship between case outcomes and the ideology of the median justice. We use case fixed effects to address the possibility of potential confounding factors that could be influencing justice votes in private enforcement cases, ranging from case characteristics (facts, parties, salience, etc.), to variation across policy areas, to the political-institutional environment, to the clarity or indeterminacy of precedent, to caseload pressures faced by the federal judiciary. The case fixed effects approach leverages only variation in the relationship between justices' ideology and their votes *within* cases to estimate the effects of ideology. This approach allows us to estimate the effects of ideology most effectively because it holds constant the influence of any variables that would take the same value for each justice vote in a case, and in this sense these estimates of the effects of ideology are net of the effects of any such variables (Greene 2003: ch. 13).

The case fixed effects approach comes at the cost that it uses only information from cases with variation across justices' votes, meaning that it can be used only for cases with at least one dissenting vote. However, as we have previously observed, we regard such cases as most informative concerning the influence of ideology on justice votes. Further, 57% of our cases (207 of 365), and 54% of our issues (218 of 404), have dissents, and thus dissents on private enforcement issues are the norm rather than the exception, and our fixed effect models use most of our data.

In addition to the direct incorporation of the ideology measure into our models, we also assess whether ideology had a greater effect on justices' votes on private enforcement issues after the mid-1990s. We do so for several reasons. First, Republicans took Congress in the 1994 elections and have held at least one chamber almost continuously since, materially reducing the probability of legislative override. The logic of this theory is that justices' votes may be constrained by the perceived threat of legislative override, and the diminution of that threat after 1994 may have widened their perceived range of policymaking discretion (Harvey and Friedman 2006: 548). Certainly, shortly prior to 1994 and in response to many of its civil rights decisions bearing on private enforcement, the Court had experienced a vigorously negative congressional response in the form of the Civil Rights Act of 1991 (Farhang 2010: 129–71).

Moreover, civil litigation retrenchment became a more salient issue in the Republican Party, and the locus of more partisan conflict, at about the same time, playing a notable role in Gingrich's "Contract with America" in the 1994 campaign, and in the Republican anti-litigation legislative program mounted in 1995 (Tobias 1998; Kaplow and Shavell 2001: 1185 & n. 533). This elevation of litigation retrenchment on the Republican Party agenda corresponded to an increasing focus on private enforcement issues by important advocacy groups associated with the Republican Party, specifically including business groups and conservative law reform organizations.

A window on this pattern can be found in amicus filings in our set of cases presenting private enforcement issues and not merits issues (summarized in Figure 4.7, and the accompanying text). In that set of cases, we identified all cases in which the United States Chamber of Commerce filed amicus briefs. The top panel of Figure 4.8 displays the annual proportion of these private enforcement cases in which the Chamber filed an amicus brief from

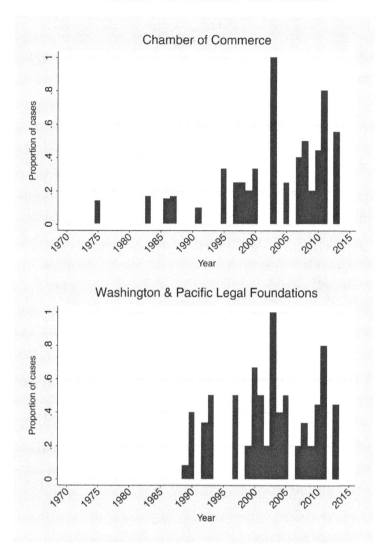

Figure 4.8   Proportion of cases with Chamber of Commerce Amicus Briefs, and with
Washington or Pacific Legal Foundation Amicus Briefs, 1970–2014

1970 to 2014 (none was filed in the 1960s). Cases in our data occurred in
each year with the result that blank years in the figure represent zero amicus
filings when there were some cases decided. By measuring amicus attention
as a proportion of cases in which a brief was filed, rather than as an absolute
number of briefs, we are better able to gauge the level of concern.

The Chamber paid modest attention to private enforcement issues before 1995. From 1970 to 1994, it filed amicus briefs in 6 of 165 (or about 4%) of these private enforcement cases. The Chamber's attention to private enforcement increased sharply in 1995. From 1995 to 2014, it filed amicus briefs in 27 of 88 (or about 31%) of these private enforcement cases. The Chamber's National Litigation Center has filed amicus briefs since it was founded in 1977 (Franklin 2009: 1023). However, the Chamber's turn to issues of procedure and court access – as contrasted with regulatory policy – was signaled by its founding in 1998 of the Institute for Legal Reform, which characterizes itself as "the country's most influential and successful advocate for civil justice reform."[39] Its focus has included limiting class actions, discovery, and damages, and promoting mandatory arbitration (Rutledge 2008; Scheuerman 2008: 881 n. 1; Beisner 2010). Growth in the Chamber's amicus filings in the mid-1990s was part of a wider, concerted campaign of litigation retrenchment.

Conservative law reform organizations also materially elevated their amicus attention to private enforcement issues in the 1990s. Among these groups, the two that participate most frequently, by far, as amicus filers in private enforcement cases are the Pacific Legal Foundation and the Washington Legal Foundation. The Pacific Legal Foundation is often characterized as the first conservative public interest law organization, founded in Sacramento in 1973 with help from members of the Reagan gubernatorial administration and with support from the California Chamber of Commerce (Zumbrun 2004: 42–3; Teles 2008: 61–2; Decker 2009: 3–5). The Washington Legal Foundation was founded in 1977, according to its mission statement, in part "to defend and promote the principles of free enterprise" (Hrina 1999: 311, n. 75). The Pacific Legal Foundation was filing amicus briefs by 1977,[40] and the Washington Legal Foundation was doing so by 1979.[41] They largely ignored private enforcement issues in the 1980s, filing only one brief in 82 (or about 1%) of these private enforcement cases in that decade. Beginning in the 1990s, and even more in the 2000s, these groups went from passive to active on private enforcement issues. From 1990 to 2014, they filed in 33 of 87 (or about 38%) of the cases. Thus, the elevation of litigation retrenchment on the Republican Party agenda in the mid-1990s appears to have been

---

[39] Available at www.instituteforlegalreform.com/about-ilr
[40] See *National Welfare Rights Organization* v. *Mathews*, 533 F.2d 637 (D.C. Cir. 1976).
[41] See *Association of National Advertisers, Inc.* v. *Federal Trade Commission*, 627 F.2d 1151 (D.C. Cir. 1979).

associated with a surge in demand for it by the Chamber of Commerce and conservative activists.[42]

We therefore create a variable that takes the value of 0 from 1961 to 1994, and 1 beginning in 1995, and interact it with the Martin-Quinn ideology score. This interaction term tests whether ideology had a different effect on justices' votes on private enforcement issues after 1994. Because Figure 4.3 suggests widening distance between liberal and conservative justices around 2000, in the appendix we examine alternative specifications placing the break in 2000 rather than 1995, and we observe very similar results in those models.

Table 4.5 reports a logit model with case fixed effects. Further details of modeling specifications and choices are provided in the appendix. The main effect of the ideology variable is statistically significant. Because of the inclusion of the interaction, this variable reflects the effect of ideology only in the period from 1961 to 1994. The marginal effect for the coefficient is −.10, which means that for each unit increase in a justice's Martin-Quinn score (which becomes more conservative as it increases), there is a corresponding reduction of 10 percentage points in the probability of a pro-private enforcement vote. To put this in substantive perspective, we translate it into the effects associated with a change from the mean Martin-Quinn score of liberal justices to that of conservative justices, as defined above (a distance of 3.5). Moving from the average liberal to conservative is associated with a 35 percentage point reduction in the probability of a pro-private enforcement vote. Of course, the effects are materially larger moving from the liberal wing to the conservative wing of the Court, as compared to moving from average liberal to average conservative.[43]

---

[42] Viewing Figure 4.7, which reflects growth in all amicus filings in our private enforcement cases, one might be tempted to conclude that growth in amicus filings by the Chamber of Commerce and the Pacific and Washington Legal Foundations merely reflect a more generalized growth in amicus filings in private enforcement cases during this period. However, this would be a mistake. When all amicus filings in our private enforcement cases are aggregated, we observe 2.6 briefs per case for the 1970–94 period, and 8.6 for the 1995–2014 period, which is 3.3 times larger. With Chamber of Commerce filings, we observe .036 briefs per case for the 1970–94 period, and .306 for the 1995–2014 period, which is 8.5 times larger.

When we compare briefs per case filed by the Pacific and Washington Legal Foundations to all briefs per case in our private enforcement cases, across the 1980–9 versus 1990–2014 periods (the comparison made in the text), the gap is even larger. Thus, even against the backdrop of strong growth in amicus filings, the growth we have documented in these last two paragraphs remains striking.

[43] For example, the distance from the most liberal to the most conservative 2014 Martin-Quinn score for sitting justices (Sotomayor to Thomas) is 5.6. This difference is 60% larger than the difference between average liberal and average conservative scores (3.5).

Table 4.5. *Logit model of justice votes in private enforcement cases, with case fixed effects, 1960–2014*

	Coefficient	Marginal effect
Ideology (Martin-Quinn)	−.80***	−.10
	(.11)	
Ideology*Post-1994 Dummy	−.39*	−.05
	(.23)	
N = 1,939		
Pseudo R^2 = .44		

***<.01; **<.05; *<.1
Standard errors in parentheses, clustered on justice

The interaction of justices' ideology scores and the post-1994 dummy is also statistically significant. The effect of ideology in the 1995 to 2014 period is given by summing the marginal effects of ideology (−.10) and its interaction with the post-1994 dummy variable (−.05), rendering a net marginal effect of −.15. In the 20-year period from 1995 to 2014, the reduction in the probability of a pro-private enforcement vote associated with moving from a liberal to a conservative justice is 53 percentage points. It is evident that the effect of ideology on private enforcement votes grew materially in the last 20 years as compared to 1961–94, exerting more powerful influence over justices' voting in private enforcement cases.[44]

We next examine the same models, but with the data divided into cases in which there was a government defendant, and cases in which there was a business defendant, each of which constitutes about half of the data. The results are presented in Table 4.6. The effects of ideology remain potent in both models, but with different temporal patterns. In the 1961–94 period, moving from a liberal to a conservative justice in government defendant cases is associated with a 53 percentage point reduction in the probability of a pro-private enforcement vote, as compared to a 25 percentage point reduction in business defendant cases. In this period, the government defendant cases were much more ideologically divisive.

---

[44] In the appendix, we discuss alternative specifications, with Segal-Cover scores substituted for Martin-Quinn scores, and with the breakpoint moved from 1995 to 2000. In both of the Segal-Cover models we observe similar results to those just discussed, but with larger growth in the effect of ideology. In the Martin-Quinn model with a 2000 break, the interaction is insignificant. As we discuss next, it is evident that growth in the influence of ideology in the recent period is driven by business defendant cases, where the interaction is significant in all alternative specifications.

Table 4.6. *Logit model of justice votes in private enforcement cases, government versus business defendant models, with case fixed effects, 1960–2014*

Government defendant cases

	Coefficient	Marginal effect
Ideology (Martin-Quinn)	−.1.44***	−.15
	(.17)	
Ideology*Post-1994 Dummy	.41*	.04
	(.24)	

N = 993
Pseudo R^2 = .53

Business defendant cases

	Coefficient	Marginal effect
Ideology (Martin-Quinn)	−.51***	−.07
	(.09)	
Ideology*Post-1999 Dummy	−.84***	−.11
	(.32)	

N = 876
Pseudo R^2 = .40

***<.01; **<.05; *<.1
Standard errors in parentheses, clustered on justice

In the 1995–2014 period, however, the picture changed significantly. Although the effect of ideology declined modestly from 53 to 39 percentage points in government defendant cases, it increased from 25 to 63 percentage points in business defendant cases. Although the effect of ideology in business defendant cases had been less than half that observed in government defendant cases in the 1961–94 period, since then it caught up to and significantly surpassed its effect in government defendant cases. The separate models show that the business defendant cases are driving the significance of the interaction in the model run on all of the cases.[45] As we have discussed, business defendant cases, where the increasing

[45] Figure 4.4 suggests that the early 1980s may be when growth in the distance between conservative and liberal justices began and thus that 1981 may be a more appropriate breakpoint in this model than 1995. We examined this possibility in alternate specifications in which we included both a 1981 interaction and a 1995 interaction. In these models the 1981 interaction was highly insignificant, and the 1995 interaction remained significant. It is critical to remember that in our models we measure justices' ideology at the individual justice level, rather than with a blunt liberal-conservative dummy variable. Model results thus will not always map neatly to our visualization of the data using the simple liberal-conservative division.

Table 4.7. *Logit model of justice votes in all federal statutory and constitutional issues (Spaeth data), with case fixed effects, 1960–2014*

	Coefficient	Marginal effect
Ideology (Martin-Quinn)	−.62***	−.09
	(.14)	
Ideology*Post-1994 Dummy	−.23	
	(.18)	
N = 4,400		
Pseudo R^2 = .35		

***<.01; **<.05; *<.1
Standard errors in parentheses, clustered on justice

effect of ideology has been concentrated in the last two decades, have at the same time grown to be the lion's share of the Court's private enforcement docket (about 72% by 2014), and the locus of rising amicus attention by the Chamber of Commerce and conservative legal organizations.[46]

For a comparative sense of the magnitude of the effects of ideology in all federal rights cases as compared to private enforcement issues, we ran the same regression on a random sample of 500 of Spaeth's federal rights issues.[47] The results, reported in Table 4.7, indicate that moving from the average liberal to the average conservative justice was associated with a 32 percentage point reduction in the probability of a liberal vote in the 1960–94 period. The interaction between justice ideology and the post-1994 dummy is insignificant, meaning that the estimated effect did not

[46] In the appendix, we discuss alternative specifications, with Segal-Cover scores substituted for Martin-Quinn scores, and with the breakpoint moved from 1995 to 2000, and find that the results are substantially similar with a larger growth effect in business defendant cases in the Segal-Cover models. In the Segal-Cover government defendant models, the effect of ideology holds constant over the full period (the interaction is insignificant), rather than declining modestly, as it does in the Martin-Quinn models. Moreover, the decline detected in the Martin-Quinn models is significant at only the .1 level. Thus, the evidence is not clear as to whether the effect of ideology in government defendant cases held constant over time or declined modestly after 1995/2000. We believe that because the litigation retrenchment project's first target was litigation against government, by 1995 or 2000 the most contentious issues in that domain had been litigated, which is consistent with the declining volume of government defendant cases on the Court's private enforcement docket.

[47] The model uses a random sample of 500 issues that are coded federal statutory or constitutional in Spaeth's issue-level database. As discussed in the appendix, sampling was necessary to facilitate use of the same regression specifications we apply to our private enforcement data.

change in the post-1994 period. Thus, the effect of ideology on private enforcement issues was similar to that in all federal rights cases in the 1960–94 period (32 percentage points in all federal rights issues, and 35 in private enforcement issues). It then grew to be substantially larger in the 1995–2014 period (32 percentage points in all federal rights issues, and 53 in private enforcement issues). Justices are now more ideologically divided over private enforcement issues than they are over federal rights issues in general. The Spaeth dataset does not contain information needed to subset business versus government defendants in the original trial court proceeding.

In the appendix, we report a similar comparison to the parallel sample of cases that match the policy distribution of our private enforcement cases and contain only votes on substantive merits issues. We find a 41 percentage point reduction in conservative justices' probability of a liberal vote throughout. The 1995 interaction was insignificant. Thus, since 1995 justice ideology has had a larger influence in our private enforcement issues – when conservative justices have been 53 percentage points less likely to vote in favor of private enforcement than liberal justices – than in votes on substantive rights in the same policy areas.

Empirical Analysis of the Federal Rules Cases

We have presented data leading us to conclude that private enforcement decisions of the Supreme Court have been substantially affected by the ideological preferences of justices, and that the influence of ideology has materially increased in recent decades. The data in question pool decisions on six issues implicating private enforcement, one of which is procedural law under the Federal Rules of Civil Procedure. For a number of reasons, decisions interpreting the Federal Rules merit discrete attention.

First, those decisions complete the picture we draw in Chapter 3 by honoring the proposition, articulated there, that the Federal Rules leave great room for judicial interpretation and discretion in the context of individual cases. They are, therefore, a necessary part of an account that recognizes the distinctive power of the federal judiciary to enlarge or constrict private enforcement through its control of procedure.

Second, only by separately considering decisions interpreting the Federal Rules can we gain traction on an important institutional question. We have seen how the rulemaking process reforms of the 1980s had the effect, and for some proponents the purpose, of assimilating that process to the administrative or legislative process, rendering significant procedural change more difficult. This insight raises the question whether, when the law of private enforcement is at issue, a similar institutional dynamic applies between the Supreme Court in its two different roles as between the Court and Congress. Put otherwise, has the Court been more successful in retrenching the law governing private enforcement when interpreting Federal Rules than it has been in promulgating them?

Third, the private enforcement issues in our data run the gamut from those that are closely tied to the substantive law – notably the existence and scope of a private right of action,[48] and attorney's fees – to those that are the bread and butter of procedure, such as pleading under the Federal Rules. For that reason, subjecting the Court's Federal Rules decisions to discrete inquiry may illuminate reasons for the enhanced influence of ideology on, and the enhanced polarization of the justices with respect to, private enforcement issues, as well as about the strategic nature of the Court's decisions on such issues.

There has been no shortage of scholarly commentary on Supreme Court decisions interpreting the Federal Rules, particularly in recent years, much of it focusing on controversial decisions concerning pleading and class actions (Burbank 2009; Spencer 2010; Resnik 2011; Klonoff 2013). Scholars have recognized the potentially substantial effect that these decisions could have on private enforcement, and, on the basis of their reading of the Court's decisions more generally, have concluded that procedure has become an important part of conservative justices' agenda in the area of litigation (Wasserman 2012; Miller 2013; Purcell 2014; Subrin and Main 2014). Reviewing some of this scholarship, political scientist Robert Kagan concluded that "[e]xperts in the law of civil procedure seem to agree that in recent decades, a conservative majority on the Supreme Court, in case after case has constricted adversarial legalism as a mechanism of enforcing public law."[49]

Justices' Votes in Federal Rules Private Enforcement Cases

As explained earlier in this chapter, our collection of Supreme Court data included identification of all cases from 1960 to 2014 in which the Court decided an issue that turned on interpretation of a Federal Rule of Civil

---

[48] In Chapter 5, we note that most of the cases that defied classification (relevant for purposes of that chapter) as between private enforcement and merits issues involved the scope of a private right of action.
[49] Robert A. Kagan, "American Adversarial Legalism in the Early 21st Century: 'Afterword' to 2nd Edition of Adversarial Legalism: The American Way of Law" 24 (Working Draft February 26, 2016).

Table 4.8. *Types of Federal Rules issues*

Federal Rules issues	Number of cases
Rule 23, class actions	23
Rule 23, policy issues	10
Rule 8, pleading	7
Rule 11, sanctions	6
Rule 56, summary judgment	5
Rule 50, judgment as a matter of law	4
Rule 15(c), relation back	3
Rule 68, offer of judgment	3
Rule 23.1, derivative actions	3
Rule 24, intervention	3
Rule 3, commencement	2
Rule 19, joinder	2
The data further included one case each for the following Rules: 4, 20, 37, 41, 48, 54, 59, 65, 83	

Procedure, where the result would either widen or narrow opportunities or incentives for private enforcement. Because we are particularly interested in class actions, we additionally included in our Federal Rules cases those that turned on an issue explicitly linked to policies underpinning Rule 23, such as tolling a statute of limitations and claim preclusion. The search yielded 78 cases, containing 80 issues, and 688 justice votes. The cases span 1961 to 2013 because none was decided in 1960 or 2014. At least one of the authors read each majority, concurring, and dissenting opinion in order to assign codes to each justice's position: anti-private enforcement ($=0$), pro-private enforcement ($=1$), and missing if the justice did not take a position on the issue.[50]

On the one hand, we acknowledge that this is a somewhat limited volume of data for empirical analysis. On the other hand, it is the full universe of Federal Rules private enforcement cases, as we have defined it, and much can be learned from it. Moreover, we reiterate that the transsubstantive nature of the Federal Rules means that such decisions are often considerably more far-reaching than decisions interpreting the private enforcement provisions of individual statutes, such as the PSLRA. Table 4.8 lists the number of issues arising under particular rules.

[50] We excluded from the dataset cases that merely cited a Federal Rule, cases in which the decision of an issue did not turn on an interpretation of a Federal Rule, habeas cases, cases not implicating private enforcement, and cases in which the interpretation of a Federal Rule could not fairly be characterized as either pro- or anti-private enforcement.

Figure 4.9 depicts estimates of the number of Federal Rules cases decided by the Court per year, and the probability that a Federal Rules case will have a dissent over time. Again, because the number of Federal Rules cases in the 1960s is limited, we focus on the figure beginning in the 1970s. The estimated number of Federal Rules cases on the Court's docket grew in the

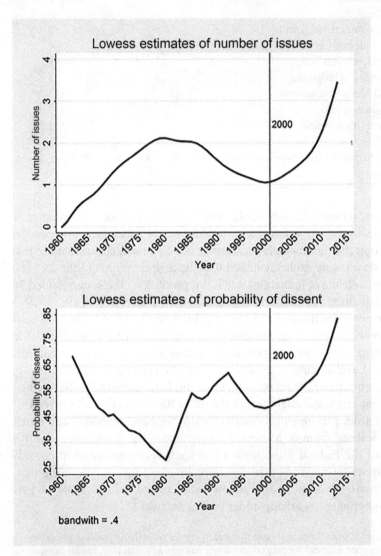

Figure 4.9   Number of Federal Rules private enforcement issues per term, and probability of dissent, 1960–2013

1970s, plateaued in the first half of the 1980s, declined until around 2000, and then spiked after around 2000. The likelihood of a dissent has increased substantially since 1980. Most significantly, after 2000 the estimated probability of a dissent grew sharply, rising from an estimated 49% in 2000 to 83% in 2013. For purposes of comparison, when all of our private-enforcement cases are pooled, the probability of a dissent at the end of the series is about 26 percentage points lower, and both the probability of dissent, and the number of issues on the docket per term, were about flat after 2000 (see Figure 4.1). Thus, among private enforcement issues in our data, the Federal Rules cases are distinctive in the growth of their presence on the Court's agenda and the likelihood of eliciting a dissent, since around 2000.

Table 4.9 lists the raw proportion of pro-private enforcement votes relative to total votes, for each justice, along with their conservative versus liberal designation according to the Martin-Quinn median, for the 40 issues (representing 348 votes) on which there was at least one dissenter. Although the specific ordering changes as compared to when we pool all of our private enforcement cases, the distribution from the lowest to highest percentage of pro-private enforcement votes is very similar. The range in the Federal Rules cases is again dramatic, with Thomas voting in the pro-private enforcement direction 6% of the time, and Kagan and Sotomayor doing so 100% of the time. The same table, but for all 80 issues (including unanimous votes), is in the appendix.

The division of justices into conservatives and liberals again does an excellent job of predicting whether a justice is above or below the median ratio of pro-private enforcement votes in Federal Rules cases. Among justices who cast at least five votes, every conservative has a lower pro-private enforcement voting rate than every liberal. Until Justice Scalia's death, the Court's conservative majority (Thomas, Roberts, Scalia, Alito, and Kennedy) were five of the seven most anti-private enforcement justices in Federal Rules cases with dissents reaching back over a half-century.

Figure 4.10 plots the estimated probability of an outcome in favor of private enforcement in the Federal Rules cases over time and the probability of votes in favor of private enforcement separately for conservative and liberal justices. As previously, these figures are intended to convey a broad descriptive sense of longitudinal patterns. This caveat is especially important in light of the smaller number of Federal Rules cases. We employ statistical models with significance tests below to formally test the effects of ideology and how they changed over time.

The figure reflects that the estimated probability of a pro-private enforcement Federal Rules outcome vacillated in the range of 50% to

Table 4.9. *Percentage of pro-private enforcement votes in Federal Rules cases with at least one dissenting vote*

Justice	Percentage of pro-private enforcement	Number of votes	Conservative	Average Martin-Quinn score
Thomas	6	17	1	3.47
Powell	8	13	1	.93
Alito	9	11	1	1.88
Stewart	17	12	1	.54
Roberts	18	11	1	1.30
Scalia	18	22	1	2.45
Kennedy	23	22	1	.68
Rehnquist	25	24	1	2.84
O'Connor	25	16	1	.88
Burger	31	13	1	1.85
White	35	20	1	.44
Blackmun	58	19	0	−0.11
Souter	60	10	0	−.93
Marshall	60	20	0	−2.83
Brennan	68	22	0	−2.88
Ginsburg	71	17	0	−1.60
Breyer	76	17	0	−1.27
Douglas	88	8	0	−6.04
Stevens	88	26	0	−1.72
Sotomayor	100	6	0	−1.92
Kagan	100	6	0	−1.66
Less than five votes				
Fortas	50	2	0	−1.11
Clark	33	3	0	.23
Black	67	3	0	−0.79
Harlan	0	4	1	1.74
Warren	25	4	0	−1.26

63% from the mid-1960s to the early 1980s, at which time it began a 20-year decline from 63% to 29% at the end of the series. As with private enforcement cases in general, the decline has been substantially driven by the votes of conservative justices in the majority, whose estimated probability of a pro-private enforcement vote declined from 56% in the mid-to-late 1980s to 18% at the end of the series. For liberal justices the probability ranged

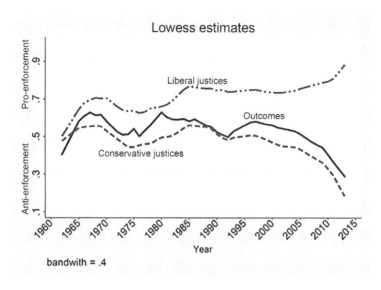

Figure 4.10   Probability of pro-private enforcement outcomes and justice votes in all Federal Rules private enforcement issues, 1960–2014

between 63% and 77% from the mid-1960s to about 2000, after which it climbed precipitously, reaching 88% by 2013. Also after about 2000, the distance between liberal and conservative justices, which had been fairly stable in the range of 20 to 25 percentage points over the previous two decades, widened markedly, reaching 70 percentage points by 2013. This degree of polarization is much greater than the 40 percentage points we observed when all private enforcement issues are pooled (Figure 4.2).

As we explained when discussing the full set of private enforcement cases, we regard cases with at least one dissent as especially informative. Such cases are most likely to present open questions regarding how the law affecting private enforcement should be applied or developed. Figure 4.11 replicates the regressions in Figure 4.10, now focusing on the 40 Federal Rules cases with at least one dissent, containing 348 justice votes. The longitudinal patterns are substantially similar, but with a sharper decline in pro-private enforcement outcomes. Beginning in 1981, the probability of such outcomes declined from 66% to 20% at the end of the series. Over the same period, the probability of a pro-private enforcement vote by conservative justices declined from 28% to 8%. Also from 1981 to 2014, the probability of a pro-private enforcement vote by liberal justices increased

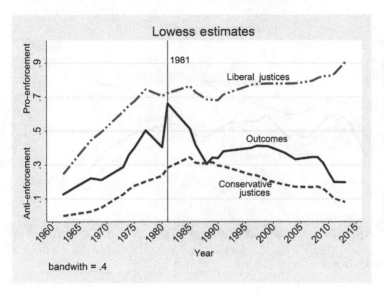

Figure 4.11   Probability of pro-private enforcement outcomes and justice votes in Federal Rules private enforcement issues with dissents, 1960–2014

materially, from 72% to 91%. Finally, the distance between liberals and conservatives grew from 44 to a remarkable 83 percentage points.

On the dimension of business versus government defendants, the Federal Rules issues stand in marked contrast to our other private enforcement issues. There are business defendants in 40% of our private enforcement issues excluding the Federal Rules issues (324 of 404 issues). For the Federal Rule issues (80 of 404 issues), the comparable statistic is 71%. Using all issues with a business or government defendant (94% of our data), Figure 4.12 depicts the estimated probability of a business versus government defendant separately for Federal Rules issues and for all remaining private enforcement issues in our data. The horizontal line at the bottom of the figure represents 100% government defendants; the horizontal line at the top of the figure represents 100% business defendants, and the horizontal line in the middle of the figure (at the value of .5) represents a 50–50 split.

The figure shows that Federal Rules cases have a consistently higher likelihood of business defendants throughout; that the share of cases with business defendants has been rising in both the Federal Rules and non-Federal Rules cases in recent decades; and that this growth in business

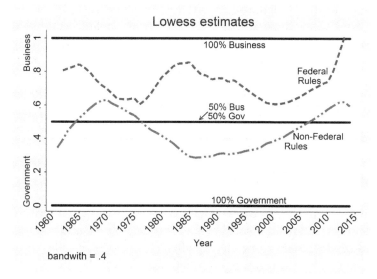

Figure 4.12   Balance between government and business defendants in Federal Rules private enforcement cases, and non-Federal Rules private enforcement cases, 1960–2014

defendants was clearly sharper in Federal Rules cases. By the end of the series, in the Federal Rules cases the estimated probability of a business defendant is 100%. When examining all of the private enforcement cases pooled, we observed that growing polarization between liberal and conservative justices in private enforcement cases in recent years corresponds to a growing focus on business regulation cases. We observe here that in recent years, when the Federal Rules cases have been distinctively ideologically contentious, they have also been distinctively focused on business regulation cases.

The Court's growing focus on business defendant Federal Rules cases since around 2000 occurred at about the time (1998) that the Chamber of Commerce founded the Institute for Legal Reform, which focuses on such issues as class actions and discovery. It also corresponds to a surge in the Chamber's amicus advocacy on private enforcement issues. We observed earlier in this chapter that from 1995 to 2014, the Chamber filed 27 briefs in 88 private enforcement cases in our data that presented a private enforcement and not a merits issue. When those cases are divided into Federal Rules and other private enforcement cases, we observe that the Chamber filed amicus briefs in 40% of the Federal Rules cases (10 of

25), as compared to 27% of the other private enforcement cases (17 of 63). Although we cannot draw strong inferences from so little data, as a descriptive matter, it is clear that the Chamber devoted proportionally more amicus attention to Federal Rules than other private enforcement issues in our data during this period.

The forgoing examination of the basic patterns in the Federal Rules cases reveals the following. Beginning around the early 1980s, there was a long decline in the probability of a pro-private enforcement vote that was sustained through 2013 (the year of the last Federal Rules case in our data). Alongside the decline in pro-private enforcement outcomes, there developed growing distance between liberal and conservative justices, with escalating polarization after around 2000. We also learned that Federal Rules private enforcement cases (much more so than other private enforcement cases), are dominated by business defendants, and that this business defendant skew grew starker after about 2000. Finally, since about the same time, the Court has devoted materially more attention to Federal Rules private enforcement issues on its docket, and those cases have elicited dissents at increasingly and notably high rates. In the past 15 years, plaintiffs are losing, and business defendants are winning, a huge majority of Federal Rules private enforcement cases, and this field is the locus of increasingly intense conflict among the justices.

Table 4.10 reports logit models with case fixed effects. The models are parallel to those presented in Table 4.5 for our full body of private enforcement cases, and discussion of the model specification is presented there. We remind the reader that fixed effects models use only cases with dissents and that they control for all law-level variables – those taking the same

Table 4.10. *Logit model of justice votes in Federal Rules private enforcement cases, with case fixed effects, 1960–2014*

	Coefficient	Marginal effect
Ideology (Martin-Quinn)	−.49***	−.06
	(.13)	
Ideology*Post-1994 Dummy	−.86***	−.11
	(.23)	
N = 348		
Pseudo R^2 = .41		

***<.01; **<.05; *<.1
Standard errors in parentheses, clustered on justice

value for each justice vote in a case. The main effect of the ideology variable is significant. Because the interaction is included, this variable reflects the effects of ideology only in the period from 1961 to 1994. The marginal effect for the coefficient is −.06, which means that for each unit increase in a justice's Martin-Quinn score, there is a corresponding reduction of about 6% in the probability of a pro-private enforcement vote.

Moving from the mean ideology score of a liberal justice to a conservative justice in our data (a Martin-Quinn distance of 3.5) is associated with a 21 percentage point reduction in the probability of a pro-private enforcement vote. The magnitude of the effect is notably less than the effect we observed in the model that pooled all of our private enforcement issues (35 percentage points), in the model of merits votes in the same policy fields as those underlying our private enforcement data (41 percentage points), and in the model of votes in all federal rights cases (32 percentage points). Thus, although there is statistically significant ideological voting on Federal Rules private enforcement issues in the 1961–94 period, the issues are characterized by a notably smaller degree of it relative to all private enforcement issues in general, federal rights issues in general, and merits votes in the policy areas underlying our private enforcement data. Put simply, during this period, procedure is different. It is less ideological.

The interaction of the justices' ideology scores and the post-1994 dummy is again statistically significant. The ideology effect for the 1995–2013 period is given by summing the marginal effects of ideology (−.06) and its interaction with the post-1994 dummy variable (−.11), rendering a net marginal effect of −.17. In the roughly two decades from 1995 to 2013, the reduction in the probability of a pro-private enforcement vote associated with moving from a liberal to a conservative justice is 60%. Remarkably, in 1995–2013, the effect of ideology on these procedure votes about tripled relative to the 1961–94 period. It went from notably less than merits votes in policy areas underlying our private enforcement data, and votes on all federal rights issues, to being 46% larger than the former, and about double the latter.[51] Overall, our results show just how far we have

---

[51] In the appendix, we observe similar results in models substituting Martin-Quinn scores, and models moving the breakpoint to 2000. In the Segal-Cover model with a 2000 break, the effect of ideology nearly quadruples. This remarkable transformation is not an artifact of how ideology is measured. Finally, we note that we have too few Federal Rules cases in general, and too few government defendant cases within them, to present separate government defendant and business defendant models, as we did in our analysis of the full dataset.

come from the traditional conception of, and rhetoric about, procedure as technical details or adjective law.[52]

In one final set of alternative specifications, we dropped class action issues from the data and re-ran all of the regressions on procedure issues. Because a disproportionate number of our Federal Rules issues concern class actions (as reflected in Table 4.8), we sought to assess whether the patterns we observed in Federal Rules cases were driven by class action issues. They are not. To the contrary, when the regression in Table 4.10 (Martin-Quinn model, with 1995 break) is replicated with class action issues excluded, the pattern is even starker. During the 1961–94 period, moving from the average liberal to conservative justice was associated with a reduction of 18 percentage points in the probability of a pro-enforcement vote, and in the 1995–2013 period it was 106 percentage points, with both the main effect and the interaction significant at better than .05.[53]

Conclusion

The data and analyses in this chapter strongly support, if they do not compel, the conclusion that the Supreme Court has been more successful than Congress or the rulemakers in changing the law governing or influencing private enforcement and thus, necessarily, that the Court has been more successful in retrenching the law governing private enforcement when acting as such rather than as a delegated lawmaker under the Rules Enabling Act. Even if so, however, they do not tell us what accounts for the Court's relative success. Nor do they tell us why, in cases with at least one dissent, the estimated probability of a pro-private enforcement outcome, and of a pro-private enforcement vote by a conservative justice, are markedly lower than the probabilities of a liberal outcome and of a liberal vote by conservative justices in the full body of the Court's civil actions asserting federal rights.

[52] Figure 4.4 suggests that the early 1980s is really when growth in the distance between conservative and liberal justices began and thus that 1981 may be a more appropriate breakpoint in this model than 1995. As with our examination of the full dataset, we evaluated alternative specifications and concluded that 1981 is not an appropriate breakpoint. See *supra* note 45 for fuller discussion.

[53] These models contained 203 judge-vote observations. The same basic pattern was detected in the Martin-Quinn model with a 2000 break, and the Segal-Cover models with the 1995 and 2000 breaks, with one exception. In the Segal-Cover model with a 1995 break, the effect of ideology in the 1961–94 period dips below significance at .1 ($p = .11$), while remaining statistically significant and very large in the 1995–2013 period.

In other words, putting other institutions out of the picture for this purpose, what makes private enforcement cases distinctive on the Supreme Court, and within that domain, what in recent years has made Federal Rules cases notably ideological and polarized? Finally – although the list of questions to be answered is much longer – analysis of our qualitative and quantitative evidence does not tell us how effective the Court has been in actually retrenching private enforcement, as opposed to retrenching law governing or influencing private enforcement.

We address these questions, as well as others, in the concluding chapter of this book. As will be evident, some of our suggested explanations draw on, and elaborate from a comparative perspective, the institutional impediments to the counterrevolution's campaign in Congress and rulemaking that we discussed in Chapters 2 and 3. Moreover, they are informed by the qualitative material in those chapters and in this one. In setting out reasons to study the results in the Court's Federal Rules cases discretely earlier in this chapter, we suggested that such an inquiry "may illuminate reasons for the enhanced influence of ideology on, and the enhanced polarization of the justices with respect to, private enforcement issues, as well as about the strategic nature of the Court's decisions on such issues." In making that suggestion, we were giving voice to our intuitions that, from the institutional perspective that drives this book (1) the Court is different from Congress and the rulemakers, (2) the Court's private enforcement cases are different from their cases involving substantive federal rights, and (3) those differences may surface most clearly in cases involving interpretation of the Federal Rules of Civil Procedure. In the next chapter, we elaborate some of the bases for these intuitions and subject them to empirical inquiry.

APPENDIX

Private Enforcement Vote Tables, All Cases

Table A.4.1 lists the raw proportion of pro-private enforcement votes, relative to total votes, for all justices in our data, and for all 404 issues in our data (containing 3,495 votes). The table also contains each justice's Martin-Quinn score and designation as conservative or liberal according to the division described in the chapter. As with Table 4.4, containing the same information for cases with dissents, the distribution from lowest to highest pro-private enforcement votes tracks the conservative-liberal dimension. When all cases are examined, focusing on justices with at least five votes, the six most pro-private enforcement scores, in order, are those of Douglas, Black, Brennan, Sotomayor, Marshall, and Stevens. The six most anti-private enforcement scores, in order, are those of Thomas, Roberts, Scalia, Alito, Rehnquist, and Powell. The scores range from Thomas voting in the pro-private enforcement direction 31% of the time, to Douglas doing so 89% of the time.

Table A.4.2 lists the same information, but restricted to the 80 Federal Rules cases (containing 688 votes). Although the specific ordering changes as compared to when we pool all of our private enforcement cases, the general distribution from the lowest to highest percentage of pro-private enforcement votes is very similar. The range in the Federal Rules cases is again large, with Alito voting in the pro-private enforcement direction 31% of the time, and Sotomayor doing so 90% of the time (based on only 10 votes).

Models of Justice Votes in Supreme Court Opinions

Because the dependent variable in these models is dichotomous, we use logistic regression, which is designed for dichotomous dependent variables (Pampel 2000). We cluster standard errors on justice because standard regression models (without clustering) treat each justice's vote in a

Table A.4.1. *Percentage of pro-private enforcement votes in all private enforcement cases, including unanimous decisions*

Justice	Percentage of pro-private enforcement	Number of votes	Conservative	Average Martin-Quinn score
Thomas	31	137	1	3.47
Roberts	32	56	1	1.30
Scalia	32	194	1	2.45
Alito	34	53	1	1.88
Rehnquist	37	299	1	2.84
Powell	38	156	1	.93
O'Connor	40	201	1	.88
Frankfurter	40	5	1	1.85
Kennedy	41	182	1	.68
Burger	43	171	1	1.85
Harlan	50	40	1	1.74
Goldberg	50	6	0	−.79
Stewart	51	145	1	.54
White	55	266	1	.44
Souter	58	119	0	−.93
Clark	58	24	0	.23
Breyer	65	122	0	−1.27
Warren	67	33	0	−1.26
Blackmun	68	238	0	−.11
Ginsburg	69	128	0	−1.60
Kagan	70	23	0	−1.66
Fortas	71	14	0	−1.20
Stevens	71	291	0	−1.72
Marshall	73	231	0	−2.83
Sotomayor	73	30	0	−1.92
Brennan	76	250	0	−2.10
Black	78	41	0	−.79
Douglas	89	80	0	−6.04
Less than five votes				
Whittaker	50	4	1	1.24

private enforcement case as independent from her vote in other private enforcement cases, but private enforcement votes by the same justices are not independent from one another. Non-independent observations add less information to regression estimates than independent observations.

Table A.4.2. *Percentage of pro-private enforcement votes in Federal Rules cases, including unanimous decisions*

Justice	Percentage of pro-private enforcement	Number of votes	Conservative	Average Martin-Quinn score
Alito	31	16	1	1.88
Thomas	33	30	1	3.47
Roberts	37	16	1	1.30
Powell	39	31	1	.93
Scalia	44	39	1	2.45
Kennedy	45	38	1	.68
Stewart	45	29	1	.54
Rehnquist	46	54	1	2.83
Harlan	50	8	1	1.74
Warren	50	6	0	−1.27
Burger	52	33	1	1.85
O'Connor	53	34	1	.88
White	57	49	1	.44
Clark	60	5	0	.23
Souter	62	21	0	−.93
Blackmun	64	44	0	−.12
Marshall	64	44	0	−2.83
Ginsburg	68	28	0	−1.60
Brennan	70	47	0	−2.10
Black	71	7	0	−.79
Breyer	71	28	0	−1.27
Stevens	77	52	0	−1.72
Douglas	81	16	0	−6.04
Kagan	89	9	0	−1.66
Sotomayor	90	10	0	−1.92
Fewer than five votes:				
Goldberg	1	1	0	−.79
Fortas	67	3	0	−1.20

Clustering standard errors on justice adjusts standard errors to account for this and thereby avoids standard errors that are too small (Woolridge 2013: ch. 14). We computed marginal effects for these models with Stata's "margins, dydx(*)" command.

Martin-Quinn Models with 2000 Break

In the models presented in Tables 4.5 (all cases) and 4.10 (Federal Rules cases), we included an interaction with a dummy variable that took the value 0 for the period 1970–94 and 1 for the period 1995–2014. We explained in the text that this dividing line was selected based on theory and evidence suggesting that the Court had greater insulation from legislative override, and that litigation retrenchment became more salient, in the latter period. Considering the distance between liberal and conservative voting on private enforcement issues in Figure 4.3 as a measure of politicization of these issues among justices, the distance appears to have begun to widen noticeably more around 2000. In alternative specifications, we moved the dividing line for the dummy variable from 1995 to 2000.

As reported in Table A.4.3, the main effects of ideology remain significant in both models. The marginal effects associated with moving from a liberal to a conservative justice for the 1960–99 period were similar for the 1960–94 period (39 percentage points in the model of all issues, and 25 in the Federal Rules model). The marginal effect of ideology for the 2000–14

Table A.4.3. *Logit model of justice votes in private enforcement cases, and in Federal Rules cases, with case fixed effects, and 2000 break*

All private enforcement cases		
	Coefficient	**Marginal effect**
Ideology (Martin-Quinn)	−.86***	−.11
	(.12)	
Ideology*post-1999 dummy	−.23	
	(.25)	
N = 1,939		
Pseudo R^2 = .44		
Federal Rules cases		
	Coefficient	**Marginal effect**
Ideology (Martin-Quinn)	−.56***	−.07
	(.15)	
Ideology*post-1999 dummy	−.77***	−.10
	(.25)	
N = 348		
Pseudo R^2 = .40		

***<.01; **<.05; *<.1
Standard errors in parentheses, clustered on justice

Table A.4.4. *Logit model of justice votes in private enforcement cases, government versus business defendant models, with 2000 break, and case fixed effects*

Government defendant cases

	Coefficient	Marginal effect
Ideology (Martin-Quinn)	−1.41***	−.15
	(.15)	
Ideology*post-1999 dummy	.47*	.05
	(.25)	

N = 993
Pseudo R^2 = .53

Business defendant cases

	Coefficient	Marginal effect
Ideology (Martin-Quinn)	−.57***	−.08
	(.11)	
Ideology*post-1999 dummy	−.67**	−.09
	(.31)	

N = 876
Pseudo R^2 = .39

***<.01; **<.05; *<.1
Standard errors in parentheses, clustered on justice

period remains 39 percentage points in the general private enforcement model, and grows to 60% in the Federal Rules model.

Table A.4.4 replicates the separate government defendant and business defendant models presented in Table 4.6, with the breakpoint moved from 1995 to 2000. The structure of the results remains the same. The effect of ideology is much larger in government than business defendant cases in the 1960–99 period, and it declines modestly in the 2000–13 period. The effect of ideology in the business defendant cases grows dramatically in the 2000–14 period, becoming even larger than in government defendant cases.

Segal-Cover Models

We replicated all of our private enforcement models substituting Segal-Cover scores for Martin-Quinn scores. Segal-Cover scores are based on pre-confirmation media coverage of justices' nominations and therefore are based on information independent of justices' voting behavior. Martin-Quinn scores are derived from justices' aggregate voting behavior in non-unanimous cases and thus are susceptible to the concern of circularity in that we are using justice votes to predict justice votes. We note in this regard that our private enforcement issues comprise a very small fraction of the total non-unanimous votes used to estimate the Martin-Quinn scores. Moreover, a key part of what we wish to understand is whether the Court's private enforcement votes actually map to the more general left–right axis on the Court that we associate with the substantive policy positions that divide it. Finally, we are especially interested in whether and how the effect of ideology on justices' votes in private enforcement cases has changed over time – which we test with the interaction term – and we see nothing in the Martin-Quinn scores that would predispose them to detecting such an effect. Still, Segal-Cover scores provide a useful robustness check.

Our replications of otherwise identical models include the models of all issues; of all issues disaggregated into government and business defendant cases; and of only Federal Rules issues. All of these models were run with a 1995 break and a 2000 break. Rather than displaying all of these models, in Table A.4.5 we summarize the percentage point change in the probability of a pro-private enforcement vote, moving from a liberal to a conservative justice, for each model. The distance between the mean Segal-Cover ideology scores of justices above and below the Segal-Cover median is .67. Defining conservative and liberal justices as those above and below the Segal-Cover median, Table A.4.5 gives the percentage point change in the probability of a pro-private enforcement vote moving from the average liberal to the average conservative justice.

The overall structure of the results is very similar with Segal-Cover scores as with Martin-Quinn scores. The main effect and the interaction are significant in the model of all private enforcement issues pooled, and when the data are subset into government versus business defendant cases, it is evident that the interaction effect is being driven by the business defendant cases. The level of growth associated with the interaction is especially large in Federal Rules cases, where the effect of ideology went from being modest to being large. The growth effect is larger with the 2000 as compared to the 1995 break.

Spaeth Comparisons

Regression on Federal Rights Issues

In Table 4.7 we presented a regression with justice votes in all federal statutory and constitutional rights issues drawn from the Spaeth database (issueArea = 1, 2, and 3). We drew a random sample of 500 issues from

Table A.4.5. *Marginal effects from models substituting Segal-Cover scores for Martin-Quinn scores*

Tables in bold contain parallel Martin-Quinn models	Reduction of probability of pro-private enforcement vote moving from conservative to liberal justice
1995 Break models	
Table 4.5	
All issues, 1960–94	29% points***
All issues, 1995–2014	73% points***
Table 4.6	
All issues, government defendants only, 1960–94	38% points***
All issues, government defendants only, 1995–2014	38% points (interaction insig.)
Table 4.6	
All issues, business defendants only, 1960–94	19% points***
All issues, business defendants only, 1995–2014	79% points***
Table 4.10	
Federal Rules issues, 1960–94	20% points***
Federal Rules issues, 1995–2014	72% points***
2000 Break Models	
Table 4.5, with 2000 break	
All issues, 1960–99	31% points***
All issues, 2000–14	78% points***
Table 4.6, with 2000 break	
All issues, government defendants only, 1960–99	40% points***
All issues, government defendants only, 2000–14	40% points (interaction insig.)
Table 4.6, with 2000 break	
All issues, business defendants only, 1960–99	21% points***
All issues, business defendants only, 2000–14	86% points***
Table 4.10, with 2000 break	
Federal Rules issues, 1960–99	21% points***
Federal Rules issues, 2000–14	80% points***

issues in which there was at least one dissenting vote. This was necessary because our fixed effects regression required incorporating a dummy variable as an explanatory variable for every case, and thus we required a dataset of manageable size in order to process that regression in Stata (the software package we used), which cannot accommodate over 3,000 independent variables, as would be required without sampling. It was critical to run the regression explicitly incorporating dummies – rather than with Stata's xt routine, which does not require explicitly incorporating dummy variables – because that routine does not allow clustering on justice, which is imperative for regressions comparable to the ones we ran on our private enforcement data. A sample of 500 issues with dissents still gives us many more cases and issues with dissents than in our private enforcement regression. The 500 Spaeth issues with dissents occurred in 443 cases and yielded 4,400 votes.

Spaeth Parallel Policy Sample

Drawing on the Spaeth data, we constructed a parallel sample of cases that match the policy distribution of our private enforcement cases and contain only votes on substantive merits issues. By "substantive merits issues," we are referring to the ultimate substantive claims in the lawsuit. If it was a civil rights, environmental, or anti-trust lawsuit, we include only cases in which the court actually reached the question whether the conduct complained of was, or could be, illegal discrimination, or pollution, or anti-competitive behavior. We say "could be" because a ruling on the appropriate legal standard would qualify as a merits ruling in our sense, even if a remand was necessary to apply the standard.

For all policy areas comprising more than 2% of our private enforcement cases (listed in Table 4.2), and that correspond to a Spaeth policy code, we included in the parallel policy sample the same number of cases as exist in our private enforcement data. The set of 312 private enforcement cases that we matched to Spaeth policy codes constitute 85% of our private enforcement cases: civil rights (133 cases), labor and employment (39), securities (36), civil liberties (34), social welfare benefits (29), antitrust (22), and environmental (19). When drawing randomly from the Spaeth case-level dataset within these policy areas in order to identify the requisite number of cases, we examined each case and included only those that ruled on the substantive merits of some part of the underlying cause of action. Having thus identified a parallel policy sample of cases, we turned to the Spaeth issue-level dataset, in which these cases yielded 434 discrete merits issue votes, with 61% (264 issues) containing a dissent.

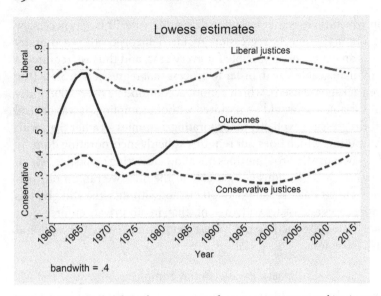

Figure A.4.1   Probability of pro-private enforcement outcomes and justice votes in parallel policy sample cases with dissents, 1960–2014

With our private enforcement issues, we replicated the regressions in Figure 4.3 (private enforcement issues with dissents), but only on the 85% of our private enforcement issues in the seven policy areas just enumerated. The resulting figure (not displayed) looks virtually identical to Figure 4.3. That is, exclusion of the 15% of our private enforcement issues from miscellaneous policy areas that are not included in the parallel policy sample does not affect outcome and voting patterns in our private enforcement issues.

Figure A.4.1 depicts the estimated probability of a liberal case outcome in the parallel policy sample of issues with at least one dissenting vote, as well as the estimated probability of a liberal vote separately for liberal and conservative justices. From 1970 to 2014, the probability of a liberal outcome looks much like all federal rights cases (Figure 4.6), and unlike private enforcement cases (Figure 4.3). It averaged 45%, ending the series at an estimated probability of 43%. At the end of the series, the estimated probabilities of a liberal outcome (43%), and of a liberal vote by conservative justices (39%), on merits issues are notably higher than the probabilities of a pro-private-enforcement outcome (14%), and of a pro-private-enforcement vote by conservative justices (10%). The difference

Table A.4.6. *Logit model of justice votes in parallel policy sample, with case fixed effects, 1960–2014*

	Coefficient	Marginal effect
Ideology (Martin-Quinn)	−.95***	−.12
	(.13)	
Ideology*post-1994 dummy	−.11	
	(.26)	
N = 2,305		
Pseudo R² = .44		

***<.01; **<.05; *<.1
Standard errors in parentheses, clustered on justice

between liberal and conservative justices' voting also looks similar to all federal rights cases, and unlike our private enforcement cases. From 1970 to 2014, there was a net decline of 2 percentage points in the estimated distance from liberals to conservatives, from 41 to 39 percentage points. We do not observe the pattern of polarization between liberal and conservative justices that is clearly evident in our private enforcement cases.

To get a comparative sense of the magnitude of the effects of ideology on merits votes as compared to private enforcement issues, we ran our regression model on the parallel policy sample votes. The regression results, reported in Table A.4.6, indicate that in the 1960–94 period moving from liberal to conservative justices was associated with a 41 percentage point reduction in the probability of a liberal vote. The interaction between justice ideology and the post-1994 dummy is insignificant, meaning that the estimated effect did not change in the post-1994 period. Thus, the effect of ideology was somewhat smaller in private enforcement cases as compared to merits votes in the same policy areas in the 1960–94 period (35 as compared to 41 percentage point reduction moving from the average liberal to the average conservative). It then grew to be larger in the 1995–2014 period (53 as compared to 41 percentage point reduction). Justices are now more ideologically divided over private enforcement issues than they are over the underlying substantive rights. Finally, when we subset these data into government and business defendant cases, the interaction remained insignificant in both models.

5

Subterranean Counterrevolution: The Supreme Court, the Media, and Public Opinion

In this chapter we explore our theory that, when seeking to retrench private enforcement, the Court benefits from strategically choosing cases that raise apparently technical and legalistic issues because the public is less likely to learn of the decisions through media coverage. The Court recognizes that public standing and perceived legitimacy are important to its institutional power, and it therefore is cognizant of the risk of straying too far or for too long from public opinion. This places limits on the feasibility of directly scaling back highly visible and popular substantive rights. From the standpoint of legitimacy, the strategy of focusing on private enforcement issues that largely fly under the public's radar has clear advantages.

The public learns about the Supreme Court's decisions from the media. Using an original dataset based on content analysis of newspaper coverage of Supreme Court decisions, we empirically investigate media coverage of decisions affecting private enforcement, such as decisions on damages, fees, and class actions, and we compare it to the coverage of rulings on substantive rights. These data demonstrate that Supreme Court decisions on laws relating to the enforcement of rights receive dramatically less press coverage than their decisions on the rights themselves. Ultimately, we argue that the Court's decisions on rights enforcement, because of their lower public visibility, are less constrained by public opinion and less tethered to democratic governance.

Why Public Opinion Matters

Theory

There is an extensive literature on what the public knows about the Court, how it comes by that knowledge, and how the knowledge translates into support or lack of support for the institution. Study after study has shown that the public knows little about the Court's decisions, but that levels of awareness differ as between the attentive public (who tend to be better educated and more interested in politics and public affairs) and the non-attentive public (Murphy and Tanenhaus 1968: 363–4; Caldeira 1991: 303). In addition, numerous studies demonstrate that most members of the public acquire the knowledge they have about the Court and its decisions from the mass media.

Research has found that the public's knowledge of the Court's decisions varies depending on a number of factors, including the extent and duration of media coverage and the perceived salience of the contested issue. "[Citizens] are much more likely to become aware of controversial issues that produce substantial and continued media coverage, while remaining ignorant of most other decisions. Only those most consistently interested in politics and the Court are likely to know of the full range of its work and decisions" (Franklin and Kosaki 1995: 366). Salience can be defined either as the perceived relevance to a person's personal circumstances (e.g., race, religion) (Murphy and Tanenhaus 1968: 362) or to his or her circumstances as a member of a geographic community (Hoekstra 2000: 97; Ginn, Searles, and Jones 2015: 176). It is also possible that "[a]n unusually controversial court decision [may be] able to cross the attention threshold of some of those for whom the judicial system is not a matter of everyday concern" (Lehne and Reynolds 1978: 901).

"Legitimacy" is a slippery term in the literature of constitutional law, so much so that Richard Fallon was moved to write an article devoted to unpacking the concept (Fallon 2005). It has the same elusive potential in political science, but far more work, theoretical and empirical, has been done that seeks to bring it to ground. Fallon focuses on what he refers to as "sociological legitimacy": "a constitutional regime, governmental institution, or official decision possesses legitimacy in a *strong* sense insofar as the relevant public regards it as justified, appropriate, or otherwise deserving of support for reasons beyond fear of sanctions or mere hope for personal reward" (1795). This is akin to what political scientists call "diffuse support," that is, support for the institution whether or not one agrees with particular products (decisions) (Easton 1965: 273). It is diffuse support, we believe, to which the late Judge Richard Arnold was referring when he stressed, as he often did, the need for the federal courts to have the "continuing consent of the governed" if they were to preserve the independence necessary for them to make unpopular decisions required by law (Arnold 1983: 5; Burbank 2005: 22). We know that diffuse support for the Supreme Court was consequential in the failure of President Roosevelt's court-packing plan (Cushman 2002; Friedman 2003).

Research suggests that diffuse support is linked to legitimizing messages about the courts, such as those that highlight the role of precedent and the rule of law ideal (Gibson, Caldeira, and Baird 1998; Scheb II and Lyons 2000; Baird and Gangl 2006).[1] It suggests that diffuse support is adversely affected by delegitimizing messages, such as those that indicate the justices consider political factors in their decision making (Christenson and Glick 2015)[2] and those that frame court decisions simply in terms of results (e.g., *Bush* v. *Gore*[3] decided the 2000 election) (Nicholson and Howard 2003). Federal courts have traditionally been able to draw on a stable, deep well of diffuse support when making unpopular decisions (Gibson and Nelson 2015: 163, 173).[4]

Political scientists often distinguish diffuse support from "specific support," that is, support based on particular products (decisions) (Easton 1965), reasoning that "[i]n principle, diffuse support differs from specific support in its sources, greater durability, and more fundamental basis" (Caldeira and Gibson 1992: 637). Those scholars most insistent on the distinction between diffuse and specific support acknowledge that there is a dynamic process at work, such that repeated decisions eroding specific support might adversely affect diffuse support (Gibson, Caldeira, and Spence 2003b: 356; Gibson and Nelson 2015: 164). Paul Gardner suggests that "ideological factors are important not only for evaluating individual Supreme Court decisions, but that they also affect support for the Supreme Court overall, at least in the short term" (2015: 16). Moreover, polls regarding confidence in leadership seem to measure a combination of specific and diffuse support, "something akin to 'presidential popularity,' rather than enduring institutional loyalty" (Gibson, Caldeira, and Spence 2003a: 555; Gibson, Caldeira, and Spence 2003b: 357).

There is also an extensive literature on the relationship between public opinion and Supreme Court behavior. The central question in the seemingly endless debate about the so-called "counter-majoritarian difficulty" is whether the Supreme Court is, in fact, unconstrained by democratic

[1] Scholars have also posited a framing effect whereby unpopular decisions are cushioned by general views about the Court and the rule of law (Gibson, Caldeira, and Spence 2003a: 553–6).

[2] Note, however, that political considerations are not necessarily incompatible with public perceptions of the Court as legitimate (Gibson and Caldeira 2011).

[3] 531 U.S. 98 (2000).

[4] A recent study suggests that the aggregate stability of diffuse support can mask "individual level changes" when those updating their ideological assessment of a highly salient case "largely canceled each other out" (Christenson and Glick 2015: 416). In sum, it appears that "individual-level support can be fluid and dynamic even if aggregate support is relatively stable" (Ginn, Searles, and Jones 2015: 177).

politics. For decades, numerous political scientists have disputed the proposition that the Supreme Court is unaccountable to the other institutions of government when deciding cases (Dahl 1957; Rosenberg 1992; McCloskey 1994). Their work, together with more recent work by scholars who take a strategic perspective, suggests that the Court does not often have the last word even on matters of constitutional interpretation (Epstein, Knight, and Martin 2004; Devins 2004), and that as a result it does not stray very far or for very long from what the majority wants. A recent study confirms that Congress seeks to override both statutory and constitutional decisions in certain circumstances, while also stressing that "Congress and the Court rarely disagree about whether the status quo should be altered" (Ulribe, Spriggs II, and Hansford 2014: 941).[5] Moreover, as Barry Friedman has observed, "there is general agreement among political scientists, and increasing recognition among legal academics, that more often than not the outcomes of Supreme Court decisions are consistent with public opinion" (2004: 114).

Why this is true remains unclear, and scholars have generated a variety of competing hypotheses concerning the causal mechanism (Unah, Rosano, and Milam 2015: 297–303 [reviewing literature]). Since writing the article quoted above, Friedman has authored a book claiming, on the basis of qualitative analysis of historical evidence, that the justices respond directly to public opinion for reasons of institutional legitimacy and effectiveness (Friedman 2009). As observed by Epstein and Martin (2010), however, studies deploying statistical analyses of quantitative data that were designed to test the effect of public opinion on the Court have yielded mixed results. Such results, of course, may be a function of the great measurement challenges implicated by the question. That said, "virtually all the studies demonstrate an *indirect* effect of public opinion via the appointments process," with the public's "role com[ing] in electing the President and the Senate, who appoint and confirm Justices reflecting the public's preferences" (270).[6]

---

[5] Barry Friedman and Anna Harvey's study of Supreme Court decisions overruling congressional statutes demonstrates "that the Court is significantly more likely to overturn congressional statutes when it faces an ideologically congenial Congress" (2003: 138). "In other words, the Court does defer to Congress, we believe, but it is more probably the sitting Congress rather than the enacting one. The sitting Congress has ample tools to discipline the Court, should Congress truly believe this is necessary" (139).

[6] Robert Dahl argued that the Court is "inevitably a part of the dominant national alliance" (Dahl 1957: 293), stressing the regularity of appointments and hence, in his view, a likely congruence of the policy preferences of a Court majority and the policy aims of the dominant political coalition (284–5). A decrease in turnover, as happened in the decade

But on the "more controversial matter . . . whether the public *directly* influences Court decisions (as Friedman claims)" (ibid.), previous studies reached different results. Departing from those studies by analyzing their data at the case level (rather than on a term-by-term basis), Epstein and Martin found "that an association exists between the public's mood and the Court's decisions" (280). However, they concluded that their study, like numerous previous studies also detecting an association between Supreme Court outcomes and public opinion, was unable to confirm Friedman's causal claim due to the extreme difficulty of including all important variables in an empirical model, and because "the same things that influence public opinion may influence the Justices, who are, after all, members of the public too" (281; *see also* Klarman 1996; Flemming and Wood 1997: 471).

We are doubtful that one should assimilate, in any simple reductive way, the justices to the general public for this purpose, particularly at a time when all of them have similar elite educational and professional backgrounds. Consider how a Supreme Court justice recently described the members of the Court:

> Judges are selected precisely for their skills as lawyers; whether they reflect the policy views of a particular constituency is not (or should not be) relevant. Not surprisingly, then, the Federal Judiciary is hardly a cross-section of America. Take, for example, this Court, which consists of only nine men and women, all of them successful lawyers who studied at Harvard or Yale Law School. Four of the nine are natives of New York City. Eight of them grew up in the east-and west-coast States . . . Not a single evangelical Christian (a group that comprises about one quarter of Americans), or even a Protestant of any denomination . . . a select, patrician, highly unrepresentative panel of nine . . .[7]

In his noted work on what audiences justices seek to satisfy, Baum (2006: 66) seemed to agree. He observed that, "[b]ecause of their pre-Court experiences, Supreme Court justices are likely to orient themselves toward elite groups rather than the general public," and that, when values held by elites differ from those of the mass public, "judges' links with their personal audiences will draw them toward the views of elites" (163).[8]

---

after Justice Breyer's appointment, "has important implications if Dahl's thesis is correct. A Supreme Court with a stable membership may be less responsive to changes in the political environment. This could result in a loss of public support over time, something that might endanger the Court's ability to perform its constitutional function" (Squire 1988: 187).

[7] *Obergefell* v. *Hodges*, 135 S. Ct. 2584, 2629 (2015) (Scalia, J., dissenting).

[8] Yet, Baum dissented from the proposition that public opinion directly affects the justices' behavior, causing them to act strategically in order to maintain the Court's institutional effectiveness, except perhaps in unusually controversial cases (2006: 63–6). As a result,

Moreover, qualitative evidence that the justices regard public standing and perceived legitimacy as important to the Court's institutional power, coupled with other recent empirical scholarship, lead us to regard this impulse as an important driver of the Court's caution about straying too far from public opinion (Friedman 2004; Clark 2011; Segal, Westerland, and Lindquist 2011).[9] This view undergirds our hypothesis that Court majorities concerned about institutional legitimacy and institutional maintenance benefit – and know that they benefit – from doing the work of retrenchment on apparently technical and legalistic terrain, where the public tends to regard decisions as more objective and neutral, if it learns of the decisions at all. As Epstein and Martin (2010: 281) suggest, to the extent that the Court is constrained by public opinion, this will be less true in legal issue areas that "fly under the public's radar screen" (see also Burbank and Friedman 2002: 3). Gardner (2015: 8–9) has summarized the situation as follows:

> Since the Court does not have electoral incentives, it is less interested in generating support for its decisions than it is in avoiding criticism or backlash. Therefore, it seeks to implement its preferred policy without generating negative attention that might decrease its legitimacy or support for its decision... The Court can achieve this either through decisions that match public preferences, or by deciding cases at odds with public opinion, but shielding themselves from public backlash by making effective journalistic coverage of those decisions significantly more difficult.

> When the Supreme Court issues opinions with ambiguous language on technical subjects, a journalist may desire to expose changes in the law that result from the opinion. Given the public demand for lower levels of sophistication in political reporting, however, journalists may not be able to simultaneously command large audience while providing sophisticated reporting. Therefore, the Supreme Court has tools to prevent the news media from reporting its decisions in such a way that the public will be well informed.

---

and notwithstanding the elite/mass opinion distinction, he deemed it "more likely that the justices' own preferences change than that the justices respond systematically to changes in mass public opinion" (70).

[9] Clark's work persuades us that this is a more likely explanation for the apparent responsiveness of the Court's decisions to the volume of court-curbing bills than is fear of congressional reprisal. As he argues, although the great majority of such bills are not credible threats to the Court, they function as signals of public displeasure. Recent work by Segal, Westerland and Lindquist reaches similar conclusions. They found that the Court's distance from Congress and the president, as well as the volume of court-curbing legislation, prompt the Court to strategically modify its behavior in the direction of the other branches. They argue that their evidence is most consistent with "institutional maintenance" concerns and suggest that the Court may regard the ideological positions of the elected branches as a proxy for public opinion (2011: 101).

Evidence

When we suggested, without data, that the lower visibility of private enforcement cases enlarged conservative justices' latitude to pursue the retrenchment project with little public notice, we encountered this objection: how do we know? After all, some private enforcement cases, such as *Wal-Mart Stores Inc.* v. *Dukes*[10] (which we discussed in Chapter 3) and *Ledbetter v. Goodyear Tire & Rubber Co.*,[11] have elicited controversy and attracted extensive public attention. Moreover, reporters covering the Court draw on sources who are highly sophisticated observers of American law, including liberal activists and representatives of public interest law organizations, many of whom are intensely aware of and aggrieved by the Court's private enforcement decisions.

There are reasons to be doubtful about the premises underlying this line of questioning. In discussing the difficulties of using newspaper coverage as a measure of case importance, the authors of a recent study observe that coverage, "being motivated by journalistic concerns, may bear little relation to the legal importance of a case." They give as an example the fact that the *New York Times* gave front page coverage to one 2009 case that has been cited in 2,160 decisions by 2015, but not to a 2009 pleading case (*Ashcroft* v. *Iqbal*, also discussed in Chapter 3) that, "[a]lthough less interesting to the average newspaper reader," has been cited "in nearly 69,000 decisions" (Epstein, Landes, and Posner 2015: 999). Gardner similarly argues that, "[f]or a media committed to large readerships and accurate reporting, conveying the nuance of these sorts of decisions may take a back seat to more sensational reporting about divided cases that may actually be less consequential" (2015: 18). The over-representation by the media of controversial or sensational cases has been well documented in empirical studies (MacCoun 2006; Haltom and McCann 2009).

Wal-Mart is an example of this dynamic. Wasserman observes that the case "involved a massive sex discrimination class action against a major nationwide corporation, making it the rare civil procedure case to draw significant scholarly and mainstream media coverage, which largely focused on its potential effect on substantive employment discrimination law" (2012: 323). More generally, he notes that, "[o]f course, having civil procedure on the doctrinal agenda will not draw the attention of the

---

[10] 564 U.S. 338 (2011).
[11] 550 U.S. 618 (2007).

popular media or the public; do not expect public calls to impeach Roberts over the scope of Rule 8(a)" (313–14).

Finding no data on the question, we undertook an empirical study to test our intuitions. Beyond that, we seek to provide concrete information about actual magnitudes of differences (if any exist), and how they vary (if they do) for distinct types of coverage, such as aggregate coverage, prominent coverage, or opinion and editorial coverage. We are also interested in longitudinal trends, and in particular whether growing ideological polarization among justices over private enforcement in recent years, which has attracted increasing attention by scholars, has garnered heightened media attention as well. These sorts of questions can only be answered with systematically collected data.

We evaluate media coverage of the Supreme Court's decisions on issues affecting the enforcement of rights, as contrasted with rights themselves. To do so we start with a set of Supreme Court cases addressing issues that have been commonly associated with private enforcement. As reported in Chapter 4, for the period 1960 to 2014, we identified all Supreme Court decisions requiring justices to vote on private enforcement issues concerning: (1) private rights of action; (2) standing; (3) the availability of attorney's fees; (4) whether an arbitration agreement forecloses access to court to enforce a federal right; (5) damages for a plaintiff who establishes the violation of a federal right; and (6) the interpretation of a Federal Rule of Civil Procedure, where the result would either widen or narrow opportunities or incentives for private enforcement. When we collected the data for this aspect of our project, we had available the cases from 1960 to 2013, of which there were 363.

From these cases, we drew 235 at random. Of these 235 cases, 149 contained a private enforcement issue but did not contain a merits issue. For each of these cases, we used the Spaeth Supreme Court database to identify a case decided at about the same time that addressed a merits issue comparable in nature to the claim underlying our private enforcement case. An example serves to illustrate. In our private enforcement data a fee issue arose in a Clean Air Act case, but the Court addressed only the fee issue and no Clean Air Act merits issue. For that reason, we searched the Spaeth database for a Clean Air Act case decided at about the same time that presented only a merits issue, or, failing that, a merits issue under another environmental statute. In the appendix we describe in detail the protocol for identifying merits companion cases for private enforcement cases that lacked merits issues. This procedure led to 149 pairs of cases, or 298 cases for analysis in total. We call these Type 1 cases.

An additional 68 cases from our random sample of 235 had both a private enforcement issue and a merits issue from the underlying claims in the litigation. We call these Type 2 cases. In the remaining 18 cases, it was not possible for us to segregate a private enforcement issue from the underlying merits issue, and thus these cases did not present an opportunity to assess differences in media coverage across the two kinds of issues.[12]

To evaluate media coverage of our issues, we constructed an issue-level dataset. For our 298 Type 1 cases, each case produced one issue with respect to which we evaluate media coverage. In accordance with the above procedure, half the cases presented private enforcement issues but not merits issues, and half presented merits issues but not private enforcement issues. The 68 Type 2 cases each presented a merits issue and a private enforcement issue, for a total of 136 issues. The total dataset, therefore, contains 434 issues, half private enforcement and half merits, which arose in 366 cases.

We conducted searches to identify articles that appeared in the *New York Times*, *Washington Post*, and *Wall Street Journal* covering cases in the data. With respect to each case, coders read all articles covering it and collected the following information on coverage of the issue in question: (1) the total number of articles discussing the issue at all; (2) the number of articles discussing the issue that were reporting *only* on the case in question, as contrasted with roundup articles that cover numerous cases; (3) the number of articles discussing the issue that were reporting only on the case in question and appeared on the front page; and (4) the number of editorial and opinion pieces covering the issue. In total, there were 1,626 episodes of an article discussing one of the issues (private enforcement or merits) that brought it into our data.

The distinctions across the four counts are important. Articles giving cursory coverage to many cases are typical in reporting on the Supreme Court. Although 80% of the cases in our data were covered, only 55% of them were covered in an article discussing only that case, and only 20% were covered in single-case articles that appeared on the front page. Thus, the count of single-case articles registers more prominent coverage than the count of total articles, and the count of front page single-case articles registers yet more prominent coverage. Nineteen percent of the cases were mentioned in at least one opinion or editorial piece. Such articles indicate whether the press is presenting issues to the public as matters of

---

[12] These were primarily cases where the Court addressed the scope of a private right of action.

particular public interest that warrant reflection and debate. Of course, a single case can receive more than one form of coverage.

We are not attempting to explain *why* the media covers private enforcement issues differently than merits issues, if in fact it does. If that were our goal, we would incorporate into statistical models independent variables intended to test explanatory theories, or to control for other factors. But that is not our goal. Rather, we wish to know the answer to the raw descriptive question: how much media coverage is garnered by the Court's decisions on private enforcement of rights, as compared to its decisions on rights themselves. Although the question *why* variation exists may be interesting, the bivariate relationship best describes the quantum of information being transmitted to the public by the media with respect to the two types of issues. Specification of models with variables to test explanatory theories would obscure what we want to know.

Table 5.1 displays the mean counts for the total number of articles, the number of single-case articles, the number of front-page, single-case articles, and the number of opinion or editorial pieces, separately for private enforcement and merits issues. The bivariate differences are large, and they increase from total articles, to single-case articles, to opinion and editorial pieces. Moving from private enforcement issues to merits issues is associated with a growth of 157%, 307%, and 400%, respectively. The difference is even greater for front-page, single-case articles (464%).

To test the statistical significance of these effects, we run negative binomial models on each count, with an indicator variable reflecting whether the issue is a private enforcement or merits issue (private enforcement = 0, merits = 1). We also include an indicator variable capturing whether the issue is from the Type 1 or Type 2 pool (Type 1 = 0, Type 2 = 1), and a linear time trend. The results are presented in Table 5.2. The effects are statistically significant, and the magnitudes are similar to those reflected

Table 5.1. *Mean values of newspaper coverage of Supreme Court decisions: private enforcement versus merits issues*

	Private enforcement	Merits	Percentage growth
Total articles	2.1	5.4	157
Single-case articles	.76	3.1	307
Opinion and editorials	.16	.80	400
Front-page, single-case articles	.11	.62	464

in Table 5.1. The marginal effect displayed in the table reflects the change in a predicted count moving from private enforcement issues to merits issues. The growth in the count is 166% for total articles, 278% for single-case articles, 371% for opinion and editorial pieces, and 464% for front-page, single-case articles.

To assess whether the difference is present across newspapers, we replicated the three models in Table 5.2 but used as the dependent variable each newspaper separately. The private enforcement coefficient is statistically significant in each of the 12 regressions. Table 5.3 summarizes the main results, displaying the marginal effect associated with moving from private enforcement to merits issues for each coefficient. Although statistical significance is always present, the marginal effects are notably smaller in the *Wall Street Journal* regressions. Examining the data reveals that the smaller effect for the *Wall Street Journal* is driven not by greater

Table 5.2. *Negative binomial model of newspaper coverage of Supreme Court decisions*

Total articles

	Coefficient	SE	Marginal effect
Merits v. private enforcement	.98***	.11	166%
Year	−.01*	.005	
Type	−.07	.14	

Single-case articles

	Coefficient	SE	Marginal effect
Merits v. private enforcement	1.33***	.14	278%
Year	−.001	.01	
Type	.35**	.18	

Opinion and editorial pieces

	Coefficient	SE	Marginal effect
Merits v. private enforcement	1.55***	.26	371%
Year	−.001	.01	
Type	.33	.27	

Front-page, single-case articles

	Coefficient	SE	Marginal effect
Merits v. private enforcement	1.73***	.26	464%
Year	−.01	.01	
Type	.97***	.24	
N = 434			

***$p < .01$; **$p < .05$; *$p < .1$
Standard errors in parentheses clustered on case

coverage of private enforcement issues, but by materially less coverage of merits issues. For example, in the single-case category, the *Wall Street Journal* had a mean value of .22 for private enforcement issues, as compared to .21 for the *Washington Post*, and .33 for the *New York Times*. For merits issues, however, the mean values are .43 for the *Wall Street Journal*, 1.1 for the *Washington Post*, and 1.6 for the *New York Times*.

We are also interested in assessing variation in media coverage of private enforcement issues over time. In Chapter 4, we find a steep long-run trend toward more anti-private enforcement outcomes in Supreme Court decisions on the private enforcement issues in our database. We also find growing ideological voting by justices on private enforcement issues, with a sharp increase in polarization between the liberal and conservative wings of the Court since the mid-to-late 1990s, such that the justices are now more divided over private enforcement issues than they are over federal rights in general or over merits issues in the policy areas covered

Table 5.3. *Marginal effects of negative binomial count models of newspaper coverage of Supreme Court decisions*

Total articles	
New York Times	189%***
Washington Post	186%***
Wall Street Journal	92%***
Single-case articles	
New York Times	344%***
Washington Post	385%***
Wall Street Journal	97%***
Opinion and editorial pieces	
New York Times	381%***
Washington Post	511%***
Wall Street Journal	239%***
Front-page, single-case articles	
New York Times	366%***
Washington Post	603%***
Wall Street Journal	None of this type of coverage of private enforcement issues
N = 434	

***$p < .01$; **$p < .05$; *$p < .1$
Robust standard errors clustered on case

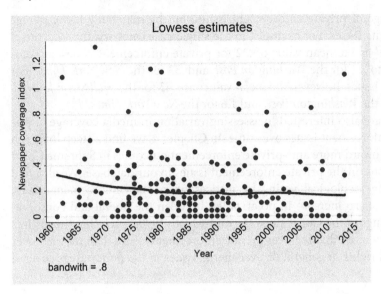

Figure 5.1   Media coverage index of private enforcement issues, 1960–2013

by our private enforcement data. Also since around 2000, there has been growing scholarly attention to the Court's anti-private enforcement posture (Law 2002; Karlan 2003; Siegel 2006; Chemerinsky 2012; Staszak 2015). We are interested in whether increasing division among the justices on these issues and mounting scholarly attention and criticism have been associated with greater press coverage of private enforcement issues.

In order to gauge that, we focus on coverage of the private enforcement issues over time. We created a composite media coverage index for each case as the mean value of the standardized counts for total articles, single-case articles, opinion and editorial pieces, and front page, single-case articles. Figure 5.1 displays that composite measure and a regression curve fit through it. The estimated values declined significantly from .33 in 1961 to .19 in the early 1980s. Since then, they continued to decline very gradually to .16 at the end of the series. There is no indication that escalating polarization on the Court over private enforcement issues since the late 1990s, or the growing attention paid to the Court's private enforcement decisions by scholars over the same period, has had any influence on the quantum of information conveyed to the public by the press.

Private Enforcement and Public Opinion

It may be cause for concern that, although the private enforcement-retrenchment campaign largely failed in democratic politics, the Court is eroding the operational meanings of rights with little notice by the public.[13] Some of the research on public opinion discussed in this chapter suggests, however, that such concerns may be misplaced. If empirical scholarship showing that the Court's decisions track public opinion is correct – regardless of the causal mechanism that produces this effect – then even if one dislikes the direction in which the Court is taking the law of private enforcement, it is likely not far from what the public wants. Our view is that the Court likely is constrained by legitimacy concerns on issues of public salience but that Court majorities have, and know that they have, greater latitude to pursue ideological agendas at odds with public preferences in more subterranean fields of law.

The suggestion that normative concerns may be misplaced and our response to that suggestion point to one further empirical question. Are the Court's private enforcement decisions just moving in tandem with public preferences? In order to test whether the Court's private enforcement decisions are merely a reflection of public opinion, we first replicate, with slight modification, a recent model of the relationship between public opinion and Supreme Court case outcomes created by Epstein and Martin (2010), and we then apply the model to our private enforcement decisions.

Epstein and Martin's case-level analysis of the empirical relationship between public opinion and Supreme Court decisions uses the Spaeth dataset of all Supreme Court opinions. Their dependent variable is the ideological direction of case outcome (conservative = 0, liberal = 1). Their key independent variable is James Stimson's influential public "mood" variable (Stimson 1991), which aggregates extensive survey data to map underlying public attitudes on a liberal-conservative continuum, with higher values associated with increasing degrees of liberalism. It is the most widely used aggregate measure of public opinion, on a liberal-conservative continuum, in empirical studies of the relationship between public opinion and Supreme Court case outcomes. It is measured quarterly. We lag it one quarter to avoid the problem that a contemporaneous quarterly mood variable would frequently be based on public opinion measured after a decision was issued. This measure extends through the first quarter of 2012.

---

[13] "Since unpopular decisions are generally short-lived, by avoiding public notice entirely, the Court is able to make small yet significant changes in the law, which may be hard to undo by the time the public takes notice" (Gardner 2015: 18).

The Epstein and Martin model incorporates a set of controls for factors well-known to be associated with the direction of case outcomes, as well as the ideological position of Congress and the President (2010: 271–5):

- **Supreme Court Ideology**. They measure the ideological position of the Court with the median Martin-Quinn scores of justices sitting in each case. Increasing Martin-Quinn values are associated with increasing conservatism.[14]
- **Lower Court Outcome**. They measure the ideological direction of the lower court outcome in the decision being reviewed. This controls for a well-known tendency of the Court to reverse.
- **Position of US Party**. Their model incorporates two variables measuring the ideological position of the United States (including federal agencies) when it is a party in the litigation. One dummy variable indicates when a US party is advocating a conservative position, and another indicates when it is advocating a liberal position. This controls for the greater success, on average, of the US as compared to other parties.
- **Policy Area**. Their model includes controls for the policy area of each case, using Spaeth policy codes. This addresses the possibility that the direction of case outcomes may be correlated with policy area, and thus outcome trends over time may be, in part, a function of changes in the policy content of the Court's docket.[15]
- **Congress and the President**. They also incorporate measures of the ideological preferences of Congress and the president, controlling for potential effects of each on the Court. As we discuss earlier in this chapter, an important line of research in political science argues that Supreme Court decision-making tracks the preferences of national political coalitions in power, whether because federal judges are drawn from it (leading to shared preferences) or because it is responsive to pressures from elected branches (Dahl 1957; Rosenberg 1992; McCloskey 1994). They rely on common space NOMINATE scores, which are continuous measures of ideology based on roll call voting behavior, and presidential positions publicly taken on issues subjected to roll calls (see Poole

[14] Martin-Quinn scores are measures of justice ideology based on the voting behavior and alignments of justices in non-unanimous decisions, and they vary for each justice each year (Martin and Quinn 2002). We use them as one of our measures of justice ideology in Chapter 4.

[15] We measure policy area with 14 policy area dummy variables based on Spaeth's "issueArea" variable.

and Rosenthal 1997).[16] In the models below, the ideological position of Congress is measured by the average of the median NOMINATE scores of the House and Senate.

We first apply this model to the Spaeth dataset for the period 1961 (the first year in our private enforcement data) through the first quarter of 2012, which is the last quarter for which the lagged Stimson public mood variable was available at the time we conducted the study. Because liberalism is coded in the positive direction for both the public mood variable and the Spaeth case outcome variable, if the two are moving in tandem, the predicted effect is a significant coefficient and a positive sign on the public mood variable. The results, presented in Model A in Table 5.4, are consistent with Epstein and Martin's results (2010: 277). The public mood variable is significant, with a marginal effect of .004. The substantive effect is modest in size. A one standard deviation (4.7) increase in public mood (moving in the liberal direction) is associated with a two percentage point increase in the probability of a liberal vote, and an increase in public mood over its full range (23) with a nine percentage point increase.[17]

The Martin-Quinn median is significant with a negative sign, indicating that a more conservative median justice is associated with a lower probability of a liberal outcome. The marginal effect is –.12, meaning that a one unit increase in the Martin-Quinn scale (which is movement in the conservative direction) is associated with a 12 percentage point reduction in the probability of a pro-private enforcement outcome. To put this magnitude in perspective, the difference between the average liberal and conservative justice (as defined in Table 4.4 and the accompanying text) from 1960 to 2014 on the Martin-Quinn scale is 3.5.[18] An increase of this magnitude is associated with a reduction of 42 percentage points in the probability of a liberal outcome. The Supreme Court is significantly more likely to reverse than affirm. Advocacy by the United States as a party, for either a conservative or liberal outcome, is statistically significantly associated with those outcomes. The ideological position of Congress also

[16] In alternative specifications, we also examined a linear time trend, which proved consistently insignificant. Epstein and Martin do not include a time trend.

[17] In an alternative specification (not displayed) we substitute Segal-Cover medians for Martin-Quinn medians as our measure of Court ideology, and the public mood variable remains significant with a comparably sized effect. Segal-Cover scores are measures of justice ideology based on pre-confirmation newspaper editorials on the nominations, and thus are independent of justices' voting behavior (Segal and Cover 1989).

[18] We illustrate the marginal effect with this quantity to be consistent with, and allow comparison to, Chapter 4's analysis of justice votes.

Table 5.4. *Logit model of Supreme Court case outcomes/justice votes, 1961–2012*

	Model A All Spaeth cases	Model B Private enforcement cases	Model C Private enforcement votes
Public mood (lag)	.02**	−.01	.02
	(.01)	(.03)	(.02)
Martin-Quinn median/score	−.51***	−.85**	−.37***
	(.08)	(.34)	(.03)
Lower court outcome	−1.15***	−.81**	−.63***
	(.07)	(.32)	(.21)
US liberal/pro-enforcement	.51***	−.16	.50
	(.08)	(.65)	(.47)
US conservative/anti-enforcement	−.44***	−.28	−.17
	(.08)	(.28)	(.25)
Congressional ideology	−.36	−2.81**	−2.19**
	(.38)	(1.25)	(.98)
Presidential ideology	−.03	−.38	−.15
	(.09)	(.29)	(.23)
Policy area fixed effects	✓	✓	✓
N =	6732	333	2875
Pseudo R² =	.11	.18	.18

***$p < .01$; **$p < .05$; *$p < .1$

Standard errors in parentheses clustered on Supreme Court term in Models A and B; and on case in Model C

barely achieves significance at the .1 level ($p = .096$), with a marginal effect of .11. A move in the conservative direction by one standard deviation of the variable (.09) is associated with only a one percentage point reduction in the probability of a liberal case outcome, and an increase over its full range (.36) is associated with a four percentage point reduction. If congressional ideology is associated with case outcomes, the association is very small.

We next apply the same model to the Court's private enforcement decisions referred to above and analyzed in Chapter 4, addressing (1) private rights of action, (2) standing, (3) attorney's fees, (4) arbitration, (5) damages, and (6) Federal Rules of Civil Procedure. Cases were included in our dataset only where resolution of the issue would predictably affect private enforcement. We coded each of the issue outcomes as pro-enforcement (=1) if it favored the plaintiff-enforcer, and as anti-enforcement (=0) if it favored the defendant. We also separately coded each justice's vote on each private enforcement issue.

A question arises about how to characterize the direction of outcomes on the conservative-liberal dimension. The anti- versus pro-enforcement coding does not necessarily correspond to conservative versus liberal, since a pro-enforcement decision may occur in a case with an ideologically conservative underlying claim. Such cases, it turns out, are relatively rare in our data. As discussed in Chapter 4, we applied the Spaeth protocol for coding conservative versus liberal outcomes to the underlying causes of action in our cases. Under this protocol, only 7% of our private enforcement issues involved conservative underlying claims. Another 8% could not be assigned an ideological direction. The remaining 85% of our private enforcement issues had liberal underlying claims. Thus, if our data are representative of private enforcement issues in general, the vast majority of private enforcement issues decided by the Supreme Court over the past half-century have been in cases asserting liberal claims. We restrict our empirical analysis to those issues in order to enable a consistent mapping between the conservative-liberal dimension of public opinion and the actual underlying ideological meaning of the anti-pro-axis of our private enforcement issues.[19] Our data contain 333 such issues, occurring in 300 cases, from 1961 to 2012.[20]

Model B replicates Model A, but with the dependent variable switched to measure anti- versus pro-enforcement outcomes in our private enforcement cases (anti = 0, pro = 1).[21] The significant correlation between public opinion and case outcomes, net of the effects of other variables, disappears. The public mood variable becomes highly insignificant ($p = .76$) with a *negative* sign. The Court's private enforcement decisions do not track public opinion.

The Martin-Quinn median is significant with a negative sign, indicating that a more conservative median justice is associated with a lower probability of a pro-private enforcement outcome. The marginal effect

---

[19] Failure to restrict the analysis in this way, we believe, would be biased toward failing to detect a correlation between public opinion and private enforcement outcomes.

[20] All of our 2012 cases were decided in the first quarter, so the Stimson public mood measure covers all of our 2012 data.

[21] The policy fixed effects in this model are each policy classification listed in Table 4.2 in Chapter 4. We also include with our policy fixed effects dummy variables that capture our private enforcement issues: private rights of action, standing, attorney's fees, arbitration, damages, and the Federal Rules.

is .16. A shift in the conservative direction by 3.5 on the Martin-Quinn scale is associated with a reduction of 56 percentage points in the probability of a pro-private enforcement outcome – a materially larger median ideology effect on case outcomes than we observed when the Court's full docket is pooled. The Supreme Court is, again, significantly more likely to reverse than affirm. Advocacy by the United States as a party is insignificant whether it is on the liberal or conservative side. The ideological position of Congress is significant, with a marginal effect of –.54. A shift in the conservative direction by one standard deviation of the variable (.09) is associated with a four percentage point reduction in the probability of a pro-private enforcement outcome. Congressional ideology has a substantively small association with outcomes.

In an alternative specification (not displayed), we substitute Segal-Cover medians for Martin-Quinn medians as the measure of Court ideology and run the otherwise identical model. The public mood variable is statistically significant ($p = .03$), *but the sign is negative*, with a marginal effect of –.013. In this model, a one standard deviation (4.7) increase in public mood (moving in the liberal direction) is associated with a six percentage point *reduction* in the probability of a pro-private enforcement vote, and an increase in public mood over its full range (23) is associated with a 30 percentage point reduction. This, of course, is the opposite of what one would expect to see if the Court's private enforcement decisions moved in tandem with public opinion. The model otherwise looks similar to Model B in Table 5.4, with median Segal-Cover score, lower court outcome, and congressional ideology statistically significant at the same level and in the same direction, and the other variables insignificant. The result reinforces the conclusion that no positive relationship exists between conservatism in public opinion and conservative Supreme Court case outcomes on private enforcement issues.

We also tested for an association between public opinion and justice votes in private enforcement cases. In Model C we replicate Model B but substitute justice votes for case outcomes as the dependent variable, and we substitute individual justice ideology scores for the median justice scores used in the case outcome models. This provides 2,875 justice votes for analysis. In this model we cluster standard errors on case.[22] Although

---

[22] We obtain very similar results with standard errors clustered on justice. We do not examine this alternative specification for the models in Table 5.5 because, when the data are subset by time period, there are an insufficient number of justices to allow clustering on justice.

Model B reveals that public mood is not positively associated with actual case outcomes on private enforcement issues, it may still be correlated with individual-level justice voting. However, in this model the public mood variable is again clearly insignificant ($p = .46$).[23] The ideological position of Congress is again significant, with a marginal effect of $-.42$, and a shift in the conservative direction by one standard deviation is again associated with a four percentage point reduction in the probability of a pro-private enforcement outcome

The data simply provide no hint that conservatism in either outcomes or justice votes in private enforcement cases is positively correlated with conservatism in public opinion. Whatever explains the significant correlation between public opinion and justice votes in highly aggregated models such as Model A, the relationship disappears or becomes negative when we focus on private enforcement decisions. This is consistent with our view that the lower-visibility character of private enforcement issues increases justices' perceived policymaking discretion. In lower visibility issue-environments, the pursuit of unpopular ideological agendas carries less risk to the Court's legitimacy and standing in the public eye. To be sure, although the models in Table 5.4 are consistent with that view, they do not demonstrate it to be true.

We note one further result and probe its meaning. In both of the private enforcement models (B and C), the measure of congressional ideology is significant, with more conservative Congresses associated with more anti-enforcement votes and outcomes. In the context of the normative question raised in this chapter, it may be significant that, although the Court's private enforcement decisions have received little public notice and are not associated with public opinion, the results on the congressional ideology variable suggest that the decisions do track the preferences of the elected representatives in Congress. It should be stressed that, although statistically significant, movement in the position of Congress explains very little variation in ultimate case outcomes, with a one standard deviation increase in congressional ideology associated with only a four percentage point reduction in the probability of a pro-enforcement outcome.

The meaning of this association, moreover, is not entirely clear. We argue in Chapter 4 that beginning around 1995 the conservative wing of the Court pushed the law of private enforcement more assertively to the right and that this may have been, in part, because nearly continuous Republican control of at least one chamber of Congress provided the Court's conservative wing

---

[23] It remains so in an alternative specification (not displayed) in which we substitute Segal-Cover scores for Martin-Quinn scores.

shelter from legislative override. To pursue this point, we first rerun Models B and C, but restricted to the 1961–94 period. This allows us to gauge whether the association between congressional ideology and the Court's private enforcement decisions existed prior to 1995, where a large majority of the data lies (71% of the data in Models B and C). There is no such relationship in the 1961–94 period; the congressional ideology variable is highly statistically insignificant (models not reported).[24] The associations detected in Models B and C appear to be driven by data in the post-1994 period.

To examine the relationship in the post-1994 period, we focus on the justice vote data, which allow us to separately model the votes of conservative and liberal justices. In the 1995–2012 period (where 29% of our data lies), Table 5.5 presents models run on all votes (Model A), the votes of only conservative justices (Model B), and the votes of only liberal justices (Model C). In models B and C, the US Pro-Enforcement variable, and several policy area dummies, were dropped due to predicting failure perfectly. We follow the definition of liberal and conservative justices set forth in Chapter 4, using the Martin-Quinn median as the dividing point (see Table 4.4 and the accompanying text). In the model of all post-1994 votes (Model A), congressional ideology is statistically significant. Relative to the model of all votes for the full 1961–2012 period (Model C in Table 5.4), the coefficient here is more than twice as large, confirming that the significance of the congressional ideology variable in the full 1961–2012 period is driven by the data after 1994.

In the model of all post-1994 votes of conservative justices (Model B), congressional ideology remains statistically significant, with a marginal effect of .78. A movement in the conservative direction by one standard deviation is associated with a seven percentage point reduction of the probability of a pro-private enforcement vote. In the model of the post-1994 votes of the liberal justices (Model C), the congressional ideology variable becomes statistically insignificant.[25] Thus, in the three and a half decades prior to Republicans taking control of Congress in 1995, there is no evidence that the Court's private enforcement decisions were correlated with congressional preferences. Starting in 1995, only the conservative justices' votes are significantly correlated with congressional ideology. Public mood is not positive and significant in any of these model specifications.

---

[24] For the congressional ideology variable, $p = .73$ in the issue-level model with 245 observations; and $p = .84$ in the vote-level model with 2,097 observations.

[25] In alterative specifications of all three models in Table 5.5 in which we substitute Segal-Cover scores for Martin-Quinn scores, these results are not materially affected.

Table 5.5. *Logit model of Supreme Court case outcomes/justice votes, 1995–2012*

	Model A All votes	Model B Conservative votes	Model C Liberal votes
Public mood (lag)	−.10	.01	.004
	(.08)	(.10)	(.09)
Martin-Quinn median	−.56***	−.22	−.34**
	(.07)	(.14)	(.13)
Lower court outcome	−1.30**	−2.23***	−1.47*
	(.50)	(.56)	(.76)
US liberal/pro-enforcement	−.20	—	—
	(.86)		
US conservative/anti-enforcement	.09	.25	.21
	(.57)	(.66)	(.86)
Congressional ideology	−6.36***	−5.60**	−4.38
	(2.19)	(2.56)	(2.88)
Presidential ideology	.71	.63	−.09
	(.58)	(.63)	(.73)
Policy area fixed effects	✓	✓	✓
N=	778	433	345
Pseudo R^2=	.32	.32	.18

***$p < .01$; **$p < .05$; *$p < .1$
Standard errors in parentheses clustered on case

Conclusion

Deploying content analysis of a large body of news articles, we demonstrate that, in fact, Supreme Court rulings on private enforcement of rights receive dramatically less press coverage than decisions concerning the rights themselves. We show that this is true with respect to the volume of total coverage, more prominent coverage, and whether issues receive editorial or opinion treatment, with increasingly large effects. The media's role in informing the public about the work of the Supreme Court declines precipitously when one moves from rulings on rights to rulings on their enforcement. This low level of coverage has been unaffected by the conservative majority's increasingly strong push against private enforcement, escalating polarization on the Court over it, and growing criticism of these developments by scholars and commentators.

Aware that, from a normative perspective, these results might not cause concern if the Court's private enforcement decisions merely tracked public opinion, we set out to test that proposition. To do this we constructed models to explore the relationship between our private enforcement data and the most widely used measure of liberalism in public opinion. In these models we find that public liberalism is highly statistically insignificant, or significant and negatively associated with case outcomes. Whatever positive association may exist between public opinion and the Court's decisions when all or large swaths of its cases are pooled, it appears to be absent in our low-visibility private enforcement cases.[26]

Finally, intrigued by results suggesting that the Court's private enforcement decisions track the preferences of Congress, we conducted further analyses. The results are consistent with, although they do not demonstrate, our hypothesis that after 1994 conservative justices were attentive to the (generally conservative) position of Congress, and the opportunities that it created for moving the law in an anti-private enforcement direction. We think it likely that many congressional Republicans during this period looked with favor on the Court's increasingly assertive retrenchment through low visibility judicial interpretation, achieving goals that they could not hope to accomplish through legislation.

---

[26] In this light, a strategy of subterranean retrenchment may have special value when, as now, the Court is badly fractured, if, as a recent study finds, "the Supreme Court responds more strongly to public opinion when the Court is more polarized than when it is not" (Unah, Rosano, and Milam 2015: 328).

APPENDIX

For each case addressing a private enforcement issue but not a merits issue, we drew a companion case from the Spaeth Supreme Court database that presented only a merits issue. We followed the procedure below to identify these companion cases.

(1) We first looked for a case under the same statute or constitutional provision in the same year. If more than one existed, we drew one randomly.

(2) If one was not present, we looked for a case under the same statute or constitutional provision in the year before and/or the year after, in random order. If more than one existed, we drew one randomly.

(3) If one was not present, we looked for one in the same *specific policy area* in the same year. The most common example of this is where a federal statutory claim was in a policy area, like environmental, there was not a specific statute match, but there was a case under another federal statute in the same policy area. For example, if our case was under the Clean Water Act, but our match case was under the Clean Air Act, we would regard that as a specific policy match.

(4) If one was not present, we looked for a case in the same *specific policy area* in the year before and/or the year after, in random order. If more than one existed, we drew one randomly.

(5) If one was not present, we looked for a case under the same statute or constitutional provision two years before and/or two years after, in random order. If more than one existed, we drew one randomly.

(6) If one was not present, we looked for one in the same *specific policy area* two years before and/or two years after, in random order. If more than one existed, we drew one randomly.

(7) In the event that these steps did not yield a match, we drew a case randomly in the same year with the same *general policy area*, defined by the Spaeth "issue" code.

After a Spaeth case was used, it was removed from the pool of data from which we drew subsequent companion cases. Using this procedure, 63% of the cases were matched on the statute or constitutional provision, 26% were matched on the specific policy area, and 11% were matched on the general policy area.

6

Rights, Retrenchment, and Democratic Governance

Why the Court Succeeded

The Supreme Court, which became increasingly conservative as a result of appointments by Republican presidents over the period we study, had greater success in advancing the goals of the counterrevolution against private enforcement than did Republican presidents, Congress, or the rulemakers. For reasons that we explore in the next section of this chapter, gauging the actual effects of the Court's decisions on private enforcement is complex and difficult. It is clear, however, that the Court was more successful than the other federal lawmakers we study in shaping law against private enforcement. The Court's posture toward private enforcement underwent a transformation from highly supportive in the early 1970s to antagonistic today. Why did the Court succeed when those sympathetic to the counterrevolution's goals in the other lawmaking sites largely failed?

In Chapter 2 we discuss a number of institutional characteristics that made retrenchment of private enforcement difficult for proponents of the counterrevolution in the elected branches. The distinctive political and electoral challenges of retrenching existing rights with broad public resonance by statutory amendment – a goal that is obvious when the proposed amendments target statutory private enforcement regimes or procedural rules known to have dramatic impact on substantive rights – coupled with the inherent stickiness of the status quo arising from America's fragmented legislative institutions, proved to be more than the movement could surmount in Congress. So long as Democrats controlled at least one chamber of Congress, Republicans' retrenchment proposals, whether initiated by the executive or the legislative branch, had little chance of success. Indeed, even when Republicans secured control of both chambers, and for a time concurrently held the presidency, their occasional successes were modest, usually required years to enact, and clustered in a few discrete policy areas. Beginning in the late 1990s, Republican proposals for legislative retrenchment began a long decline to the point that they are negligible in number today. The issue has essentially disappeared from the legislative agenda.

In Chapter 3 we uncover similar dynamics affecting court rulemaking, delegated legislative activity that was a powerful engine driving private enforcement through the 1960s, most notably in the 1966 amendments to Rule 23 (class actions). We show that rulemaking became the focus of retrenchment efforts starting in 1971, under the leadership of the first of a succession of Chief Justices appointed by Republican presidents. However, once its potential for that purpose became apparent, rights-oriented interest groups and Democratic members of Congress who favored private enforcement quickly responded. Their efforts ultimately led to reforms in the rulemaking process that made the process itself more transparent, more accessible to public participation, and stickier. These reforms to the rulemaking process, in turn, made major retrenchment under its auspices more difficult, even by committees increasingly dominated by judges appointed by Republican presidents and corporate attorneys. On one view, the history of the 2015 amendments to the discovery rules suggests that those barriers can be overcome when leaders within the judiciary who are predisposed to the goals of the counterrevolution believe that concerns about the perceived legitimacy of the Enabling Act process can safely be subordinated to the desire to exercise power. On another view, that history confirms the difficulty of effecting ambitious retrenchment through rulemaking and highlights the importance of the struggle for influence on judicial interpretation.

In Chapter 4, we show that, although the counterrevolution largely failed in the elected branches and was only modestly successful in the domain of court rulemaking, it flourished in the federal courts. Having learned that retrenching rights enforcement by statute was politically and electorally perilous – and unlikely to succeed – the proponents of the counterrevolution pressed federal courts to interpret, or reinterpret, existing federal statutes and court rules to achieve the same purpose. They found a sympathetic audience in courts that were increasingly staffed by judges appointed by Republican presidents. Some of these judges were ideologically sympathetic to the retrenchment project; some were connected to the conservative legal movement that had given birth to the counterrevolution, and some had even participated in or promoted the Reagan administration's failed efforts to retrench private enforcement of federal rights through legislation.

Incrementally at first but more boldly in recent years, conservative majorities of the Supreme Court have transformed federal law over the past four decades, making it less and less friendly, if not hostile, to the enforcement of rights through private lawsuits. This branch of the campaign for retrenchment achieved victories in a long succession of decisions interpreting statutory private enforcement regimes, reshaping standing and private rights of action doctrine, and interpreting the Federal Rules of Civil Procedure. Even if such apparently technical and legalistic rulings do not attract the notice of the American public, their importance is plain to the members of the Supreme Court. Or at least that is how we interpret our findings that both non-procedural private enforcement cases and, even more so, cases calling for interpretation of the Federal Rules of Civil Procedure, have emerged in recent years as axes of ideological conflict among the justices even more factious than conflicts over substantive rights.

This fact is especially striking when viewed alongside the legislative story. At the same time that retrenchment of private enforcement has essentially disappeared from the legislative agenda, ideological polarization on the issue is at its highest point ever on the Supreme Court. Moreover, as suggested by the data on amicus filings that we present in Chapter 4, the issue remains a high priority of the Chamber of Commerce and conservative law reform organizations. On the surface this may appear anomalous. But from the institutional perspective we advance in this book, it is readily explicable. By the late 1990s, it must have become evident to congressional Republicans that major retrenchment of private enforcement would not come from Congress. The institutional hurdles were simply too high. At the same time, it must have become clear to the conservative justices that significant retrenchment would come from the Supreme Court or not at all. As the conservative wing of the Court has granted review and prevailed in cases that are more and more polarizing, congressional Republicans have focused their legislative efforts elsewhere, knowing that, as we observed about class action retrenchment in Chapter 4, the counterrevolution is in the hands of those best equipped institutionally to achieve its goals.

In Chapter 5, drawing on institutional theory, we argue that the ostensibly technical and legalistic qualities of the Court's decisions on issues affecting private enforcement, and the gradual, evolutionary nature of case-by-case decision-making, opened a pathway of judicial retrenchment that was remote from public view as compared to legislative politics, court rulemaking after the reforms of the 1980s, and Supreme Court decisions on highly salient issues. We show that the Court's decisions on private enforcement issues are, indeed, covered much less than decisions on the pertinent merits issues by major newspapers, that the differences increase as coverage moves from round-up articles to single-case articles, to opinion and editorial pieces, and to front-page single-case articles. We also find no evidence that either heightened polarization on the Court over private enforcement issues or growing criticism of the Court's private enforcement decisions by scholars has influenced the amount of information that the press conveys to the public. Finally, we find no evidence that those decisions tracked public opinion.

The preceding chapters thus highlight a host of distinguishing institutional characteristics that theory and our evidence suggest are pertinent when comparing the results of the counterrevolution's project to change law governing or influencing private enforcement across lawmaking sites. We believe that four have the greatest explanatory value in assessing the reasons for the Supreme Court's success in implementing that project.

First, as contrasted with the institutional fragmentation of the legislative and rulemaking processes, the Court is governed by a more streamlined decisional process and simple voting rules, making it comparatively more capable of unilateral action on controversial issues (Whittington 2007: 124–34). Four justices suffice to put an issue on the Court's agenda, and bare majorities routinely win in decided cases, although they rarely do to enact legislation (or to send forward Federal Rules). Indeed, in Chapter 4 we suggest that the growing polarization between conservative and liberal justices over private enforcement issues, which is particularly striking in the Court's Federal Rules decisions, may reflect a narrow but determined conservative majority pressing its advantage in pursuit of the counterrevolution's goals, and the liberal justices' response. Justice Kagan said as much when, in a passage we quote in Chapter 4, she dissented from one of the Court's decisions upholding arbitration clauses that prohibit party aggregation, which collectively pose an existential threat to private enforcement of small claims under federal (and state) law: "To a hammer everything looks like a nail. And to a Court bent on diminishing the usefulness of Rule 23, everything looks like a class action, ready to be dismantled."[1]

Second, legislators and presidents are democratically accountable through elections. This accountability limits their ability to retrench existing rights that enjoy broad popularity (Pierson 1994: 17–19; Graber 1993). Retrenching rights is electorally dangerous. By reason of the phenomenon of "negativity bias" (or an "endowment effect"), people are substantially more likely to mobilize to avoid losing existing rights and interests than

---

[1] *American Express Co. v. Italian Colors Restaurant*, 133 S. Ct. 2304, 2314 (2013) (Kagan, J., dissenting).

they are to secure new ones. Politicians understand that, for the same reason, voters are more likely to punish those who have impaired their interests than to reward those who have benefited them (Pierson 1994: 39–46; Eskridge and Ferejohn 1995: 1560–2). Chapter 2's account of the birth of the counterrevolution in the first Reagan administration, which is grounded in original archival research, demonstrates that prominent among the influences that doomed the administration's legislative initiatives was the fear, abetted by extensive press coverage of its fee-capping bill, that the public would regard the bills as further evidence that it was hostile to civil rights and punish the bills' elected sponsors in the 1984 elections.

Members of the Advisory Committee on Civil Rules are not elected. Yet, as we observe in Chapter 3, rulemaking under the Enabling Act involves the exercise of delegated legislative power. We also note there that, concerned by rulemaking controversies that were fueled by the 1983 amendments to Rule 11 and the 1983 and 1984 proposals to amend Rule 68, Chief Justice Burger was prepared to disengage the Supreme Court from the process. His concern was about the effects of those controversies on the perceived legitimacy of the Court as such. Similar concerns, we suggest, may have contributed to the restraint evident in rulemaking during much of the period following the process reforms of the 1980s. Widespread public perception that the members of the Advisory Committee, including in particular its Article III judge members, are engaged in ordinary politics (Burbank 2007) might not cause them to lose their rulemaking jobs directly. It could, however, bring the process itself into disrepute, putting at risk the major source of the federal judiciary's power to craft rules of procedure. Moreover, if that were to happen, the damage might extend to the public's view of the judiciary – the problem that concerned Burger.

Federal judges (when acting as such, rather than serving as rulemakers) are far more insulated from the forces and incentives of democratic politics than elected officials or rulemakers, which gives the Court greater freedom to act decisively on divisive issues (Graber 1993; Gillman 2002). As Mark Graber observes, the Court's electoral insulation and streamlined decisional rules are especially advantageous in pursuit of a policy agenda as to which elements of a potential legislative coalition are internally divided. As we show in Chapter 2, that was true of Republicans in their attitudes towards the Reagan administration's fee-capping bill.

To be sure, as we discuss in Chapter 5, the Court is not immune to public opinion. Its power in the long run – its independence – depends on the continued existence of a well of diffuse support, the depth of which could be adversely affected by a series of unpopular decisions, including in particular decisions perceived to deprive people of rights enjoying broad support. Therein lies the brilliance of the counterrevolution's judicial strategy as implemented by conservative majorities of the Court in the cases that are the subject of Chapter 4. The justices understand that the Constitution's formal protections would not effectively shield the federal judiciary against a concerted attack by an inflamed Congress (Burbank and Friedman 2002). The strategy of retrenching private enforcement of rights, rather than the rights themselves, enables justices who share the goals of the counterrevolution to avoid eroding diffuse support for the Court, even when the decisions in question do not track public opinion, because the public is unlikely to be aware of them.

Third, in an era of divided government and party polarization, the Court has faced less credible threats of statutory override, and correspondingly has enjoyed a wider range of policymaking discretion (Eskridge 1991a; Eskridge 1991b; Whittington 2007: ch. 5). With Republicans controlling at least one chamber of Congress nearly continuously since 1994, the prospect of Congress overriding the decisions of a conservative majority of the Court has usually been vanishingly small (Harvey and Friedman 2006: 548; Hasen 2012). The growth of the influence of ideology on justices' votes on private enforcement issues, both procedural and non-procedural, after 1994, which we discuss in Chapter 4, is consistent with the hypothesis that the Court has exercised wider policy-making discretion during this period, with the conservative majority pushing the law of private enforcement more assertively in the anti-enforcement direction, eliciting greater opposition from the liberal minority.

The reduced threat of statutory override since 1995 also appears to be salient for proposed amendments to the Federal Rules of Civil Procedure. In Chapter 3, we suggest that this consideration has influenced some leaders who favored the goals of the counterrevolution (including Chief Justice Roberts). Even if sharing the concern about the legitimacy and effectiveness of the Enabling Act process that contributed to rulemaking's restraint throughout much of the period since the 1980s process reforms, we believe that these leaders read the reduced threat of override to mean that legitimacy was a concern that could safely be subordinated to the desire to exercise power. Nor is this surprising. Legitimacy concerns among rulemakers about the Enabling Act process are motivated in part by a desire to maintain control of procedural lawmaking by the judiciary. Threats to a proposed amendment that the Court promulgates, and to the Enabling Act itself, have a common source: Congress.

Finally, the Court's success was fostered by the lower visibility of its retrenchment efforts as compared to those of Congress or the Advisory Committee. A number of scholars have suggested that when potentially controversial issues must be addressed, the judiciary can be a less visible and politically safer policymaking site, lowering the probability of public notice and controversy (Graber 1993: 42–3; Frymer 2008: 7, 14). Two inter-related institutional features of courts promote the comparatively low visibility of their decisions relative to legislation and rulemaking: the potential for highly incremental change, and the obscuring effects of legalistic justification.

Courts can (although they need not) move policy very slowly and incrementally over long time-horizons through case-by-case adjudication. The six issue areas in our data encompassed 404 issues. And these are but a subset of a wider constellation of the Court's jurisprudence affecting private enforcement. Moreover, the lower federal courts, inevitably called on to implement these decisions, decided many more cases in the same private enforcement issue domains over the same period. The story of retrenchment of private enforcement by court decision is one of substantial change effected in large part by many comparatively small acts of lawmaking over decades, few of which garnered much public or press attention.

Efforts at legal change through legislation and rulemaking stand in marked contrast. Like the Reagan administration's fee-capping bill, they are often characterized by high levels of policy disjuncture. For legislators or rulemakers to accomplish the level of retrenchment achieved by the Supreme Court, a much smaller number of larger interventions would have been required. In addition, like both the fee-capping bill and the proposals that led to the 2015 discovery amendments, legislative and rulemaking proposals often present (or appear to present) stark alternatives that trigger powerful interest group mobilization and attract press coverage. This increases the probability that they will be obstructed.

A second institutional feature of courts that diminishes visibility concerns the nature of legal justification. Courts benefit from popular "belief that judicial decisions are based on autonomous legal principles" and "that cases are decided by application of legal rules formulated and applied through a politically and philosophically neutral process of legal reasoning," with outcomes framed in "legalistic" terms dictated by such sources as detailed legal text, legislative history, and precedent. Political scientists call these beliefs "the myth of legality" (Scheb and Lyons 2000: 929; see also Gibson, Caldeira, and Baird 1998: 345; Ginsburg 2003: 32). When courts elect a strategy of incremental and evolutionary change, their opinions will typically frame each step using this style of legal justification. Moreover, survey research suggests that "elite acceptance of [these beliefs] conditions public discourse about the Court" (Scheb and Lyons 2000: 929 (citing Casey 1974)). The media, we believe, likely pay less attention to decisions that they regard as merely applying well-established legal rules of a technical nature.

Congress and the rulemakers (who act in a legislative capacity) are not similarly insulated. A bill or rule proposal to amend existing law, by its explicit form, is a proposal offered to change (or occasionally to clarify) the legal status quo, and cannot feasibly be characterized as dictated by existing law. Moreover, the nature of legislative and rulemaking hearings, convened to evaluate the wisdom and desirability of such changes, frequently will lead to public ventilation of substantive policy tradeoffs implicated by the proposed change – tradeoffs that can be obscured by legalistically framed court decisions. Indeed, we argue in Chapter 3 that one effect of the Enabling Act reforms of the 1980s, which contributed to a more inclusive and participatory rulemaking process, was to diminish the capacity of rulemakers to present consequential rule changes as merely technical. As contrasted with court opinions that use doctrinal and legalistic justifications to present decisions as dictated by existing law, we believe that the products of the legislative and rulemaking processes, where the merits of proposed legal change are openly contested, will receive more attention from the press and the public.[2]

We have been discussing institutional differences between the Supreme Court on the one hand, and Congress and the rulemakers on the other, as they relate to the visibility of their retrenchment efforts. The discussion of the role of legal justification is also important in highlighting how the question of visibility may shape the justices' strategic calculus regarding how best to pursue their agendas. Specifically, we believe that the "hypothesis . . . that judges . . . play to public opinion in the visible cases while pursuing their agendas in less visible ones" (Burbank and Friedman 2002: 3) has substantial explanatory power for our work. If the Court's public standing and legitimacy are important to its institutional power (Stephenson 2004; Friedman 2009; Clark 2011), the need for broad public support and concern about negativity bias place some limits on its discretion to scale back

---

[2] We emphatically do not maintain that beliefs associated with the "myth of legality" are universally shared, nor do we doubt that many regard courts as political institutions. We maintain only that the press and the public are more likely to regard judicial decision-making as legalistic, technical, and neutral, than to so regard policymaking by legislatures or rulemakers since the process reforms of the late 1980s.

highly visible substantive statutory rights directly. From the standpoint of legitimacy, the strategy of focusing on private enforcement issues, particularly those implicated in the Federal Rules of Civil Procedure, is preferable.

Scholarship highlights how, to some degree, judges can strategically tap into the beliefs about the objectivity and neutrality of courts by self-consciously "framing" decisions in legalistic and technical terms (Gibson, Caldeira, and Baird 1998: 345; Scheb and Lyons 2000: 929). Although we agree that this is true, we believe that it is much more likely in some types of cases than others. As contrasted with substantive merits decisions (where the court may feel constrained by public opinion), decisions focused on private enforcement issues in general, and procedural issues in particular, offer justices more opportunities for technical and legalistic forms of legal justification. They therefore allow justices more effectively to harness beliefs about the objectivity and neutrality of courts, and to deflect attention from substantive policy consequences, minimizing press interest and public attention, and helping to forestall public perceptions that justices are legislators in black robes.

> The expressive consequences of rules and decisions are matters of social meaning which do not turn solely on the purposes of the rules or the decisionmaker's intent. Means matter. Facially neutral procedural and evidentiary rules that make liability more difficult to prove minimize the appearance of overt tradeoffs [of values and interests]. And it is these overt tradeoffs that the public is likely to see as morally and expressively offensive.
> (Bierschbach and Stein 2005: 1779)

The results we report in Chapter 5 are consistent with this theory. They support our view that a large transformation in law governing or influencing private enforcement resulted from a succession of hundreds of court decisions, distributed over decades, few of which may have appeared monumental in isolation. Focusing on welfare state retrenchment, Jacob Hacker (2004) has noted that, because of obstacles to overtly retrenching rights and programs with a substantial base of support, developments toward retrenchment in the welfare state have taken the form of strategically chosen "subterranean," "covert," and "hidden" processes that often involve lower-visibility decisions of bureaucrats in the course of administering a statute without formally changing it. Similarly, Paul Pierson has suggested that, in contrast with attempting change through legislation at one or a few moments in time, slow-moving and low-visibility historical processes of policy change may be capable of overcoming the obstacles to retrenching rights in a democratic polity. As Pierson puts it, such slow-moving processes of retrenchment may be "invisible at the surface" while producing "long-term erosion" – like "termites working on a foundation" (Pierson 2007: 33).[3]

How to Measure Success (and Failure)

We have been careful to specify that success and failure, as we use those terms, relate only to changing law that directly governs or predictably influences private enforcement of federal law. We believe that law matters and that changes in legal rules limiting standing, private rights of action, attorney's fees, damages, and procedural rules such as those governing class actions and discovery, will limit the private enforcement of federal rights. This is especially likely in a legal system in which private enforcement is largely fueled by plaintiffs' attorneys' expectations of being paid from the proceeds of, or on the basis of success in, litigation. The consequences thus should be greatest for plaintiffs least able to pay for legal representation. Although there is surely uncertainty about the effects of this or that change in the law of private enforcement, we feel no uncertainty that hundreds of decisions over more than 40 years restricting private rights of action, standing, attorney's fees, damages, the ability to litigate rather than arbitrate, and access under Federal Rules – *cumulatively* – have diminished private enforcement of federal rights.

However, the focus of this book has been the substance of law rather than its effects. We have not sought to measure the extent to which lawmakers have actually succeeded in affecting the incidence or qualitative impact of private enforcement of federal rights. Such an undertaking would require another book, and that book might not succeed, for the measurement challenges are monumental. Figure 1.1 shows the growth of private litigation enforcing federal statutes from the late 1960s to the present. Some might be tempted to conclude from it that the Court's anti-private enforcement decisions have not been consequential. However, we caution against this inference. Statistics reporting termination or filing rates are notoriously unreliable for judging how extensively cases are actually litigated (Burbank, Plager, and Ablavsky 2012: 23–5). Many influences independent of legal rules can affect whether people seek to enforce

---

[3] Staszak (2015) emphasizes the low visibility of retrenchment through procedural law in general (across institutional settings). In contrast, we maintain that retrenchment of private enforcement through rulemaking and legislation can in fact be highly visible in ways that have importantly limited its success, and that distinctive institutional properties of courts facilitate lower visibility retrenchment by the Court as compared to Congress or the rulemakers.

rights through litigation, such as economic performance (Donohue and Siegelman 1991; Jacobi 2009), media coverage of litigation (McCann 1992; MacCoun 2006), and changes in culture and social relations (Friedman 1994; Schudson 1999), among many others. Pinning down the effects of specific causes is difficult. Moreover, we note several confounding features when one seeks to determine the effects of changes in law governing private enforcement on litigant behavior.

The work of Jonah Gelbach shows that measuring the effects on judicial behavior of changes in law with obvious salience to private enforcement (e.g., the Supreme Court's pleading decisions that we discussed in Chapter 4) is inadequate for a well-grounded understanding of the effects of such changes on litigation and those involved in it (2012; 2014). Indeed, Gelbach demonstrates that, even for the limited purpose of assessing changes in judicial behavior, one needs to understand and measure the selection effects that may be induced by legal change. A plaintiff who would have filed a lawsuit prior to the *Twombly* decision may not do so after *Twombly/Iqbal* (plaintiff selection effects). A defendant who would not have filed a motion to dismiss prior to *Twombly* may do so after *Twombly/Iqbal* (defendant selection effects). And cases that might have progressed through discovery prior to *Twombly* may settle before discovery after *Twombly/Iqbal* (settlement selection effects).

Finally, Gelbach (2016) demonstrates that, depending on the question to be answered, the task of empirically studying the effects of decisions like *Twombly/Iqbal* can be even more challenging than his work considering selection effects suggests. That is because, even assuming away the most troublesome selection effects, sophisticated empirical work does not yield, and probably cannot yield, clear answers to some questions that are critical to understanding the effects of private enforcement decisions (i.e., the effects of *Twombly/Iqbal* on the mix of non-meritorious cases that nonetheless reach discovery, and meritorious cases that should reach discovery but are dismissed). Simply looking at filing rates (or in the case of the Court's pleading decisions, grant rates on motions to dismiss) leaves most questions about the effects of private enforcement decisions unanswered.

A further confounding feature for one studying the federal private enforcement landscape results from the fact that, as we state in Chapter 1, "even during periods of significant Republican legislative power, while calls for retrenchment were emanating from some quarters of the Republican Party, there was net growth in the private enforcement infrastructure." At the same time that Republicans in Congress were working to retrench private enforcement of some laws through changes to the private enforcement infrastructure, they were sponsoring or supporting (albeit at a lower rate than Democrats) the creation of other private enforcement regimes favorable to Republican constituencies, or at least not inconsistent with their preferences. As we discuss in Chapter 2, the potential tension between those policy stances ripened into conflict when Republican (small business) support for the Equal Access to Justice Act contributed to the failure of the Reagan administration's fee-capping bill.

Aggregate litigation rates do not differentiate between the types of litigation primarily targeted by the forces of retrenchment and the types they favor (or toward which they are indifferent). Thomas Keck describes a similar phenomenon in the domain of constitutional litigation (judicial review), which, as we discuss later in this chapter, we regard as presenting discrete normative questions. Keck emphasizes that "rights-based litigation is rampant on the right as well as the left ... The choice faced by movement advocates is not whether to fight for their policy priorities in court or through elected legislatures. The choice, rather, is whether these issues will be brought to court, and hence legally framed, by themselves or by their adversaries" (2014: 242).

This is just one illustration of a more general danger in using aggregate litigation rates to judge the success of retrenchment by the Court. Aggregate rates combine many types of claims and in doing so can mask contrary movement in rates across different fields of law, or even within the same field (Galanter 1988). We provide another illustration by focusing on civil rights. In addition to demonstrating what aggregate litigation rates can conceal, civil rights cases are of particular interest because they constitute a large share of the federal courts' civil statutory docket and have been a critical site of conflict over private enforcement. According to Administrative Office of US Courts data, since 1981, when the counterrevolution began in earnest, civil rights have accounted for an annual average of 21% of federal statutory actions.[4] Over the same period, the civil rights classifications enumerated in Table 4.2 amounted to 36% of the Supreme Court's private enforcement decisions in our data. If we classify all Section 1983 actions – which seek damages for the violation of any federal right by a state officer – as civil rights (as the Administrative Office does), then 43% of the Court's private enforcement decisions since 1981 fall into the civil rights category. What is primarily added by including all Section 1983 actions, in addition to the civil rights categories in

[4] Administrative Office of the United States Courts, Judicial Business of the United States Court, Table C-2, 1981–2015.

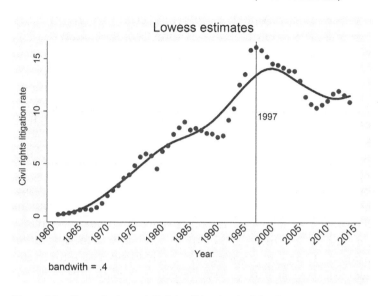

Figure 6.1 Rate of private civil rights litigation in federal court, 1961–2014

Table 4.2, is the subset of Section 1983 actions that are brought to enforce rights under federal social welfare statutes. It is notable that, under this broader definition, from 1981 to 2014 civil rights accounts for more than double the share of the Supreme Court's private enforcement docket than it does of the federal courts' civil statutory docket.[5] Some combination of litigant behavior and Supreme Court decisions to grant review have led to a disproportionate level of Supreme Court attention to private enforcement issues in civil rights cases. This has been true over the period during which the Court has grown ever more likely to limit opportunities and incentives for private enforcement.

Figure 6.1 reflects the population-adjusted annual filing rate for cases classified as private civil rights by the Administrative Office from 1961 to 2014. The smoothed estimates reflect that the rate grew fairly steadily from the late 1960s to the mid-to-late1990s, when it turned and began a 15-year decline to the present. Although private federal statutory litigation rates in general have continued growing over the past 15 years (see Figure 1.1), focusing on aggregate figures conceals the fact that the civil rights litigation rate turned down and declined over that period. This has been the

---

[5] If we examine only the 79% of our cases asserting a federal statutory claim, it remains the case that civil rights (under the expanded definition) accounts for 44% of them.

first sustained decline in private civil rights enforcement actions since they began to grow shortly following passage of the Civil Rights Act of 1964, and the reduction has been substantial. From a high of 16.1 per 100,000 in 1997, the rate declined to 10.9 by 2014, for a net rate reduction of 32%. We do not make a causal claim here about the effects of the Court's decisions. As we have discussed, such claims are fraught with difficulty. However, we do observe that the patterns in this large and important field of federal litigation, which has been a focal point of the Court's private enforcement jurisprudence, are consistent with the hypothesis that the Court's jurisprudence has consequentially curtailed filings.

The discussion to this point has focused on the difficulties of measuring "success" and on the Supreme Court's private enforcement decisions that are the subject of Chapter 4. The other side of the coin is, of course, "failure." In Chapter 2 we describe the experience of the counterrevolution that we chronicle there – by tracking more than 40 years of anti-private-enforcement legislative activity on issues selected because of their obvious importance for that purpose – as largely one of failure. In doing so, we again focus on changes in legal rules. As we discuss in Chapter 2, very few of the bills in our data set were enacted, and, more importantly, very few of those that were enacted involved legal changes of broad import, although bills containing such changes were certainly introduced. Indeed, perhaps the only bills that can properly be so described – those that led to the Class Action Fairness Act of 2005 – facilitated legal change by the judiciary through the development of restrictive class action doctrine.[6]

Although we are comfortable with the conclusion that the counterrevolution largely failed in Congress on the metric of consequential changes in legal rules, we note two clarifications. First, in so concluding, we are not making any implicit comparative claim about legislative reform in other policy areas. That is to say, we are not suggesting that the proponents of the counterrevolution fared any worse than others who have sought to retrench rights through legislation. On the contrary, the clear implications of our discussion of institutional influences in Chapter 2 are that legislation in general is difficult to enact and that legislation abridging broadly popular rights is especially difficult to enact.

Second, it appears that for some purposes the existence of introduced bills may be consequential, with the result that failure of enactment cannot

---

[6] The only other major bills that were enacted, the Private Securities Litigation Reform Act of 1995 and the Prison Litigation Reform Act of 1996, involved legal change in discrete substantive or institutional contexts.

properly be deemed failure in terms of those purposes. Tom Clark's work on court-curbing bills (2011) suggests that, even if they have no chance of passage, such bills may serve as signals of public concern or dissatisfaction that prompt the Court to moderate decisions for reasons of institutional maintenance, fearing the erosion of public support. The type of court-curbing bills Clark focuses on frequently concern controversial issues with high public salience, such as abortion, school busing, school prayer, reapportionment, and flag burning. We see no comparable argument in the private enforcement context, however. We show in Chapter 5 that the public receives little information about the Court's private enforcement decisions; we argue that this materially mitigates the constraining effects of justices' concerns about institutional legitimacy and maintenance; and we find that the Court's private enforcement decisions are not correlated with public opinion.

An alternative signaling account might be that the Court was influenced by a signal reflecting the importance of private enforcement issues and the retrenchment agenda to congressional Republicans. As we show in Chapter 4, however, when all cases are viewed together (Figure 4.2), conservative justices led a long and steep decline in the probability of a pro-private enforcement outcome starting from about the time they held a majority of the Supreme Court in the early 1970s, nearly a decade before their ideological compatriots launched the counterrevolution in Congress in the early 1980s. Moreover, our qualitative evidence in Chapter 3 confirms that retrenchment of private enforcement was on the radar of some conservative justices in the 1970s (especially Burger, but also Powell). Not surprisingly, perceived excessive private enforcement litigation was a matter of concern to conservatives on the Court before it became part of the agenda of Republicans in Congress and in the White House. They needed no signal of congressional conservatives' antipathy to private enforcement.

At the same time, focusing on cases most likely to have presented substantial legal questions (those with dissents), the early 1980s was an important turning point on the Court in an anti-private enforcement direction (Figures 4.3 and 4.4). Although justices did not learn about private enforcement issues from Congress, they may well have been cognizant of and influenced by the elevation of private enforcement as the source of a salient partisan cleavage when the Reagan administration began to advocate legislative retrenchment and congressional Republicans quickly followed suit. Indeed, we so suggest in Chapter 3 when discussing Chief Justice Burger's public rhetoric about litigation.

If congressional bill activity constituted such a signal, it must have been reinforced by the Reagan administration's concurrent amicus campaign against private enforcement, which we discuss in Chapter 4. Indeed, political scientists have suggested that federal judges are sometimes attuned to providing assistance, through decisions, to their co-partisans in the elected branches who face difficulty achieving goals through the legislative process (Graber 1993; McMahon 2000; Whittington 2005). If this is true, perhaps the legislative retrenchment project had indirect success by accelerating an anti-enforcement trend already underway on the Court by signaling that it had become an important part of the Republican Party's agenda that could benefit from judicial assistance – a "friendly hand," as Whittington puts it (2005). This, of course, is speculative.

Finally, we note that if there is any signaling story to be told, its effects were, as one might expect, entirely asymmetric. Even assuming liberal justices cared about a signal of Republican displeasure in bills to amend federal statutory law or Federal Rules – perhaps because of a perceived threat of legislative override of a decision or a Federal Rule[7] – they do not appear to have received the messages. As we note in Chapter 4, the probability of a pro-private enforcement vote by liberal justices was stable and high from 1981–2014.

Just as rulemaking under the Enabling Act occupies intermediate lawmaking space, so does our evaluation of the Advisory Committee's work in Chapter 3. We are operating under the same constraints that put measuring the impact of legal change effected by Supreme Court decisions beyond the reach of this book. We conclude that the committee's proposals salient to private enforcement, almost all of which ultimately became law, create a record of what we call modest and episodic success from the perspective of the goals of the counterrevolution. At the least, that judgment reflects the fact that, since 1970, more proposals changed the Federal Rules in ways that predictably would disfavor private enforcement than favor it, and since 2000 the anti-enforcement skew has been very pronounced, with 10 out of 11 proposals disfavoring private enforcement. We note, however, that in the 1970s the Advisory Committee's proposals favored private enforcement, and in both the 1980s and the 1990s there was a relatively

---

[7] In Chapter 3 we briefly discuss the implications of the signal sent to the rulemakers by discovery hearings that a conservative Republican convened. It could not have been that the failure to retrench would lead to legislation. Rather, it was more likely confirmation (if needed) that retrenchment would not prompt override.

evenly balanced mix between the number of pro- and anti-enforcement proposals. It took decades for the Advisory Committee's current clear anti-enforcement cast to emerge.

At various points in Chapter 3 we also offer qualitative judgments about the likely potential effects of the committee's proposals that became law. These include the judgment that, at least after the rulemaking process reforms of the 1980s, the work of the committee has usually lacked the ambition of rulemaking in the 1960s, which, of course, took place under a very different process. We also offer the judgments that the anti-private enforcement potential of the 1980s proposals in that direction "swamped the contrary tendencies of" the pro-private enforcement proposals, and that, in the mix of pro- and anti-private enforcement proposals produced in the 1990s, the potential impact of the latter seems to us obviously more significant. Finally, our account of the 2015 discovery amendments, which resulted from proposals within our study period, suggests that, with encouragement from the Chief Justice and changed leadership on the relevant committees, rulemaking may have entered another period of ambition from the perspective of the goals of the counterrevolution.

Retrenchment and Democracy

Our empirical findings and qualitative analysis raise normative questions. One set of questions concerns how the Court's success in retrenching law governing or influencing private enforcement should be understood from the standpoint of democracy. Here, it is important to emphasize that a majority of the cases in our data involved the interpretation of private enforcement regimes in federal statutes, and that in 79% of the cases, plaintiffs were asserting federal statutory rights. We regard this as an important feature that distinguishes the cases in our study from cases triggering judicial review under the Constitution. The American constitutional tradition, if not the constitutional text itself, enables the federal judiciary legitimately to invalidate majoritarian legislative (and other) actions. Of course, even in the context of judicial review normative democratic concerns are implicated, but they are typically couched as an argument that federal judges should be sparing in their exercise of judicial review, rather than as an argument against judicial review itself (Thayer 1893; Bickel 1962; Ely 1980).

The role of courts in statutory implementation, we believe, is a very different normative environment. It is one in which the primary questions concern the appropriate means and methods for implementing ordinary statutory commands where no questions of constitutionality are implicated.

234 RIGHTS, RETRENCHMENT, AND DEMOCRATIC GOVERNANCE

The American constitutional order contemplates democratic control of leg-islative rules. The first clause of the first section of the first article of the Constitution provides that "[a]ll legislative powers herein granted shall be vested in a Congress of the United States." By design, the Congress, in which the founders lodged "all legislative powers," is the branch of government most tied to the people – through decentralized geographic representation and periodic elections. Federal judges, by contrast, are appointed and enti-tled to serve for life absent removal through the impeachment process. In this respect, on the dimension of democratic control and accountability, the Supreme Court is the antithesis of the House of Representatives. Judicial resistance to legislative will is, in our view, more problematic when Article I lawmaking is indisputably constitutional than when there is an appropriate occasion for judicial review. As Judge Robert Katzmann recently observed:

> Statutes, after all, are expressions by the people's representatives of this nation's aspirations, its challenges, and approaches to those challenges. That has been so throughout our country's experience, across a whole range of issues, mundane and dramatic, bearing on the very fabric of our values. That has been true as Congress enacted laws, for example, addressing civil rights, the environment, health care, voting rights, the economy, national security, and gender discrimination. When judges interpret the words of statutes, they are not simply performing a task. They are maintaining an unspoken covenant with the citizenry on whose trust the authority and vitality of an independent judiciary depend, decisions that strive to be faithful to the work of the people's representatives, memorialized in statutory language. (2014: 104–5)

One need not subscribe to naïve or simplistic views of federal courts as wholly beyond democratic control, or of Congress as resembling a New England town meeting, in order to believe that judicial subversion of legis-lation raises troubling questions from the standpoint of democratic values. We recognize that in countless ways – including several highlighted in the literatures we turn to later in this discussion – federal courts are squarely embedded in American democracy; they do not exist above or outside it. We also recognize that representation in Congress is often parochial, and that some (powerful) interests receive far greater representation and solicitude than other (less powerful) interests. However, in a world painted in shades of grey, one can still discern meaningful variation. Rejection of ideal types – judges who are independent of politics and representa-tives who are perfectly in tune with and faithful to the preferences of their constituents – need not lead to the view that the Supreme Court is as democratically accountable and responsive as the House of Representatives. To us, such a view is no less preposterous than the ideal types we reject.

As we note in Chapter 5, the "counter-majoritarian difficulty" is among the most enduring debates in American law. There is an enormous literature, which continues to grow, addressing the question whether the Court is responsive to the preferences of the elected branches and to public opinion. This literature reflects a widespread belief, at least among scholars, that serious normative issues of democratic governance would arise if the Court's decisions on important issues of public policy were not associated with the preferences of the elected branches or the public. Although most prominent in work discussing judicial review, these normative issues are, in fact, most salient when federal courts interpret indisputably constitutional statutes.

Federal courts have long faced democratic legitimacy challenges when making important new public policy through the interpretation of statutes. A number of scholars have questioned whether this democratic challenge is well-founded, highlighting how, in many areas in which the Court has been attacked on these grounds, one might better regard it as wielding purposefully delegated legislative power (Graber 1993; Lovell 2003; Frymer 2007; see also Salzberger 1993). Focusing on major Supreme Court interpretations of statutes in the fields of antitrust, labor, and civil rights, this work highlights how Congress intentionally and knowingly failed to resolve foreseeable and controversial issues for strategic reasons, delegating (or punting) policymaking authority to courts.

Read together, this line of work suggests the following explanation for such implicit delegations. In some circumstances, the ruling coalition is internally divided and not capable of coordinating on a specific policy, and yet its capacity to govern would be disrupted by allowing the issue to remain unresolved on the agenda. A majority of legislators may seek electoral or policy benefits from "doing something" in response to public pressures for legislative action, while wishing to avoid the political costs of actually resolving some core controversial issues. Indeed, in some circumstances seeking to resolve important issues could make legislation impossible to pass (Rodriguez 1992; Mashaw 1997: 155–6; Lovell 2003). Thus, vague legislation is passed that intentionally empowers courts – and effectively requires them – to legislate through interpretation. From this perspective, regarding the ensuing judicial policymaking as undemocratic is mistaken. Democratically accountable legislators intentionally licensed courts to resolve issues left unaddressed. The existence of a more insulated (unelected, life-tenured) policymaking venue, allowing the resolution of issues that cause the elected branches to seize up, actually facilitates democratic governance rather than frustrating it.

This influential line of work offers an important perspective. However, it serves to highlight, rather than resolve, the normative questions we raise. It is manifestly a rebuttal of critiques of courts as undemocratic founded on the notion that elected officials licensed courts to make controversial decisions. This account does not fit the Court's increasingly assertive anti-private enforcement posture. There is no legislative license for retrenchment through judicial interpretation. To the contrary, the private enforcement infrastructure on which the Litigation State is founded was the product of self-conscious legislative design. The design was animated by the goal of promoting enforcement of statutory mandates.

Scholarship shows that Congress chooses private enforcement for a variety of reasons, including these:

- **Presidential Subversion.** When Congress is concerned that the president will subvert bureaucratic enforcement of congressional preferences, typically in a period of divided government, Congress is more likely to incorporate private lawsuits, with financial incentives, into implementation regimes as insurance against executive underenforcement (Melnick 1994, 2005; Kagan 2001: 48–9; Burke 2002: 14–15, 173; Farhang 2010, 2012).

- **Bureaucratic Drift.** Legislative coalitions sometimes lack faith that bureaucracy will enforce legislation aggressively because they perceive bureaucrats as politically timid, apathetic, careerist, and vulnerable to capture. They therefore advocate in the legislative process for private rights of action in court as insurance against bureaucratic failure (Vogel 1981; Melnick 2004; Farhang 2010: 40–2, 69–70).

- **Budget Constraints.** Lack of adequate tax revenue, or the political costs of raising it, encourages Congress to achieve public policy goals through private lawsuits because it shifts substantial implementation costs away from the state to private parties. Further, the costs borne by the judiciary are less traceable to particular legislative enactments than appropriations for agencies. This implementation strategy thus can attract a broader support-coalition in a tax-averse political environment (Kagan 2001: 15–16; Burke 2002: 15–16; Melnick 2005; Farhang 2010: 154–5).

- **Antistatism.** In the United States' relatively "antistatist" political culture, reliance on private lawsuits often can attract a broader support coalition than is possible with bureaucratic implementation requiring administrative state-building (Lipset 1996: 21; Kagan 2001: 15–16, 50–1, 193–4; Burke 2002: 13–14, 172–3; Farhang 2010: 155).

Although this list is not exhaustive, the key point is that the Litigation State has been produced by self-conscious legislative design-choices whose purpose was to mobilize private lawsuits as a central – and often the primary – vehicle of regulatory enforcement. The bulk of the laws were passed by Democratic Congresses distrustful of an administrative state under Republican presidential leadership (Farhang 2010). The conservative wing of the Court's campaign against private enforcement has been mounted with the goal of demobilizing those private lawsuits. Rather than carrying out an implicit legislative mandate to make policy choices that Congress sought to avoid (Graber 1993; Salzberger 1993; Lovell 2003), the conservative wing of the Court is better understood as seeking to enfeeble legislative policy with which it disagrees.

As we note earlier in this discussion, there is a second, perhaps more prominent, line of research in political science and law that questions democratic-legitimacy challenges to federal judicial power. As discussed in Chapter 5, numerous political scientists have disputed the proposition that the Supreme Court is unaccountable to the other institutions of government when deciding cases (Dahl 1957; Rosenberg 1992; McCloskey 1994; Peretti 1999; Devins 2004). Taken together, this work suggests that federal judges are drawn from, often share the preferences of, and are responsive to pressures by, political coalitions in power in the elected branches, and that the Court therefore does not often stray very far or for very long from what the majority wants. Moreover, as Barry Friedman puts it, "there is general agreement among political scientists, and increasing recognition among legal academics, that more often than not the outcomes of Supreme Court decisions are consistent with public opinion" (Friedman 2004: 114; see also Klarman 1996; Epstein and Martin 2010 [reviewing political science studies]). If the Court's decisions track what the public wants, the argument goes, this takes the bite out of the counter-majoritarian critique.

This literature provides an important perspective on debates over the extent to which democratic concerns about federal judicial power are warranted. However, it again serves to heighten rather than dissipate the concerns about democratic legitimacy and accountability raised in this book. We argue in Chapter 5 that the oft-observed correlation between public opinion and Supreme Court decision-making is likely explained, in part, by the Court's incentive to maintain institutional legitimacy, and that this incentive is significantly diluted in fields of law with lower levels of public visibility. The Court recognizes that its public standing is not hurt by decisions that the public does not learn about. We show empirically that the public receives dramatically less information about decisions governing private enforcement than decisions addressing underlying substantive rights. We also show that, although the Court's full docket of decisions may be correlated with long-run trends in "public mood," its private enforcement decisions are not.

Further, this argument against the urgency of the counter-majoritarian difficulty focuses on the preferences of the current coalition in power and the current public that put them there. On Dahl's classic formulation, to the extent that the Court is reflecting the preferences of the current governing coalition as it develops constitutional law when engaging in judicial review, it will be unlikely to do harm to the current majority's governing project by negating the laws they pass. In this sense judicial review does not present a real threat to democracy because the current majority is being allowed to govern through enactment of legislation. Critically, in this literature the *successful enactment of legislation* is regarded as the core democratic expression of the polity's preferences, and hence invalidation of legislation by an unelected court gives rise to counter-majoritarian difficulty.

The domain that we have investigated in this book is primarily legislative. The normative issues we have raised are rooted specifically in the fact that current governing coalitions were *not* able to muster the consensus necessary to pass legislation to achieve the counterrevolution's goals, due in part to apprehension concerning how the public would vote in response. We reject the notion – and in fact have never seen it maintained – that when interpreting legislation courts may legitimately privilege the will of a current legislative coalition unable to enact its preferences over the will of an earlier one that was. Although this may be an accurate positive account of what has happened, in our view it provides no normative shelter.[8]

The literatures on delegation of policymaking discretion to courts on controversial issues, the Court's responsiveness to the political branches, and the Court's responsiveness to public opinion, all offer responses to normative democratic challenges to certain exercises of federal judicial power. The responses are that the power has been intentionally delegated

---

[8] Peretti (1999) suggests that in the "pluralist" American political system, in which diverse groups contend in multiple institutional domains, it need not offend democratic values if the Court serves as an "institutional recourse for legislative or administrative losers," providing "a desirable redundancy in the process of developing policies that command widespread agreement" (219). She suggests that this may be defensible where the Court provides a venue for groups systematically excluded from the legislative or administrative process, or where the Court is merely fine-tuning public policy by adapting it to specific contexts and transmitting feedback to lawmakers. Neither justification, even if one were inclined to accept it, appears apposite here.

by democratically legitimate actors seeking to govern, that the Court is exercising the power substantially in conformity with the preferences of the elected branches, or that it is largely giving the public what they want. None of these responses, we believe, accurately describes the Court's private enforcement decisions, and thus they do not mitigate the concerns we have raised.

Although we emphasize here normative questions grounded in democratic values that emerge from the Supreme Court's private enforcement decisions involving statutory interpretation, such questions are not confined to that domain. Chapter 3 raises a number of similar questions about rulemaking under the Enabling Act. We suggest there that the controversies about class actions that arose shortly after the 1966 amendments to Rule 23 might have been avoided had the process that yielded them been more inclusive and transparent. That suggestion, however, speaks to the epistemic foundations of the amendments and, more generally, to whether they represented good public policy, which is a discrete question. It is not clear to us that critiques founded in democratic values, which crystallized as a result of experience with the proposed Federal Rules of Evidence in the early to mid-1970s, can fairly be applied to the 1966 amendments, which took essentially final form in early 1964. Put otherwise, such critiques may suffer from hindsight bias.

When the 1960s Advisory Committee was at work on Rule 23, it was not yet clear that the landscape of federal civil litigation was undergoing a profound transformation, one that would soon fill the federal courts with private lawsuits brought as a result of conscious legislative choices to stimulate private enforcement of federal law. Those choices, we show in Chapter 2, led to the birth of the counterrevolution in the first Reagan administration. It was not until the political and ideological valence of private enforcement became apparent that questions about democratic values in rulemaking, presaged in debates about the proposed Federal Rules of Evidence, became obvious and insistent. It was this democratic deficit, in part, to which the 1980s reforms were addressed, seeking to make rulemaking more open, accessible, and susceptible to congressional oversight.

The same dispensation is not available, however, for the Supreme Court decisions we discussed in Chapter 4 – *Twombly/Iqbal* (pleading) and *Wal-Mart* (class actions) – that effectively amended Federal Rules under the guise of interpretation. Although the costs of such decisions in terms of democratic values are less obvious than the costs of the Court's private enforcement decisions that subvert statutory policy choices, they are hardly insignificant (Burbank 2009; Burbank and Subrin 2011).

As we point out in Chapter 4, in *Ortiz* v. *Fibreboard Corp.*,[9] the Court provided an interpretive criterion "for distinguishing permissible judicial interpretation of Federal Rules from impermissible judicial amendment of them outside the legislatively mandated Enabling Act process. In order to protect that process, the statute's limitations on rulemaking, and the power it accords Congress to review and, if it so desires to block, prospective procedural policy choices, the Court disclaimed the freedom to treat as mere interpretation (or reinterpretation) giving meaning to a Federal Rule that is different from the meaning the Court understood 'upon its adoption.'"[10] By failing to engage that criterion in the cases in question, the Court was able to accomplish under Article III results that would have been, or had already proved to be, unattainable through legislation or the delegated legislation of rulemaking, which prompted us to call them the "new undemocratic legislation" (Burbank and Farhang 2014: 1603).[11]

In Chapter 3 we also observe that whether the difficulty of making major changes to the Federal Rules affecting private enforcement since the reforms of the 1980s "is counted a benefit depends on one's normative views about the need for, or the desirability of, major changes, and about the appropriate relationship between court rulemaking and legislative policy concerning private enforcement." Recognition that the Court's Federal Rules decisions circumventing the Enabling Act process may have been motivated by its perception that the changes sought were unlikely to be achievable through rulemaking may complicate the normative question as to the legitimacy of the decisions. Some may regard amendment through interpretation as more justifiable in the face of inaction by a rulemaking process with a heavy institutional bias toward the status quo. But in our view it does not change the answer.

To be sure, it would be ironic if the 1980s rulemaking process reforms, which were designed in part to make Federal Rules more democratically legitimate and more deeply grounded in evidence, contributed to Supreme Court decisions that are neither. It would be equally ironic if one focused on the apparent purpose of some interest groups and legislators who were involved in the 1980s lawmaking process to insulate the (pro-private-enforcement) status quo. Whatever one may conclude generally

---

[9] 527 U.S. 815 (1999).

[10] *Ortiz*, 527 U.S. at 861. *See also Amchem Products, Inc.* v. *Windsor*, 521 U.S. 591, 620 (1997).

[11] Apart from their democratic deficits, these decisions also exemplify the risks of rulemaking masquerading as adjudication for the quality of public policy (Burbank 2009: 116).

about the normative trade-offs when major procedural change is deemed necessary but is difficult or impossible to obtain through rulemaking, however, respect for democratic values requires that existing statutory policy choices concerning private enforcement be respected. It therefore requires that changes to Federal Rules that are potentially consequential for those policy choices be affected through rulemaking rather than (re)interpretation.

Only in that way can Congress be provided the opportunity to review, and if deemed appropriate to block, proposed policy choices before they become effective. This opportunity assumes special importance because of the Enabling Act's supersession clause, under which a valid Federal Rule supersedes pre-existing statutory law with which it is inconsistent (Burbank 1986: 437). Amendment of a Federal Rule through reinterpretation permits five justices to change federal law that was developed pursuant to a process prescribed by Congress and that was previously presented to Congress for potential override when the understanding of its meaning was different. If the Federal Rule postdates federal statutory law with which, as reinterpreted, it is inconsistent, the supersession clause directs that the reinterpreted Federal Rule applies.

Moreover, only through the prescribed rulemaking process can law with obvious implications for private enforcement be made on the basis of an evidentiary record, and on a base of public participation, sufficient to augur wise public policy. As John Roberts wrote when he was in the Reagan Justice Department seeking retrenchment through legislative channels:

> Not only are unelected jurists with life-tenure less attuned to the popular will than regularly elected officials, but judicial policymaking is also inevitably inadequate or imperfect policymaking. The fact-finding resources of courts are limited – and inordinately dependent upon the facts presented to the courts by the interested parties before them. Legislatures, on the other hand, have extensive fact-finding capabilities that can reach far beyond the narrow special interests urged by parties in a lawsuit. Legislatures can also devise comprehensive solutions beyond the remedial powers of courts.[12]

---

[12] Draft Article on Judicial Restraint, National Archives & Records Administration, Record Group 60: Department of Justice, Accession # 60-89-372, Box 30 of 190, Folder: John G. Roberts, Jr. Misc. The article was written by John Roberts for Attorney General William French Smith. *See* Sheryl Gay Stolberg and David E. Rosenbaum, "Court Nominee Prizes 'Modesty,' He Tells the Senate," *New York Times*, August 3, 2005. It appeared under Smith's name in a public articulation of the Reagan Justice Department's philosophy published in the *American Bar Association Journal* in January 1982, vol. 68: 59–61.

More recently, Judge Anthony Scirica, who played a prominent role in rulemaking described in Chapter 3, observed:

> The primary responsibility of the Standing Rules Committee on Practice and Procedure is to implement the Rules Enabling Act. The Act was a brilliant solution to the making of procedural law. Described as a treaty between the legislative and judicial branches, it provides a dispassionate, neutral forum that allows procedural law to be written in a deliberate and thoughtful manner. Key members of the Executive Branch (such as the Deputy Attorney General and the Solicitor General) have seats on the Rules Committees. The openness mandated by Congress invites public comment, and new rules are enacted only after approval by the Judicial Conference, adoption by the Supreme Court, and after a [seven]-month interval while Congress considers whether to permit the rules to become law. All of this ensures the rigorous scrutiny and public review essential to establish the credibility and legitimacy of the rulemaking process.[13]

Other Normative Questions

Finally, we take up two other, related, normative questions that arise from our study of rulemaking in Chapter 3. We have noted that Chief Justice Burger was willing to extricate the Court from the Enabling Act process in the early 1980s because of the threat that rulemaking controversies posed to the perceived legitimacy of the Court as such. That stance was probably easy for him to take because of the minimal role (other than symbolic) that the Court plays in the process of formulating the content of the Federal Rules and in exercising independent judgment about their promulgation.[14] More importantly, Burger knew that he would not thereby surrender the real source of power: appointments to the rulemaking committees. Our data on the appointments that Burger and his successors have made to the Advisory Committee raise (at least) two troubling questions, both concerned with imbalances among the members of the committee that at times have been extreme.

---

[13] Interview, To Speak with One Clear Voice: The Executive Committee's Role in the Judiciary (interview of Anthony J. Scirica), 41 THE THIRD BRANCH 10, 11 (December 2009).

[14] The proposed 1993 amendments to the Federal Rules, which contained controversial amendments to Rule 11 and Rule 26, encountered resistance at the Supreme Court, with the Chief Justice indicating that Court promulgation did not mean that "the Court itself would have proposed these amendments," and with "four other Justices indicat[ing] their agnosticism about, lack of competence to evaluate or disagreement with, one or more of the amendments" (Burbank 1993: 842).

In Chapter 3, we present data on the mix of practitioner members. Acknowledging the limitations of our data, we observe quite consistent dominance of lawyers who represent primarily businesses and corporations. We acknowledge that the trends we perceive may, to some extent, reflect larger trends in practice toward an increasing share of the bar working in business and corporate practice that scholars studying Chicago lawyers have documented. We note, however, that, even if representative of large city practice, the Chicago bar may differ from the bar in other locations where federal litigation occurs, and we point out that it does differ in that regard with respect to solo practitioners.

As a normative matter, this is not, of course, to suggest that the Chief Justice should search for solo practitioners to appoint to the Advisory Committee. Most of them probably lack, if not the requisite expertise in federal litigation, then the time for what is a demanding volunteer position. The latter consideration might also be daunting for members of very small public interest law firms with limited resources. Yet, in Chapter 3 we also note studies demonstrating "growth in the number, size, and budgets of public interest law firms." Given the importance of such firms (across the ideological spectrum) to private enforcement, and the recurrent questions about the impact of rules proposals on congressional policy in that domain that have arisen in recent decades, one can question the absence of non-profit public interest lawyers on the Advisory Committee.

More generally, even if we are approaching a national bar in important swaths of federal litigation, a more heterogeneous practitioner group on the Committee (including more lawyers who represent individuals rather than classes) might diminish the phenomenon of Federal Rules that are crafted to address problems in high-stakes, complex cases being applied in simpler cases for which they are manifestly unsuited. This is a cost of trans-substantive procedure to which the trends in practitioner membership on the Advisory Committee that we document may contribute (Burbank 2009; Thornburg 2016).

There may also be concern on that score as a result of evidence that, in both 1975 and 1995, Chicago lawyers "were considerably more supportive of big business than was the general population" (Heinz et al. 2005: 200). The same scholars suggest that the "increase in the lawyers' expression of support for big business may correspond to the change in their clientele," noting that the "lawyers' views, sharply divided even on fundamental issues concerning the virtues of the free market, appear to be generally congruent with those of their clients" (200–01; see Gordon 2003: 1191; Galanter and Henderson 2008). This work suggests that business/corporate attorneys are inclined to identify with and support business interests, which are a primary target of private enforcement.

Readers of this book are likely to be more surprised by the imbalances in the appointment and service of Article III judges on the Advisory Committee that our data very clearly establish. Without reference to data, James Pfander has suggested that "[w]hatever the validity of the attitudinal model in this (or other) contexts, the specter of a politicized appointments process will linger as long as the Chief Justice makes the appointments himself" (2013: 1135). Since the reconstitution of the Advisory Committee in 1971, a series of Chief Justices, all of whom were appointed by Republican presidents, have not only ensured that Article III judges dominated the committee. They have ensured that a greatly disproportionate share of those appointments went to judges who were themselves appointed by Republican presidents. Moreover, they have ensured that an astonishingly disproportionate share of appointments as chair of the committee, a powerful position because of the chair's ability to influence if not control its agenda, went to judges appointed by Republican presidents.

We do not believe that this imbalance makes a difference for the great majority of the committee's work. As discussed in Chapter 3, however, we expect ideological differences about the content of Federal Rules to surface precisely in that part of the landscape of litigation procedure where ideological and political valence has been inescapable since the birth of the counterrevolution in the first Reagan administration – private enforcement of federal law – and in the terrain with which it merged not long thereafter, the project of tort reform. In addition, it is difficult to escape the possible influence on the current Chief Justice's appointments to the Advisory Committee (as well as the Standing Committee) of the personal ideological preferences that animated his role in the birth of the counterrevolution. As we show in Chapter 2, that role included advocating for an attorney's fee-capping bill that others in the administration regarded as politically dangerous, and initiating legislative proposals to dilute Section 1983, one of the most important civil rights statutes, and one that can only be enforced by private plaintiffs. Our data revealing Chief Justice Roberts as one of the most anti-private enforcement justices in over 50 years do not suggest that his preferences have changed. Nor, of course, does his encouragement to move ahead with rulemaking in an area of intense controversy (discovery) or, once amendments in that area became effective, his decision to use the Chief Justice's entire 2015 annual report on the federal judiciary to emphasize his view of (or hopes concerning) their importance and to support training designed to make sure they are effective.

Scholars have observed that justices may serve long after the party of the president who appointed them has lost the presidency, Congress, or both, which has the potential to undermine democratic control of policymaking through periodic elections (e.g., Calabresi and Lindgren 2006: 809–13; but see Burbank 2006b). When one considers the power of Chief Justices to appoint all members of Judicial Conference committees, and to make many other significant appointments (Ruger 2004; 2006; 2007; Resnik and Dilg 2006), the lag assumes greater importance, particularly if one believes that Chief Justices wish to, and can effectively, time their retirements to facilitate ideological succession. In the case of the Chief Justice, then, the size of the gift that keeps giving long after regimes have changed is bigger than is usually recognized. If one concludes on the basis of our quantitative and qualitative research that it is too big, a number of reform strategies might be considered. We briefly discuss two of them.

One strategy would be to change the locus of the power to make appointments to all Judicial Conference committees that participate in the exercise of delegated legislative power under the Enabling Act.[15] Article II of the Constitution empowers Congress to vest the appointment of "inferior" officers in the President acting alone, in the heads of departments, and in the "Courts of Law." James Pfander has suggested that membership on rulemaking committees may be "the sort of inferior office that the Court itself must oversee," as opposed to the Chief Justice alone (2013: 1179). The Supreme Court as a whole appointed the original Advisory Committee in 1935.[16] Congress could by statute restore the original system, extending it to include all of the Conference's rulemaking committees. Objections are predictable, but so long as Congress did not seek to regulate other Judicial Conference committees (i.e., those not involved in rulemaking) in this respect, arguments founded in inherent judicial power or separation of powers should fail (Burbank: 2004a).

The Chief Justice would have a hefty advantage even in such a new system because of the involvement of the Administrative Office of US (AO) Courts in gathering/screening the names of potential members. More generally, the Chief Justice would have an advantage unless the Court delegated front-line responsibility to a committee of justices, which would control the agenda and, for this purpose, monitor the relevant activities of

---

[15] As we note in Chapter 3, imbalances as to the appointment of Article III judges similar to those we find on the Advisory Committee exist on other Judicial Conference committees as well (Chutkow 2014).

[16] For the order appointing the original Advisory Committee, see 295 U.S. 774 (1935).

the AO.[17] Even if the Chief Justice retained leadership, however, collective responsibility might encourage at least those justices who were interested to develop alternative sources of prospective members and to monitor the Chief Justice's suggestions.

Instead of, or in addition to, altering the locus of appointment power, Congress could seek to prevent imbalances that it regarded as salient by prescribing appointment criteria. Perceived imbalances in the composition of the rulemaking committees were central to some of the critiques of rulemaking in the 1970s, and they were a prominent source of criticism at the 1983 and 1984 House Hearings, both of which we discussed in Chapter 3. The House addressed the matter to a limited extent in the bill that was the foundation of the 1988 amendments to the Enabling Act. A requirement that "[e]ach such committee shall consist of a balanced cross section of bench and bar, and trial and appellate judges" was part of the House bills that passed in 1985 and 1988.[18] The provision was not part of the 1988 legislation, however, which substituted the language in the Senate bill: "Each such committee shall consist of members of the bench and professional bar, and trial and appellate judges."[19] Of course, the effect of deleting "a balanced cross-section" was to give judges double (or triple) billing. It is significant, nevertheless, that a reform of this type has been on the legislative agenda before.

We are uncertain whether statutory requirements of this sort could be sufficiently prescriptive to have much impact. To be sure, some progress might be made redressing the imbalances among practitioners that prompt the normative concerns we raise earlier in this chapter – if, for instance, Congress required that certain rulemaking committees include lawyers who represent primarily individuals and/or plaintiffs and lawyers from non-profit public interest law firms (again recognizing that such firms span the ideological spectrum). Yet, even if Congress required that the committees comprise specified numbers or percentages of judges, practitioners, and academics – or established acceptable ranges – so long as one person appointed the members, and if that person privileged

---

[17] As we note in Chapter 2, Jonathan Rose, who recently served as Secretary of the Standing Committee and Chief, Rules Committee Support Office in the AO, was a colleague of the Chief Justice in the first Reagan Administration, deeply involved both in the birth of the counterrevolution and in the effort to screen federal judge prospects to ensure ideological alignment with administration policy priorities.

[18] See H.R. 3550, 99th Cong., § 2 (1985); H.R. 4807, 100th Cong., § 2 (1988).

[19] Judicial Improvements and Access to Justice Act, Pub. L. No. 100–702, § 401, 102 Stat. 4642, 4649, ___ (1988), 28 U.S.C. § 2073(a)(2) (2006) (hereinafter 1988 Act).

ideology in making such appointments, other normative concerns raised here would remain. Indeed, even if Congress required a specified mix of Article III members appointed by presidents of different parties (Stempel 2001: 248–9), our (anecdotal) evidence suggests that a sufficiently determined and strategic Chief Justice could find individuals whose preferences were congenial. If this is true, it suggests that specification of criteria seeking balance on salient dimensions would be most effective in conjunction with, rather than as an alternative to, moving the appointment authority from the Chief Justice to the full Court.

Apart from the question of efficacy, the judiciary would vigorously oppose legislation of this sort, and the opposition would likely be most intense if it were proposed to require a mix of Article III judges appointed by presidents of different parties. We understand the sources of discomfort that (non-strategic) opposition to such a proposal would reflect, which have to do with the awkwardness of Article III judges acknowledging the pertinence of ideological preferences to their appointment or performance of their duties as judges, and their consequent reluctance to be part of a public controversy perceived as political, let alone partisan, when acting as rulemakers. We also understand, therefore, that a distinction between judging and rulemaking would provide insufficient comfort.

We are left where we were when responding to the Chief Justice's call – in his 2015 annual report about discovery – "to ensure that our legal culture reflects the values we all ultimately share." As we observed at the end of Chapter 3, "[i]f the data on decisions interpreting Federal Rules that we present in Chapter 4 tell us anything, it is that, when those rules have obvious implications for private enforcement, shared values have become increasingly hard to find." At the end of the day, appointment by the Court as a whole may be the best way to submerge the sources of discomfort that Article III judges may feel when asked to acknowledge what these data demonstrate clearly: When procedure is a source of power to determine whether rights are enforced, the influence of ideology cannot be denied.

BIBLIOGRAPHY

Aberbach, Joel D. *Keeping a Watchful Eye: The Politics of Congressional Oversight.* Washington, DC: Brookings Institution, 1990.

Arnold, Richard S. "Judges and the Public." *Litigation* 4 (1983): 5–7.

Bagenstos, Samuel R. "Who Is Responsible for the Stealth Assault on Civil Rights?" *Michigan Law Review* 114 (2016): 893–911.

Baird, Vanessa A. and Amy Gangl. "Shattering the Myth of Legality: The Impact of the Media's Framing of Supreme Court Procedures on Perceptions of Fairness." *Political Psychology Review* 27 (2006): 597–614.

Barnes, Jeb. "Courts and the Puzzle of Institutional Stability and Change: Administrative Drift and Judicial Innovation in the Case of Asbestos." *Political Research Quarterly* 61 (2008): 636–48.

Barnes, Jeb and Thomas F. Burke. *How Policy Shapes Politics: Rights, Courts, Litigation and the Struggle over Injury Compensation.* New York: Oxford University Press, 2015.

Baum, Lawrence. *Judges and Their Audiences: A Perspective on Judicial Behavior.* Princeton: Princeton University Press, 2006.

Beisner, John H. "Discovering a Better Way: The Need for Effective Civil Litigation Reform." *Duke Law Journal* 60 (2010): 547–96.

Bickel, Alexander M. *The Least Dangerous Branch: The Supreme Court at the Bar of Politics.* Indianapolis: Bobbs-Merrill, 1962.

Bierschbach, Richard A. and Alex Stein. "Overenforcement." *Georgetown Law Journal* 93 (2005): 1743–81.

Bradt, Andrew. "A Radical Proposal: The Multidistrict Litigation Act of 1968." *University of Pennsylvania Law Review* 165 (forthcoming 2016).

Brady, David W. and Craig Volden. *Revolving Gridlock Politics and Policy from Jimmy Carter to George W. Bush*, 2nd edn. Boulder: Westview Press, 2005.

Brown, Winifred R. *Federal Rulemaking: Problems and Possibilities.* Washington, DC: Federal Judicial Center, 1981.

Burbank, Stephen B. "The Rules Enabling Act of 1934." *University of Pennsylvania Law Review* 130 (1982): 1015–197.

   "Sanctions in the Proposed Amendments to the Federal Rules of Civil Procedure: Some Questions About Power." *Hofstra Law Review* 11 (1983): 997–1012.

"Afterwords: A Response to Professor Hazard and a Comment on Marrese." *Cornell Law Review* 659 (1985): 659–65.

"Proposals to Amend Rule 68 – Time to Abandon Ship." *University of Michigan Journal of Law Reform* 19 (1986): 425–40.

"The Costs of Complexity." *Michigan Law Review* 85 (1987): 1463–87.

"The Transformation of American Civil Procedure: The Example of Rule 11." *University of Pennsylvania Law Review* 137 (1989a): 1925–67.

"Hold the Corks: A Comment on Paul Carrington's 'Substance' and 'Procedure' in the Rules Enabling Act." *Duke Law Journal* (1989b): 1012–46.

"Ignorance and Procedural Law Reform: A Call for a Moratorium." *Brooklyn Law Review* 59 (1993): 841–56.

"Implementing Procedural Change: Who, How, Why, and When?" *Alabama Law Review* 49 (1997): 221–50.

"Semtek, Forum Shopping, and Federal Common Law." *Notre Dame Law Review* 77 (2002): 1027–55.

"Procedure, Politics and Power: The Role of Congress." *Notre Dame Law Review* 79 (2004a): 1677–744.

"Vanishing Trials and Summary Judgment in Federal Civil Cases: Drifting towards Bethlehem or Gomorrah?" *Journal of Empirical Legal Studies* 1 (2004b): 591–626.

"Judicial Accountability to the Past, Present, and Future: Precedent, Politics and Power." *University of Arkansas at Little Rock Law Review* 28 (2005): 19–62.

"Aggregation on the Couch: The Strategic Uses of Ambiguity and Hypocrisy." *Columbia Law Review* 106 (2006a): 1924–54.

"Alternative Career Resolution II: Changing the Tenure of Supreme Court Justices." *University of Pennsylvania Law Review* 154 (2006b): 1511–50.

"Judicial Independence, Judicial Accountability, and Interbranch Relations." *Georgetown Law Journal* 95 (2007): 909–27.

"The Class Action Fairness Act of 2005 in Historical Context: A Preliminary View." *University of Pennsylvania Law Review* 156 (2008): 1439–552.

"Pleading and the Dilemmas of Modern American Procedure." *Judicature* 93 (2009): 109–20.

"On the Study of Judicial Behaviors: Of Law, Politics, Science, and Humility." In *What's Law Got to Do with It? What Judges Do, Why They Do It, and What's at Stake*, edited by Charles Gardner Geyh, 41–70. Palo Alto: Stanford University Press, 2011.

Burbank, Stephen B. and Sean Farhang. "Litigation Reform: An Institutional Approach." *University of Pennsylvania Law Review* 162 (2014): 1543–618.

"Federal Court Rulemaking and Litigation Reform: An Institutional Approach." *Nevada Law Journal* 15 (2015): 1559–96.

"The Subterranean Counterrevolution: The Supreme Court, the Media, and Litigation Reform." *DePaul Law Review* 65 (2016a): 293–321.

"Reforming Civil Rights Litigation: Why the Court Succeeded Where Congress Failed." In *The Rights Revolution Revisited*, edited by Linda Dodd. Cambridge: Cambridge University Press, 2016b.

Burbank, Stephen B., Sean Farhang, and Herbert Kritzer. "Private Enforcement." *Lewis and Clark Law Review* 17 (2013): 637–722.

Burbank, Stephen B. and Barry Friedman. "Reconsidering Judicial Independence." In *Judicial Independence at the Crossroads: An Interdisciplinary Approach*, edited by Stephen B. Burbank and Barry Friedman, 9–42. Thousand Oaks: SAGE Publications, 2002.

Burbank, Stephen B., S. Jay Plager, and Gregory Ablavsky. "Leaving the Bench, 1970–2009: The Choices Federal Judges Make, What Influences Those Choices, and Their Consequences." *University of Pennsylvania Law Review* 161 (2012): 1–102.

Burbank, Stephen B. and Stephen N. Subrin. "Litigation and Democracy: Restoring a Realistic Prospect of Trial." *Harvard Civil Rights-Civil Liberties Law Review* 46 (2011): 399–414.

Burbank, Stephen B. and Tobias Barrington Wolff. "Redeeming the Missed Opportunities of *Shady Grove*." *University of Pennsylvania Law Review* 159 (2010): 17–76.

Burger, Warren. "The State of the Judiciary." *American Bar Association Journal* 56 (1970): 929–34.

"Address Before the Fifth Circuit Judicial Conference." *Journal of Public Law* 21 (1972): 271–80.

"Agenda for 2000 A.D. – A Need for Systematic Anticipation." In *The Pound Conference: Perspectives on Justice in the Future*, edited by A. Leo Levin and Russell R. Wheeler, 23–35. St. Paul: West Publishing Co, 1979.

"Isn't there a Better Way?" *American Bar Association Journal* 68 (1982): 274–7.

"Using Arbitration to Achieve Justice." *The Arbitration Journal* 40 (1985): 3–6.

Burke, Thomas. *Lawyers, Lawsuits, and Legal Rights: The Battle over Litigation in American Society*. Berkeley: University of California Press, 2002.

Calabresi, Steven C. and James Lindgren. "Term Limits for the Supreme Court: Life Tenure Reconsidered." *Harvard Journal of Law and Social Policy* 29 (2006): 769–877.

Caldeira, Gregory A. "Courts and Public Opinion." In *The American Courts: A Critical Assessment*, edited by John B. Gates and Charles A. Johnson, 303–34. Washington, DC: CQ Press, 1991.

Caldeira, Gregory A. and James L. Gibson. "The Etiology of Public Support for the Supreme Court." *American Political Science Review* 36 (1992): 635–64.

Cameron, A. Colin and Pravin K. Trivedi. *Regression Analysis of Court Data*, 2nd edn. New York: Cambridge University Press, 2013.

Carrington, Paul D. "Renovating Discovery." *Alabama Law Review* 49 (1997): 51–78.

"Politics and Civil Procedure Rulemaking: Reflections on Experience." *Duke Law Journal* 60 (2010): 597–667.

Chemerinsky, Erwin. "Closing the Courthouse Doors to Civil Rights Litigants." *University of Pennsylvania Journal of Constitutional Law* 5 (2003): 537–57.

"Closing the Courthouse Doors." *Denver University Law Review* 90 (2012): 317–30.

Chen, Anthony S. *The Fifth Freedom: Jobs, Politics, and Civil Rights in the United States, 1941–1972.* Princeton: Princeton University Press, 2009.

Christenson, Dino P. and David M. Glick. "Chief Justice Roberts's Health Care Decision Disrobed: The Microfoundations of the Supreme Court's Legitimacy." *American Journal of Political Science* 59 (2015): 403–18.

Chutkow, Dawn. "The Chief Justice as Executive: Judicial Conference Committee Appointments." *Journal of Law and Courts* 2 (2014): 301–25.

Clark, Tom C. "Foreword (1969)." In *4 Federal Practice and Procedure*, edited by Charles Alan Wright, Arthur R. Miller, and Adam N. Steinman, xvii–xx. St. Paul: West Publishing Company, 2015.

Clark, Tom S. *The Limits of Judicial Independence.* New York: Cambridge University Press, 2011.

Coffee, John C., Jr. *Entrepreneurial Litigation: Its Rise, Fall, and Future.* Cambridge: Harvard University Press, 2015.

Collins, Paul M., Jr. "Interest Groups and Their Influence on Judicial Policy." In *New Directions in Judicial Politics*, edited by Kevin T. McGuire, 221–37. New York: Routledge, 2012.

Cooper, Edward H. "Revising Civil Rule 56: Judge Mark R. Kravitz and the Rules Enabling Act." *Lewis and Clark Law Review* 18 (2014): 591–614.

Council for Public Interest Law. *Balancing the Scales of Justice: Financing Public Interest Law in America.* Washington, DC: Council on Public Interest Law, 1976.

Cox, Adam B. and Thomas J. Miles. "Judging the Voting Rights Act." *Columbia Law Review* 108 (2008): 1–54.

Cramton, Roger C. "Crisis in Legal Services for the Poor." *Villanova Law Review* 26 (1981): 521–56.

Cross, Frank B. "Law Is Politics." In *What's Law Got to Do with It? What Judges Do, Why They Do It, and What's at Stake*, edited by Charles Gardner Geyh, 92–113. Palo Alto: Stanford University Press, 2011.

Cushman, Barry. "Mr. Dooley and Mr. Gallup: Public Opinion and Constitutional Change in the 1930s." *Buffalo Law Review* 50 (2002): 7–102.

Davis, Richard. *Decisions and Images: The Supreme Court and the Press.* Englewood Cliffs: Prentice Hall, 1994.

Dahl, Robert A. "Decision-Making in a Democracy: The Supreme Court as a National Policy-Maker." *Journal of Public Law* 6 (1957): 279–95.

Decker, Jefferson. "Lawyers for Reagan: The Conservative Litigation Movement and American Government, 1971–87." Ph.D. dissertation, Columbia University, 2009.

Derfner, Armand. "Background and Origin of the Civil Rights Attorney's Fee Awards Act of 1976." *Urban Law 37* (2005): 653–62.

Derfner, Mary Frances. "One Giant Step: The Civil Rights Attorney's Fees Awards Act of 1976." *Saint Louis University Law Journal* 21 (1977): 441–51.

Devins, Neal. "Is Judicial Policymaking Countermajoritarian?" In *Making Policy, Making Law: An Interbranch Perspective*, edited by Mark C. Miller and Jeb Barnes, 189–201. Washington, DC: Georgetown University Press, 2004.

Dodd, Lynda G. "The Rights Revolution in the Age of Obama and Ferguson: Policing, the Rule of Law, and the Elusive Quest for Accountability." *Perspectives on Politics* 13 (2015): 657–79.

Donohue, John J. III, and Peter Siegelman. "The Changing Nature of Employment Discrimination Litigation." *Stanford Law Review* 43 (1991): 983–1033.

Dunham, Kenneth F. "The Future of Court-Annexed Dispute Resolution is Mediation." *Jones Law Review* 5 (2001): 35–49.

Easton, David. *A Systems Analysis of Political Life*. New York: John Wylie and Sons, 1965.

Ely, John Hart. *Democracy and Distrust: A Theory of Judicial Review*. Cambridge: Harvard University Press, 1980.

Epp, Charles R. *The Rights Revolution: Lawyers, Activists, and Supreme Courts in Comparative Perspective*. Chicago: University of Chicago Press, 1998.

Epstein, Lee, Jack Knight, and Andrew D. Martin. "Constitutional Interpretation from a Strategic Perspective." In *Making Policy, Making Law: An Interbranch Perspective*, edited by Mark C. Miller and Jeb Barnes, 170–188. Washington, DC: Georgetown University Press, 2004.

Epstein, Lee, William A. Landes, and Richard A. Posner. "How Business Fares in the Supreme Court." *Minnesota Law Review* 97 (2013a): 1431–73.

  The Behavior of Federal Judges: A Theoretical and Empirical Study of Rational Choice. Cambridge: Harvard University Press, 2013b.

  "The Best for Last: The Timing of U.S. Supreme Court Decisions." *Duke Law Journal* 64 (2015): 991–1022.

Epstein, Lee and Andrew D. Martin. "Does Public Opinion Influence the Supreme Court? Possibly Yes (But We're Not Sure Why)." *University of Pennsylvania Journal of Constitutional Law* 13 (2010): 263–82.

Eskridge, William N., Jr. "Reneging on History – Playing the Court/Congress/President Civil Rights Game." *California Law Review* 79 (1991a): 613–84.

  "Overriding Supreme Court Statutory Interpretation Decisions." *Yale Law Journal* 101 (1991b): 331–456.

Eskridge, William and John Ferejohn. "Virtual Logrolling: How the Court, Congress, and the States Multiply Rights." *Southern California Law Review* 68 (1995): 1545–64.

Fallon, Richard H., Jr. "Legitimacy and the Constitution." *Harvard Law Review* 118 (2005): 1787–853.

Farhang, Sean. *The Litigation State: Public Regulation and Private Lawsuits in the U.S.* Princeton: Princeton University Press, 2010.

———. "Legislative-Executive Conflict and Private Statutory Litigation in the United States: Evidence from Labor, Civil Rights, and Environmental Law." *Law and Social Inquiry* 37 (2012): 657–85.

Farhang, Sean and Gregory Wawro, "Institutional Dynamics on the U.S. Court of Appeals: Minority Representation under Panel Decision Making." *Journal of Law, Economics, and Organization* 20 (2004): 299–330.

Farley, John J. III. "Robin Hood Jurisprudence: The Triumph of Equity in American Tort Law." *Saint John's Law Review* 65 (1991): 997–1021.

Firth, David. "Bias Reduction of Maximum Likelihood Estimates." *Biometrika* 80 (1993): 27–38.

Flemming, Roy B. and B. Dan Wood. "The Public and the Supreme Court: Individual Justice Responsiveness to American Policy Moods." *American Journal of Political Science* 41 (1997): 1224–50.

Franklin, Charles H. and Liane C. Kosaki. "Media, Knowledge and Public Evaluations of the Supreme Court." In *Contemplating Courts*, edited by Lee Epstein, 352–66. Washington, DC: CQ Press, 1995.

Franklin, David L. "What Kind of Business-Friendly Court – Explaining the Chamber of Commerce's Success at the Roberts Court." *Santa Clara Law Review* 49 (2009): 1019–57.

Friedenthal, Jack. "The Rulemaking Power of the Supreme Court: A Contemporary Crisis." *Stanford Law Review* 27 (1975): 673–86.

Friedman, Barry. "Mediated Popular Constitutionalism." *Michigan Law Review* 101 (2003): 2596–636.

Friedman, Barry. "History, Politics and Judicial Independence." In *Judicial Integrity*, edited by András Sajó, 99–114. Leiden: M. Nijhoff, 2004.

Friedman, Barry. *The Will of the People: How Public Opinion Has Influenced the Supreme Court and Shaped the Meaning of the Constitution.* New York: Farrar, Straus & Giroux, 2009.

Friedman, Barry and Anna L. Harvey. "Electing the Supreme Court." *Indiana Law Journal* 78 (2003): 123–51.

Friedman, Lawrence. *Total Justice.* New York: Russell Sage Foundation, 1994.

Frymer, Paul. *Black and Blue: African Americans, the Labor Movement, and the Decline of the Democratic Party.* Princeton: Princeton University Press, 2007.

Galanter, Marc. "Why the 'Haves' Come Out Ahead: Speculations on the Limits of Legal Change." *Law & Society Review* 9 (1974): 95–160.

———. "The Life and Times of the Big Six, or, the Federal Courts since the Good Old Days." *Wisconsin Law Review* (1988): 921–54.

———. "Planet of the Aps: Reflections on the Scale of Law and Its Users." *Buffalo Law Review* 53 (2006): 1369–418.

Galanter, Marc. "More Lawyers than People: The Global Multiplication of Legal Professionals." In *The Paradox of Professionalism: Lawyers and the Possibility of Justice*, edited by Scott L. Cummings, 68–89. New York: Cambridge University Press, 2011.

Galanter, Marc and William Henderson. "The Elastic Tournament: A Second Transformation of the Big Law Firm." *Stanford Law Review* 60 (2008): 1867–920.

Galanter, Marc and David Luban. "Poetic Justice: Punitive Damage and Legal Pluralism." *American University Law Review* 42 (1993): 1393–464.

Gardner, Paul J. "The Effect of Media Framing on Public Support for the Supreme Court" (January 9, 2015).

Gelbach, Jonah B. "Locking the Door to Discovery – Assessing the Effects of *Twombly* and *Iqbal* on Access to Discovery." *Yale Law Journal* 121 (2012): 2270–345.

"Can the Dark Arts of the Dismal Science Shed Light on the Empirical Reality of Civil Procedure?" *Stanford Journal of Complex Litigation* 2 (2014): 223–65.

"Material Facts in the Debate over *Twombly* and *Iqbal*." *Stanford Law Review* 68 (2016): 369–424.

George, Warren E. "Development of the Legal Services Corporation." *Cornell Law Review* 61 (1976): 681–730.

Gibson, James L. and Gregory A. Caldeira. "Has Legal Realism Damaged the Legitimacy of the U.S. Supreme Court?" *Law and Society Review* 34 (2011): 195–219.

Gibson, James L., Gregory A. Caldeira, and Vanessa A. Baird. "On the Legitimacy of National High Courts." *American Political Science Review* 92 (1998): 343–58.

Gibson, James L., Gregory A. Caldeira, and Lester Kenyatta Spence. "The Supreme Court and the U.S. Presidential Election of 2000: Wounds, Self-Inflicted or Otherwise?" *British Journal of Political Science* 33 (2003a): 535–56.

"Measuring Attitudes toward the United States Supreme Court." *American Journal of Political Science* 47 (2003b): 354–67.

Gibson, James L. and Michael J. Nelson. "Is the U.S. Supreme Court's Legitimacy Grounded in Performance Satisfaction and Ideology?" *American Journal of Political Science* 59 (2015): 162–74.

Gillman, Howard. "How Political Parties Can Use Courts to Advance Their Agendas: Federal Courts in the United States 1875–1891." *American Political Science Review* 96 (2002): 511–24.

Ginn, Martha H., Kathleen Searles, and Amanda Jones. "Vouching for the Court? How High Stakes Affect Knowledge and Support of the Supreme Court." *Justice System Journal* 36 (2015): 163–79.

Ginsburg, Tom. *Judicial Review in New Democracies: Constitutional Courts in Asian Cases*. New York: Cambridge University Press, 2003.

Goldman, Sheldon. *Picking Federal Judges: Lower Court Selection from Roosevelt through Reagan*. New Haven: Yale University Press, 1997.

Gordon, Robert W. "A New Role for Lawyers? Corporate Counsel after Enron." *University of Connecticut Law Review* 35 (2003): 1185–216.

Gossett, William T., Bernard G. Segal, and Chesterfield Smith. "Foreword." In *The Pound Conference: Perspectives on Justice in the Future*, edited by A. Leo Levin and Russell R. Wheeler, 7–16. St. Paul: West Publishing Company, 1979.

Graber, Mark. "The Nonmajoritarian Difficulty: Legislative Deference to the Judiciary." *Studies in American Political Development* 7 (1993): 35–73.

Greene, William. *Econometric Analysis*, 5th edn. Upper Saddle River: Pearson Publishing, 2003.

Greve, Michael S. "Why 'Defunding the Left' Failed." *Public Interest* 89 (1987): 91–106.

Hacker, Jacob S. "Privatizing Risk Without Privatizing the Welfare State: The Hidden Politics of Social Policy Retrenchment in the United States." *American Political Science Review* 98 (2004): 243–60.

Haltom, William and Michael McCann. *Distorting the Law: Politics, Media, and the Litigation Crisis*. Chicago: University of Chicago Press, 2009.

Handler, Joel F., Betsy Ginsberg, and Arthur Snow. "The Public Interest Law Industry." In *Public Interest Law: An Economic and Institutional Analysis*, edited by Burton Weisbrod, 42–79. Berkeley: University of California Press, 1978.

Harvey, Anna and Barry Friedman. "Pulling Punches: Congressional Constraints on the Supreme Court's Constitutional Rulings, 1987–2000." *Legislative Studies Quarterly* 28 (2006): 247–80.

Hasen, Richard L. "End of the Dialogue: Political Polarization, the Supreme Court, and Congress." *Southern California Law Review* 86 (2012): 205–61.

Hazard, Geoffery C., John Gedid, and Stephen Solwe "An Historical Analysis of the Binding Effect of Class Suits." *University of Pennsylvania Law Review* 146 (1998): 1849–948.

Heinz, John P., Robert L. Nelson, Rebecca L. Sandefur, and Edward O. Laumann. *Urban Lawyers: The New Social Structure of the Bar*. Chicago: University of Chicago Press, 2005.

Higginbotham, A. Leon, Jr. "The Priority of Human Rights in Court Reform." In *The Pound Conference: Perspectives on Justice in the Future*, edited by A. Leo Levin and Russell R. Wheeler, 87–110. St. Paul: West Publishing Co., 1979.

Higginbotham, Patrick E. "Foreword." *Alabama Law Review* 49 (1997): 4–6.

"Iron Man of the Rules." *University of Michigan Journal of Law Reform* 46 (2013): 627–30.

Hirschl, Ran. *Towards Juristocracy: The Origins and Consequences of the New Constitutionalism*. Cambridge: Harvard University Press, 2004.

Hixson, Everett L. "All Losers Should Pay in Tennessee: How to Amend T.C.A. Section 20-12119 to Deter Meritless Claims." *University of Memphis Law Review* 44 (2013): 183–228.

Ho, Daniel E. and Kevin M. Quinn. "Did a Switch in Time Save Nine?" *Journal of Legal Analysis* 2 (2010): 69–113.

Hoekstra, Valerie J. "The Supreme Court and Local Public Opinion." *American Political Science Review* 94 (2000): 89–100.

   Public Reaction to Supreme Court Decisions. New York: Cambridge University Press, 2003.

Hrina, David J. "The Future of IOLTA: Has the Death Knell Been. Sounded for Mandatory IOLTA Programs?" *Akron Law Review* 32 (1999): 301–26.

Immergut, Ellen M. "The Rules of the Game: The Logic of Health Policy-Making." In *Structuring Politics: Historical Institutionalism in Comparative Analysis*, edited by Sven Steinmo, Kathleen Thelen, and Frank Longstreth, 57–89. New York: Cambridge University Press, 1992.

Jacobi, Tania. "The Role of Politics and Economics in Explaining Variation in Litigation Rates in the U.S. States." *Journal of Legal Studies* 38 (2009): 205–33.

Jacobson, Gary. "Partisan Polarization in Presidential Support: The Electoral Connection." *Congress and the Presidency* 30 (2003): 1–36.

Joseph, Gregory P. "An Instinct for the Capillary." *Litigation* 38 (2012): 9–10.

Kagan, Robert A. *Adversarial Legalism: The American Way of Law.* Cambridge: Harvard University Press, 2001.

Kalven, Harry Jr. and Maurice Rosenfield. "The Contemporary Function of the Class Suit." *University of Chicago Law Review* 8 (1941): 684–721.

Kaplan, Benjamin. "Continuing Work of the Civil Committee: 1966 Amendments of the Federal Rules of Civil Procedure (I)." *Harvard Law Review* 81 (1966): 356–416.

   "A Prefatory Note." *Boston College Industrial and Commercial Law Review* 10 (1969): 497–500.

Kaplow, Louis and Steven Shavell. "Fairness versus Welfare." *Harvard Law Review* 114 (2001): 961–1388.

Karlan, Pamela S. "Disarming the Private Attorney General." *University of Illinois Law Review* (2003): 183–210.

Katzmann, Robert A. *Judging Statutes.* New York: Oxford University Press, 2014.

Keck, Thomas M. *Judicial Politics in Polarized Times.* Chicago: University of Chicago Press, 2014.

Kersch, Ken I. "The Reconstruction of Constitutional Privacy Rights and the New American State." *Studies in American Political Development* 16 (2002): 61–87.

Kessler, Daniel P. *Regulation versus Litigation: Perspectives from Economics and Law.* Chicago: University of Chicago Press, 2011.

Kirkham, Francis R. "Complex Litigation – Have Good Intentions Gone Awry?" In *The Pound Conference: Perspectives on Justice in the Future*, edited by A. Leo Levin and Russell R. Wheeler, 209–20. St. Paul: West Publishing Company, 1979.

Klarman, Michael. "Rethinking the Civil Rights and Civil Liberties Revolutions." *Virginia Law Review* 82 (1996): 1–67.

Klonoff, Robert H. "The Death of Class Actions." *Washington University Law Review* 90 (2013): 729–838.

Kravitz, Mark R., David F. Levi, Lee H. Rosenthal, and Anthony J. Scirica, "They Were Meant for Each Other: Professor Edward Cooper and The Rules Enabling Act." *University of Michigan Journal of Law Reform* 46 (2013): 495–526.

Krent, Harold J. "Explaining One-Way Fee Shifting." *Virginia Law Review* 79 (1993): 2039–89.

Kritzer, Herbert M. and Mark J. Richards. "The Influence of Law in the Supreme Court's Search-and-Seizure Jurisprudence." *American Politics Research* 33 (2005): 33–55.

Landes, William M. and Richard A. Posner. "An Independent Judiciary in an Interest-Group Perspective." *Journal of Law and Economics* 18 (1975): 875–901.

Law, Sylvia A. "In the Name of Federalism: The Supreme Court's Assault on Democracy and Civil Rights." *University of Cincinnati Law Review* 70 (2002): 367–432.

Lazarus, Simon and Joseph Onek. "The Regulators and the People." *Virginia Law Review* 57 (1971): 1069–108.

Lehne, Richard and John Reynolds. "The Impact of Judicial Activism on Public Opinion." *American Journal of Political Science* 22 (1978): 896–904.

Lemos, Margaret H. "Special Incentives to Sue." *Minnesota Law Review* 95 (2011): 782–845.

Lipset, Seymour Martin. *American Exceptionalism: A Double-Edged Sword.* New York: W.W. Norton & Company, 1996.

Litan, Robert and William Nordhaus. *Reforming Federal Regulation.* New Haven: Yale University Press, 1983.

Lovell, George I. *Legislative Deferrals: Statutory Ambiguity, Judicial Power, and American Democracy.* New York: Cambridge University Press, 2003.

Lyles, Kevin L. *The Gatekeepers: Federal District Courts in the Political Process.* Westport: Praeger, 1997.

MacCoun, Robert J. "Media Reporting of Jury Verdicts: Is the Tail (of the Distribution) Wagging the Dog?" *DePaul Law Review* 55 (2006): 539–62.

Marcus, David. "The Past, Present, and Future of Trans-Substantivity in Federal Civil Procedure." *DePaul Law Review* 59 (2010): 371–429.

"Trans-Substantivity and the Processes of American Law." *Brigham Young University Law Review* (2013a): 1191–250.

"The History of the Modern Class Action, Part I: Sturm und Drang, 1953–1990." *Washington University Law Review* (2013b): 587–652.

Marcus, Richard. "Shoes That Did Not Drop." *University of Michigan Journal of Law Reform* 46 (2013): 637–50.

"'Looking Backward' to 1938." *University of Pennsylvania Law Review* 162 (2014): 1691–730.

Martin, Andrew D. and Kevin M. Quinn. "Dynamic Ideal Point Estimation via Markov Chain Monte Carlo for the U.S. Supreme Court, 1953–1999." *Political Analysis* 10 (2002): 134–53.

Mashaw, Jerry L. *Greed, Chaos, and Governance: Using Public Choice to Improve Public Law*. New Haven: Yale University Press, 1997.

McCann, Michael. "Reform Litigation on Trial." *Law and Social Inquiry* 21 (1992): 457–82.

McCarty, Nolan, Keith T. Poole, and Howard Rosenthal. *Polarized America: The Dance of Ideology and Unequal Riches*. Cambridge: MIT Press, 2006.

McCloskey, Robert G. *The American Supreme Court*, 2nd edn. Chicago: University of Chicago Press, 1994.

McCubbins, Mathew D. and Thomas Schwartz. "Congressional Oversight Overlooked: Police Patrols Versus Fire Alarms." *American Journal of Political Science* 28 (1984): 165–79.

McGarity, Thomas O. "Regulatory Reform in the Reagan Era." *Maryland Law Review* 45 (1986): 253–73.

McKay, Robert B. *Nine for Equality under Law: Civil Rights Litigation: A Report to the Ford Foundation*. New York: Ford Foundation, 1977.

McMahon, Kevin J. "Constitutional Vision and Supreme Court Decisions: Reconsidering Roosevelt on Race." *Studies in American Political Development* 14 (2000): 20–50.

McNollgast. "Administrative Procedures as Instruments of Political Control." *Journal of Law, Economics, & Organization* 3 (1987): 243–78.

"The Political Origins of the Administrative Procedure Act." *Journal of Law, Economics & Organization* 15 (1999): 180–217.

Melnick, R. Shep. *Between The Lines: Interpreting Welfare Rights*. Washington, DC: Brookings Institution, 1994.

Melnick, R. Shep. "Courts and Agencies." In *Making Policy, Making Law: An Interbranch Perspective*, edited by Mark C. Miller and Jeb Barnes, 89–106. Washington, DC: Georgetown University Press, 2004.

Melnick, R. Shep. "From Tax and Spend to Mandate and Sue: Liberalism after the Great Society." In *The Great Society and the High Tide of Liberalism*, edited by Sidney Milkis and Jerome M. Mileur, 387–410. Amherst: University of Massachusetts Press, 2005.

Melnick, R. Shep. "Courts and Agencies in the American Civil Rights State." In *The Politics of Major Policy Reform in Postwar America*, edited by Jeffrey Jenkins and Sidney Milkis, 77–102. New York: Cambridge University Press, 2014.

Mezey, Susan and Susan Olson, "Fee Shifting and Public Policy: The Equal Access to Justice Act." *Judicature* 77 (1993): 13–20.

Miller, Arthur R. "Of Frankenstein Monsters and Shining Knights: Myth, Reality, and the 'Class Action Problem.'" *Harvard Law Review* 92 (1979): 664–94.

The August 1983 Amendments to the Federal Rules of Civil Procedure: Promoting Effective Case Management and Lawyer Responsibility. Washington, DC: Federal Judicial Center, 1984.

"Simplified Pleading, Meaningful Days in Court, and Trials on the Merits: Reflections on the Deformation of Federal Procedure." *New York University Law Review* 88 (2013): 286–372.

Moe, Terry M. "Political Institutions: The Neglected Side of the Story." *Journal of Law, Economics & Organization* 6 (1990): 213–53.

Moore, Patricia H. "The Anti-Plaintiff Pending Amendments to the Federal Rules of Civil Procedure and the Pro-Defendant Composition of the Federal Rulemaking Committees." *University of Cincinnati Law Review* 83 (2015): 1083–154.

Morriss, Andrew P., Bruce Yandle, and Andrew Dorchak. *Regulation by Litigation.* New Haven: Yale University Press, 2008.

Murphy, Bruce A. *Scalia: A Court of One.* New York: Simon & Schuster, 2014.

Murphy, Walter F. "Reagan's Judicial Strategy." In *Looking Back on the Reagan Presidency*, edited by Larry Berman, 207–37. Baltimore: Johns Hopkins University Press, 1990.

Murphy, Walter F. and Joseph Tanenhaus. "Public Opinion and the United States Supreme Court: Mapping of Some Prerequisites for Court Legitimation of Regime Changes." *Law and Society Review* 2 (1968): 357–84.

Nash, Jonathan R. "Interparty Judicial Appointments." *Journal of Empirical Legal Studies* 12 (2015): 664–85.

Nicholson, Stephen P. and Robert M. Howard. "Framing Support for the Supreme Court in the Aftermath of Bush v. Gore." *Journal of Politics* 65 (2003): 676–95.

Nielsen, Laura Beth and Catherine Albiston. "The Organization of Public Interest Practice: 1975-2004." *North Carolina Law Review* 84 (2006): 1591–622.

Niemeyer, Paul V. "Here We Go Again: Are the Federal Discovery Rules Really in Need of Amendment?" *Boston College Law Review* 39 (1998): 517–24.

Note. "Limiting the Section 1983 Action in the Wake of Monroe v. Pape." *Harvard Law Review* 82 (1969): 1486–511.

O'Brien, David M. "The Reagan Judges: His Most Enduring Legacy?" In *The Reagan Legacy: Promise and Performance*, edited by Charles O. Jones, 60–101. London: Chatham House, 1988.

O'Connor, Karen and Lee Epstein. "Rebalancing the Scales of Justice: Assessment of Public Interest Law." *Harvard Journal of Law & Public Policy* 7 (1984): 483–506.

Pampel, Fred C. *Logistic Regression: A Primer.* Thousand Oaks: Sage Publications, 2000.

Percival, Robert and Geoffrey Miller. "The Role of Attorney Fee Shifting in Public Interest Litigation." *Law and Contemporary Problems* 47 (1984): 233–48.

Peretti, Terri Jennings. *In Defense of a Political Court.* Princeton: Princeton University Press, 1999.

Pfander, James E. "The Chief Justice, the Appointment of Inferior Officers, and the 'Court of Law' Requirement." *Northwestern University Law Review* 107 (2013): 1125–80.

Pickerill, Mitchell and Cornell Clayton. "The Rehnquist Court and the Political Dynamics of Federalism." *Perspectives on Politics* 2 (2004): 233–48.

Pierson, Paul. *Dismantling the Welfare State? Reagan, Thatcher, and the Politics of Retrenchment.* Cambridge: Cambridge University Press, 1994.

Pierson, Paul. "The Rise and Reconfiguration of Activist Government." In *The Transformation of American Politics: Activist Government and the Rise of Conservatism*, edited by Paul Pierson and Theda Skocpol, 19–38. Princeton: Princeton University Press, 2007.

Poole, Keith T. and Howard Rosenthal. *Congress: A Political-Economic History of Roll Call Voting.* New York: Oxford University Press, 1997.

Purcell, Edward A., Jr. "From the Particular to the General: Three Federal Rules and the Jurisprudence of the Rehnquist and Roberts Courts." *University of Pennsylvania Law Review* 162 (2014): 1731–65.

Quayle, Dan. "Civil Justice Reform." *American University Law Review* 41 (1992): 559–70.

Quigley, William P. "The Demise of Law Reform and the Triumph of Legal Aid: Congress and the Legal Services Corporation from the 1960s through the 1990s." *Saint Louis University Public Law Review* 17 (1998): 241–64.

Ragozin, Arlene S. "The Waiver of Immunity in the Equal Access to Justice Act: Clarifying Opaque Language." *Washington University Law Review* 61 (1986): 217–44.

Remus Dana A. "The Institutional Politics of Federal Judicial Conduct Regulation." *Yale Law and Policy Review* 31 (2012): 33–78.

Resnik, Judith. "Fairness in Numbers: A Comment on AT&T v. Concepcion, Wal-Mart v. Dukes, and Turner v. Rogers." *Harvard Law Review* 125 (2011): 78–171.

Resnik, Judith and Lane Dilg. "Responding to a Democratic Deficit: Limiting the Powers and the Term of the Chief Justice of the United States." *University of Pennsylvania Law Review* 154 (2006): 1575–664.

Rhode, Deborah L. "Public Interest Law: The Movement at Midlife." *Stanford Law Review* 60 (2008): 2027–86.

Rifkind, Simon. "Are We Asking Too Much of our Courts?" In *The Pound Conference: Perspectives on Justice in the Future*, edited by A. Leo Levin and Russell R. Wheeler, 23–35. St. Paul: West Publishing Company, 1979.

Rodriguez, Daniel B. "Statutory Interpretation and Political Advantage." *International Review of Law and Economics* 12 (1992): 217–31.

Rodriguez, Daniel and Barry R. Weingast, "The Positive Political Theory of Legislative History." *University of Pennsylvania Law Review* 151 (2003): 1417–542.

Rosenberg, Gerald. "Judicial Independence and the Reality of Political Power." *Review of Politics* 54 (1992): 369–98.

Ruger, Theodore W. "The Judicial Appointment Power of the Chief Justice." *University of Pennsylvania Journal of Constitutional Law* 7 (2004): 341–402.

"The Chief Justice's Special Authority and the Norms of Judicial Power." *University of Pennsylvania Law Review* 154 (2006): 1551–74.

"Chief Justice Rehnquist's Appointments to the Foreign Intelligence Surveillance Act Court: An Empirical Perspective." *Northwestern University Law Review* 101 (2007): 239–58.

Rutledge, Peter B. "Arbitration – A Good Deal for Consumers: A Response to Public Citizen." *U.S. Chamber of Commerce Institute for Legal Reform*, 2008.

Salzberger, Eli M. "A Positive Analysis of the Doctrine of Separation of Powers, or: Why Do We Have an Independent Judiciary?" *International Review of Law and Economics* 13 (1993): 349–79.

Scheuerman, Sheila B. "Two Worlds Collide: How the Supreme Court's Recent Punitive Damages Decisions Affect Class Actions." *Baylor Law Review* 60 (2008): 880–940.

Schiller, Reuel E. "Rulemaking's Promise: Administrative Law and Legal Culture in the 1960s and 1970s." *Administrative Law Review* 53 (2001): 1139–88.

Scheb II, John M. and William Lyons. "The Myth of Legality and Public Evaluation of the Supreme Court." *Social Sciences Quarterly* 81 (2000): 928–40.

Schudson, Michael. *The Good Citizen: A History of American Civil Life*. Cambridge: Harvard University Press, 1999.

Segal, Jeffrey A. and Albert D. Cover. "Ideological Values and the Votes of U.S. Supreme Court Justices." *American Political Science Review* 83 (1989): 557–65.

Segal, Jeffrey A. and Harold J. Spaeth. *The Supreme Court and the Attitudinal Model Revisited*. New York: Cambridge University Press, 2002.

Segal, Jeffrey A., Chad Westerland, and Stefanie A. Lindquist. "Congress, the Supreme Court, and Judicial Review: Testing a Constitutional Separation of Powers Model." *American Journal of Political Science* 55 (2011): 89–104.

Shapiro, Martin M. *Who Guards the Guardians? Judicial Control of Administration*. Athens: University of Georgia Press, 1988.

Shefter, Martin. *Political Parties and the State: The American Historical Experience*. Princeton: Princeton University Press, 1994.

Shugart, Matthew S. and John M. Carey. *Presidents and Assemblies: Constitutional Design and Electoral Dynamics*. New York: Cambridge University Press, 1992.

Siegel, Andrew M. "The Court against the Courts: Hostility to Litigation as an Organizing Theme in the Rehnquist Court's Jurisprudence." *Texas Law Review* 84 (2006): 1097–202.

Sisk, Gregory C. "The Essentials of the Equal Access to Justice Act: Court Awards of Attorney's Fees for Unreasonable Government Conduct." *Louisiana Law Review* 55 (1994): 217–360.

Spencer, A. Benjamin. "The Restrictive Ethos in Civil Procedure." *George Washington University Law Review* 78 (2010): 353–73.

Squire, Peverill. "Politics and Personal Factors in Retirement from the United States Supreme Court." *Political Behavior* 10 (1988): 180–90.

Staszak, Sarah. "Realizing the Rights Revolution: Litigation and the American State." *Law & Social Inquiry* 38 (2013): 222–45.

———. *No Day in Court: Access to Justice and the Politics of Judicial Retrenchment.* New York: Oxford University Press, 2015.

Steinman, Adam N. "The End of an Era: Federal Civil Procedure after the 2015 Amendments." *Emory Law Journal* 66 (2016): 1–53.

Steinmo, Sven H. "American Exceptionalism Reconsidered: Culture or Institutions?" In *The Dynamics of American Politics: Approaches and Interpretations*, edited by Lawrence C. Dodd and Calvin Jillson, 106–31. Boulder: Westview Press, 1994.

Stempel, Jeffrey W. "Politics and Sociology in Federal Civil Rulemaking: Errors of Scope." *Alabama Law Review* 52 (2001): 529–637.

Stephenson, Matthew. "Court of Public Opinion: Government Accountability and Judicial Independence." *Journal of Law, Economics, and Organization* 20 (2004): 379–99.

Stewart, Richard. "The Reformation of American Administrative Law." *Harvard Law Review* 88 (1975): 1669–813.

Stimson, James. *Public Opinion in America: Moods, Cycles, and Swings.* Boulder: West View Press, 1991.

Subrin, Stephen. "How Equity Conquered Common Law: The Federal Rules of Civil Procedure in Historical Perspective." *University of Pennsylvania Law Review* 135 (1987): 909–1002.

Subrin, Stephen and Thomas O. Main. "The Fourth Era of American Civil Procedure." *University of Pennsylvania Law Review* 162 (2014): 1839–95.

Sunderland, Edison R. "An Appraisal of English Procedure." *Michigan Law Review* 24 (1925): 109–29.

———. "Discovery before Trial under the New Federal Rules." *Tennessee Law Review* 15 (1939): 737–57.

Sundquist, James L. "Needed: A Political Theory for the New Era of Coalition Government in the United States." *Political Science Quarterly* 103 (1988–89): 613–35.

Sunstein, Cass R., David Schkade, Lisa Ellman, and Andres Sawicki. *Are Judges Political? An Empirical Analysis of the Federal Judiciary.* Washington, DC: Brookings Institution Press, 2006.

Taylor, Paul. "The Federalist Papers, the Commerce Clause, and Federal Tort Reform." *Suffolk Law Review* 45 (2012): 357–94.

Teles, Steven M. *The Rise of the Conservative Legal Movement: The Battle for Control of the Law.* Princeton: Princeton University Press, 2008.

Thayer, James B. "The Origin and Scope of the American Doctrine of Constitutional Law." *Harvard Law Review* 7 (1893): 129–56.

Thornburg, Elizabeth G. "Cognitive Bias, the 'Band of Experts,' and the Anti-Litigation Narrative." *DePaul Law Review* 65 (2016): 755–92.

Tobias, Carl. "Reforming Common Sense Legal Reforms." *Connecticut Law Review* 30 (1998): 537–68.

Tonsing, Mike. "Symposium on Proposed Changes to FRCP: An Introduction." *Federal Lawyer* (September 2004): 22–5.

Trubek, Louise. "Public Interest Law: Facing the Problem of Maturity." *University of Arkansas at Little Rock Law Review* 33 (2011): 417–34.

Ulribe, Alicia, James F. Spriggs, II, and Thomas G. Hansford. "The Influence of Congressional Preferences on Legislative Overrides of Supreme Court Decisions." *Law and Society Review* 48 (2014): 921–46.

Unah, Isaac, Kristen Rosano, and K. Dawn Milam. "U.S. Supreme Court Justices and Public Mood." *Journal of Law and Politics* 30 (2015): 293–340.

Viscusi, W. Kip. *Regulation through Litigation*. Washington, DC: AEI-Brookings Joint Center for Regulatory Studies, 2002.

Vogel, David. "The 'New' Social Regulation in Historical and Comparative Perspective." In *Regulation in Perspective*, edited by Thomas K. McCraw, 155–85. Cambridge: Harvard University Press, 1981.

Vogel, David. *Fluctuating Fortunes: The Political Power of Business in America*. New York: Beard Books, 1989.

Wallace, Clifford J. "Judicial Reform and the Pound Conference of 1976." *Michigan Law Review* 80 (1982): 592–96.

Wasserman, Howard. "The Roberts Court and the Civil Procedure Revival." *Review of Litigation* 31 (2012): 313–52.

Weaver, Kent R. and Burt A. Rockman. "Assessing the Effects of Institutions." In *Do Institutions Matter?*, edited by Kent R. Weaver and Burt A. Rockman, 1–41. Washington, DC: Brookings Institution, 1993.

Weinstein, Jack B. *Reform of Court Rulemaking Procedures*. Columbus: Ohio State University Press, 1977.

Weisbrod, Burton A. *Public Interest Law: An Economic and Institutional Analysis*. Berkeley: University of California Press, 1978.

Whittington, Keith. "'Interpose Your Friendly Hand': Political Supports for the Exercise of Judicial Review by the United States Supreme Court." *American Political Science Review* 99 (2005): 583–96.

 Political Foundations of Judicial Supremacy: The Presidency, the Supreme Court, and Constitutional Leadership in U.S. History. Princeton: Princeton University Press, 2007.

Wilson, James Q. "The Bureaucracy Problem." *The Public Interest* 6 (1967): 3–9.

Witcover, Jules. *Party of the People: A History of the Democrats*. New York: Random House, 2003.

Woolridge, Jeffrey M. *Introductory Econometrics: A Modern Approach*, 5th edn. Mason: South-Western Cengage Learning, 2013.

Yeazell, Stephen C. *From Medieval Group Litigation to the Modern Class Action*. New Haven: Yale University Press, 1987.

"Judging Rules, Ruling Judges." *Law & Contemporary Problems* 61 (1998): 229–52.

"Unspoken Truths and Maligned Interests: Political Parties and the Two Cultures of Civil Litigation." *University of California Los Angeles Law Review* 60 (2013): 1752–91.

Zemans, Frances K. "Fee Shifting and the Implementation of Public Policy." *Law and Contemporary Problems* 47 (1984): 187–210.

Zumbrun, Ronald A. "Life, Liberty, and Property Rights." In *Bringing Justice to the People: The Story of the Freedom-Based Public Interest Law Movement*, edited by Lee Edwards, 41–53. Berwyn Heights: Heritage Books, 2004.

INDEX

ABA. *See* American Bar Association

ABA Section of Litigation, 124

ABA Special Committee, 101, 103

ACLU. *See* American Civil Liberties Union

administrative adjudicatory powers, 9

administrative agencies. *See* regulatory agencies

administrative capture, 10

administrative enforcement, 28

Administrative Office of the US Courts, 59, 228, 245

Administrative Procedure Act, 110

administrative process, 110

administrative state, 4–8, 237
  limitations, 4–5

Advisory Committee, 19–20, 65–129, 132, 221, 232–33, 239
  administrative process, 19
  history, 70–77

Advisory Committee members, 77–82
  academics, 19, 71, 77–79, 98, 113, 246
  appointments process, 97, 113, 242–47
  federal judges, 77–79
    and party affiliation, 126–27
    Republican-appointed, 19–20, 66–67, 82–91, 104, 113, 116, 218, 244
  practitioners, 19, 71, 77–79, 246
    corporate attorneys, 19–20, 66–67, 81, 116, 218, 244
    plaintiffs' attorneys, 81
    types, 79–82, 126, 242–43

Advisory Committee on Civil Rules. *See* Advisory Committee

Alito, Samuel, 150, 173, 182

Alliance for Justice, 12, 53, 107

Amchem Products, Inc. v. *Windsor*, 74

American Bar Association, 101, 102, 103, 107

American Civil Liberties Union, 53, 96, 107, 110

American College of Trial Lawyers
  Federal Civil Procedure Committee, 115

American Enterprise Institute
  Regulation magazine, 34, 59

American Rule, 8, 105
  common fund exception, 75

amicus briefs
  fee-shifting
    Marek v. *Chesny*, 134
  private enforcement cases, 22, 160
    Bush I administration, 61
    Carter administration, 60
    Nixon-Ford administrations, 60
    Reagan administration, 59, 60–61, 232

Anti-Injunction Act, 117

anti-litigation proposals
  civil damages, 48
  fee-shifting, 48
  loser pays rule, 48

anti-litigation reform, 15

anti-private enforcement
  legislative proposals, 34–46
  rulemaking proposals, 103–25, 233

antistatism, 236

arbitration
  retrenchment
    jurisprudence, 21, 141

Arnold, Richard S., 193

Article III judges. *See* federal judges
Article III powers, 65, 83, 120, 130,
　138, 143–44, 240
Ashcroft v. *Iqbal*, 137–38, 143, 198,
　227, 239
attorney's fees, 8
　anti-litigation proposals, 47
　as part of costs, 133–34
　common fund, 74
　retrenchment
　　jurisprudence, 21
　　legislation, 17, 29, 31, 34, 53, 132
attorney's fees
　retrenchment
　　jurisprudence, 21
　　legislation, 17

backlash, 20, 66, 197
Balancing the Scales of Justice, 12–13
Barnes, Jeb, 138
Baum, Lawrence, 196
Becker, William H., 96
Bell Atlantic Corp. v. *Twombly*, 137–38,
　143, 227, 239
bicameralism, 50
big business, 57, 243
bill data models, 63
Blackmun, Harry A., 134, 152
Brennan, William J., 134, 150–52, 182
Burger, Warren E., 19–20, 66–67, 79,
　85, 97–107, 113, 120, 133–34,
　221, 231, 242
Bush II administration
　Department of Justice, 49
Bush v. *Gore*, 194
Bush, George H. W., 38, 114
Bush, George W., 6
business defendants, 114, 130, 155–57,
　168, 176–78
business interests, 4, 26, 56, 244
business regulation cases, 22, 157, 177

CAFA. *See* Class Action Fairness Act
　of 2005
Campbell, Robert S., Jr., 115
Carter administration, 15, 37, 45, 139
　Department of Justice, 44, 101
Carter, Jimmy, 113

case-by-case policy change, 23, 68,
　138, 219
Center for Individual Rights, 27
Chamber of Commerce, 22, 96, 157
　anti-private enforcement amicus
　　briefs, 162–65, 177
checks and balances, 105
Chief Justices
　appointment power, 19, 77, 89, 91,
　　245–46
　Republican-appointed, 3, 19–20, 66,
　　112, 218, 244
civil liberties, 36, 146, 189
Civil Rights Act of 1871, 17, 29, 30
Civil Rights Act of 1964, 9, 10–12, 17,
　29, 33, 134, 229
　Title VII
　　class actions, 142
　　fee-shifting, 11, 13
　　private enforcement regimes, 9,
　　　13–15, 62
Civil Rights Act of 1991, 162
civil rights actions
　definition, 228
Civil Rights Attorney's Fees
　　Awards Act of 1976, 10, 31,
　　36, 48, 133
civil rights bar, 12
civil rights cases, 58, 147, 228–29
civil rights groups, 9–11, 96
civil rights laws, 9, 10–11, 17, 52, 133
civil rights legislation. *See* civil rights
　laws
civil rights litigation, 31, 54, 86, 229
Clark, Tom S., 231
Class Action Fairness Act of 2005, 48,
　117, 139, 230
class actions
　1966 amendments, 42–43, 72–77,
　　100, 138, 218, 239
　anti-litigation proposals, 48
　cases, 171, 198
　Federal Rules of Civil Procedure,
　　18, 72
　legislation, 1
　retrenchment
　　jurisprudence, 21, 23, 68, 119,
　　　138–43, 170

legislation, 34–37, 41–50, 99–101, 140, 230
    rulemaking, 72–77, 100–101, 101, 103, 113–14, 116–17, 118–19, 226
    transsubstantive limits, 141
class actions (small claims)
    1966 amendments, 42, 73–76
    retrenchment
        jurisprudence, 220
        legislation, 44, 101, 139
Clean Air Act of 1963, 199, 215
Clinton, Bill, 38, 46
Coffee, John C., Jr., 143
Conference on Civil Litigation. *See* Duke Conference
Conley v. *Gibson*, 118, 135
conservative legal movement, 3, 17, 21, 29, 218
    public interest law groups, 22, 25, 26–27
Contract with America (1994), 114, 162
cost-shifting, 92, 105, 114
Council for Public Interest Law, 12
Council of the Administrative Conference of the United States, 60
Council on Competitiveness, 115
counter-majoritarian critique, 194, 235, 237–38
counterrevolution, 2–4, 45, 65–67, 72, 83, 97, 99, 102, 115, 119, 130, 141, 181, 217–26, 228, 229–33, 238, 239, 244
    institutional framework, 16–24
Court of Appeals judges, 89
court-curbing, 231
CRA of 1871. *See* Civil Rights Act of 1871
CRA of 1964. *See* Civil Rights Act of 1964
CRA of 1991. *See* Civil Rights Act of 1991
Cuban Liberty and Democratic Solidarity (Libertad) Act of 1996, 15

Dahl, Robert A., 238
damages
    anti-litigation proposals, 48, 114
    retrenchment
        jurisprudence, 20–21, 23
        legislation, 17, 29–30, 31, 34, 36–38, 41, 43, 46, 49, 226
D.C. Circuit
    pro-fee award decisions, 34
    Scalia appointment, 59
Decker, Jefferson, 28
DeConcini, Dennis, 44
defendant selection effects, 227
defense lawyers, 79, 98, 115
delegated legislative power, 109, 143, 221, 235, 245
Delta Airlines v. *August*, 134
demobilization
    of administrative regulatory enforcement, 28
    of private enforcement, 16, 32–34, 237
Democratic Congresses, 3, 6, 15, 110, 237
democratic governance, 4, 23, 192, 235
Democratic Party, 9
Democratic Party coalition, 5–6
democratic values, 234, 239–41
discovery
    1938 rules, 68–70
    abuse of, 101–3
        lack of evidence for, 115
    administrative subpoena power, 70
    amendments
        1970, 77
        1980, 103, 114
        2000, 92, 115–16
        2015, 66, 67, 121–25, 233
    cost-shifting, 114–15, 122–23
    retrenchment
        rulemaking, 101, 104, 114, 122, 226
    scope, 102, 114, 121–25
district judges, 35, 89, 100
divided government, 5–7, 22, 123, 222, 236
DOJ. *See* Department of Justice *under presidential administration name*

Domestic Council Review Group on
    Regulatory Reform, 60
Douglas, William O., 150, 152, 182
Duke Center for Judicial Studies, 124
Duke Conference, 121–25
Dunne, Finley Peter, 211

EEOC. See Equal Employment
    Opportunity Commission
Eisenhower, Dwight D., 113
Enabling Act. See Rules Enabling Act
    of 1934
Epstein, Lee, 147, 195–96, 197, 205–7
Equal Access to Justice Act of 1980,
    57, 62
Equal Employment Opportunity
    Commission, 27
  adjudicatory powers, 9
executive branch, 43, 242

Fallon, Richard H., Jr., 193
federal judges
  Republican-appointed, 21, 218
Federal Judicial Center, 106, 118, 127
Federal Rules of Civil Procedure, 16,
    65–72, 125, 130
  cases, 22, 169–81
  interpretation, 218–19
  private enforcement issues,
    18–19, 21
  retrenchment
    rulemaking, 3, 222
  Rule 4. See service of process
  Rule 8. See pleadings
  Rule 11. See sanctions
  Rule 15. See amended pleadings
    under pleadings
  Rule 23. See class actions
  Rule 23(b)(3). See class actions
    (small claims)
  Rule 26. See discovery
  Rule 54(d), 105
  Rule 56. See summary judgment
  Rule 68. See offers of judgment
  transsubstantive scope, 68, 110, 112,
    140, 171, 243
Federal Rules of Evidence, 100, 106,
    239

Fielding, Fred, 53–55
Ford Foundation, 11
Ford, Gerald R., 60
Fox, Francis, 115
Frankfurter, Felix, 152
Franks, Trent, 123
FRCP. See Federal Rules of Civil
    Procedure
Friedman, Barry, 195–96, 237

Galanter, Marc, 1
Gardner, Paul J., 194, 197–98
Gelbach, Jonah B., 227
Gignoux, Edward T., 108
Gingrich, Newt, 114, 162
government defendants, 29, 114,
    155–57, 168, 176
Graber, Mark, 58
Greve, Michael S., 27–28, 32

Hacker, Jacob S., 225
Hatch, Orrin, 57–58
Hickman v. Taylor, 135
Higginbotham, A. Leon, Jr., 102
Higginbotham, Patrick E., 113, 118
Honoring America's Veterans and
    Caring for Camp Lejeune
    Families Act of 2012, 16
Horowitz, Michael, 29, 32–33
House Judiciary Committee, 106, 123
House of Representatives, 107, 234
House Tea Party Caucus, 123

institutional theory, 50
interventionist state, 5
Iqbal. See Ashcroft v. Iqbal

Johnson administration, 9, 10
Johnson, Frank, 113
Judicial Conference of the
    United States, 70, 92, 98, 115,
    121, 242
  committee appointments, 245–47
judicial review, 50, 111, 228, 233–35,
    238
Justice Department. See Department
    of Justice under presidential
    administration name

Kagan, Elena, 142, 150, 173, 182, 220
Kagan, Robert A., 170
Kastenmeier, Robert, 106–8, 113
Katzmann, Robert A., 234
Keck, Thomas M., 228
Kennedy administration, 9
Kennedy, Anthony M., 173
Kennedy, Edward M., 44

Lawyers' Committee for Civil Rights Under Law, 11
Leatherman v. *Tarrant County Narcotics Intelligence & Coordination Unit*, 138
Ledbetter v. *Goodyear Tire & Rubber Co.*, 198
Legal Fee Equity Act of 1984, 58
legal services, 30, 54
legislative costs, 20, 109, 111
Library of Congress, 36, 43
Limitation of Legal Fees Awards Act of 1981, 17, 29–30
litigation costs, 2, 8, 104–5, 114, 128, 132–34, 141
litigation explosion, 2, 96, 99
Litigation Highway, 67–77
Litigation State, 2, 4–16, 18, 45–48, 50, 61, 65, 235–37
loser pays rule
   anti-litigation proposals, 114

Marek v. *Chesny*, 133–34
Marshall, Thurgood, 134, 182
Martin, Andrew D., 195–96, 197, 205–7
MDLA. *See* Multi-District Litigation Act of 1968
Meese, Edwin, 33, 59
Moe, Terry M., 51
Morrison, Alan, 108
Multi-District Litigation Act of 1968, 96

NAACP, 53
NAACP Legal Defense Fund, 10
Nader, Ralph, 108
National Archives, 29

National Association of State Attorneys General, 55
National Conference on the Causes of Popular Dissatisfaction with the Administration of Justice. *See* Pound Conference
National Institute of Municipal Law Officers, 55
National Labor Relations Board, 9
negative value claims, 73
   economic costs, 75
Neuborne, Burt, 107–8, 110
New Deal, 4, 110
New Deal Democrats, 110
New York Times, 198, 200, 203
Niemeyer, Paul V., 114, 113–15
Nixon, Richard M., 6, 10, 27
Nixon-Ford administrations, 59
NLRB. *See* National Labor Relations Board
NOMINATE scores for legislator ideology, 63, 206

Obama, Barack, 46
offers of judgment
   retrenchment
      jurisprudence, 132–35
      legislation, 34, 35
      rulemaking, 104–8
Office for Improvements in the Administration of Justice, 44
Office of Legal Policy, 30, 52, 59
Office of Management and Budget, 26, 29
O'Neill, Tip, 33
Ortiz v. *Fibreboard Corp.*, 240

Pacific Legal Foundation, 27
   anti-private enforcement amicus briefs, 164
Partial-Birth Abortion Ban Act of 2003, 16
party polarization, 5–7, 22, 222
Paul, Weiss, Rifkind, Wharton and Garrison, 102
Pfander, James E., 244, 245
Pierson, Paul, 51, 226

pleadings, 135, 199
  1938 rules, 68–70
  amended pleadings
    rulemaking, 104
  fact pleading, 135
    definition, 69
  notice pleading, 102, 118, 135, 137
    definition, 69
  retrenchment
    jurisprudence, 135
policymaking
  congressional oversight, 68
Posner, Richard A., 133
Pound Conference, 101–3, 121, 124
Pound, Roscoe, 102, 103
Powell, Lewis F., Jr., 96, 103, 107, 182, 231
Prison Litigation Reform Act of 1996,
    49, 139
private enforcement infrastructure,
    10–16
  attacks on, 29–32
private enforcement of federal rights,
    2–10, 15, 17, 21, 26, 30, 75, 219,
    226, 236–37, 239
  civil rights model, 9–10
private enforcement regimes, 1
  attorney's fees, 27, 42, 57
  damages, 8, 13–16, 35, 42–43
  economic incentives, 76
  fee-shifting, 7–12, 13–16, 26,
    133, 134
  private rights of action, 8, 15–16,
    27, 28
  rationales
    budget constraints, 236
    bureaucratic drift, 6, 236
    standing, 8
private rights of action, 236
  retrenchment
    jurisprudence, 21, 219
    legislation, 226
Private Securities Litigation Reform
    Act of 1995, 48, 139
PSLRA. See Private Securities
    Litigation Reform Act of 1995
Public Citizen, 53
Public Citizen Litigation Group, 108
public mood variable, 205–7, 209–11

Quayle, Dan, 114

Reagan administration, 3, 17–18, 21,
    65, 132, 140, 218, 221, 231, 239, 244
  anti-civil rights, 52, 54
  appointments, 25, 27
  Department of Justice, 30–31, 33,
    51–52, 58–60, 137, 241
    appointments, 58
  deregulation strategy, 25–28, 33
  fee-cap bill, 29, 32–34, 50, 52, 54–58,
    59–62, 137
  hostility to Legal Services
    Corporation, 28–29
  judiciary
    appointments, 58
  retrenchment of private enforcement
    rights
    legislation, 17–18, 25–64
  Tort Policy Working Group, 29
Reagan Library, 29
Reagan, Ronald, 25–28, 33, 38, 173
  hostility to liberal public interest
    lawyers, 27
Reagan-Bush years, 46
regulatory agencies, 5, 108–10,
    206, 236
  congressional oversight, 7, 20
  judicial review, 7
regulatory state, 2, 17
Rehnquist court
  hostility to litigation generally,
    130–31
Rehnquist, William H., 67, 103, 111,
    134, 136, 150, 182
Republican anti-litigation legislative
    program, 162
Republican Party, 3, 4, 14–15, 17–18,
    41, 46, 55, 61, 86, 104, 162, 227,
    232
Republican Study Committee, 123
retrenchment of private enforcement
    rights, 1–24, 27–29, 216–47
  by statutory interpretation, 58–61,
    239
  failure, 229–33
  in the private sector, 57
  institutional framework, 1–24

jurisprudence, 20–24, 130–91, 197, 198, 205, 217, 218–20, 222
and democracy, 233–42
institutional framework, 219
social and economic regulation, 20
legislation, 132, 217–18, 231, 232, 241
failure, 46–58
fee-shifting, 35, 107
litigation, 139, 150, 173
transsubstantive scope, 47–48
litigation, 34, 41, 63, 99, 103, 104, 114–15, 135, 138, 162, 185, 228
political costs, 18, 51–54, 61, 62, 110, 235
rulemaking, 18–20, 23, 65–129, 132, 137–38, 141, 218–20, 240
fee-shifting, 106
social and economic regulation, 17, 147–49
substantive rights, 3, 25
success, 226–29
welfare state, 51, 225
Rifkind, Simon, 102
Roberts, John G., 33–34, 67, 124, 137, 150, 152, 173, 182, 199, 222, 241, 244
Section 1983 changes, 30–31
Roosevelt, Franklin D., 110
court-packing plan, 193
Rose, Jonathan, 59–61
Rosenthal, Lee H., 118
rulemaking process, 66, 70, 77, 95–120, 133, 136, 169, 218, 220, 233, 240–42
congressional oversight, 111, 239
institutional reforms, 20
Rules Committee Support Office, 59
Rules Enabling Act of 1934, 44, 65, 66–68, 70, 83, 103, 104, 130, 136, 138, 143, 181, 218, 221, 222, 232, 239–42
1988 amendments, 110–11, 245–46
proposed rules changes, 92
rulemaking as legislative process, 120–21
substantive rights, 100–101, 106–8, 111, 116–19, 121, 132–35

sanctions
retrenchment
legislation, 34–35, 37, 41, 48
rulemaking, 92, 104, 103–7, 127, 221
Scalia, Antonin, 34, 59, 142, 150, 173, 182
Schmults, Edward Charles, 59–61
School Aid Act of 1971, 10
Scirica, Anthony J., 241–42
Section 1983, 17, 36, 59
amendments, 30–32, 33, 49–50, 51–52, 61
civil rights actions, 133, 137, 228
dilution, 244
Section 1988, 133–34
service of process, 104
Siegel, Andrew H., 131–32
small business, 48, 57, 62
opposition to Reagan fee-cap bill, 56–57
support for Equal Access to Justice Act of 1980, 62, 228
Smith William French, 53–55
social and economic regulation, 5–6
Sotomayor, Sonia, 150, 182
Souter, David H., 152, 173
Spaeth Supreme Court Database
comparisons of federal rights and private enforcement decisions with dissents, 187–89
definition of liberal Supreme Court decisions, 147
federal rights cases with dissents, 157–60
ideology effects on justice votes, 167–69
private enforcement cases lacking merits issues, 199
Special Committee for the Study of Discovery Abuse. See ABA Special Committee
standing
retrenchment
jurisprudence, 20–21, 23, 219
legislation, 17, 226

Standing Committee on Rules of
    Practice and Procedure, 71, 97,
    99, 108, 113, 117
  appointments, 244
  proposals affecting private
      enforcement rights, 91–92
  scope of discovery, 121–24
Starr, Kenneth
  Section 1983 changes, 30–31
Staszak, Sarah, 2, 138
Stevens, John Paul, 150–52
Stewart, Potter, 103
Stimson, James, 205
Stockman, David Alan, 29, 33
Subcommittee on Abuse of Discovery,
    101
substantive rights, 16
  abridgement, 100–101
summary judgment
  1993 amendments, 92
  retrenchment
    rulemaking, 117
Sunderland, Edson R., 69
Supreme Court
  and civil rights, 3, 22
  anti-private enforcement posture,
    204, 231, 236
  appointments, 152, 195, 217
  delegitimizing messages, 194
  diffuse support, 193–94, 221
  private enforcement decisions
    and public opinion, 192–216
    anti-private enforcement, 144,
      170–80, 203, 226
    arbitration, 143–44, 199, 208
    attorney's fees, 143–44, 170, 199,
      208, 226
    class actions, 144, 192, 239
    congressional ideology, 211–13
    damages, 143–44, 192, 199, 208,
      226, 228
    dataset, 143–69
    dissents, 21, 134, 142, 143–68,
      170–80, 220, 231
    Federal Rules of Civil Procedure,
      143–44, 208
    litigation, 226

pleading, 239
pleadings, 135–38
private rights of action, 143–44,
  170, 199, 208, 226
pro-private enforcement, 144,
  158–61, 170–80, 209, 231
standing, 143–44, 199, 208, 226
Supreme Court justices
  anti-private enforcement, 34, 244
  conservative, 3, 22, 67, 130–31,
    141–43, 149, 150–59, 165–69,
    170, 173–81, 182–87, 190–91,
    198, 203, 207, 209, 211–14, 217,
    220, 222, 231, 237
  ideology scores
    Martin-Quinn models, 149, 152,
      165–67, 173, 179, 180, 182–87,
      206, 207, 209–10, 212
    Segal-Cover models, 149, 166–67,
      180, 186–87, 210
  liberal, 131–32, 143, 150–59, 165–69,
    173–81, 182–87, 190–91, 203,
    212–13, 220, 222, 232
  votes
    anti-private enforcement, 144,
      149, 150, 154–55, 171–73, 182
    case outcomes, 148–61
    ideology, 22, 161–69, 170–80
    pro-private enforcement, 149,
      150–58, 170–80, 182, 187, 210,
      212, 232
Supreme Court of the United States.
  See Supreme Court
Swierkiewicz v. Sorema N.A., 138

Taft-Hartley Act of 1947, 15
Thomas, Clarence, 136, 150, 173, 182
TILA. See Truth in Lending Act
  of 1968
tort reform, 29, 40, 244
Truth in Lending Act of 1968, 42, 48,
  138
Twombly. See Bell Atlantic Corp. v.
  Twombly

United States Conference of Mayors, 56
University of Chicago, 34

Vogel, David, 5
Voting Rights Act Amendments of
  1975, 10

Wall Street Journal, 57, 200, 202–3
Wal-Mart Stores, Inc. v. *Dukes*, 142–43,
  198, 239
Warren, Earl, 71, 77, 98
Washington Legal Foundation

anti-private enforcement amicus
  briefs, 164
Washington Post, 11, 53, 200, 203
Wasserman, Howard, 198
White & Case, 60
White, Byron R., 152
Whittington, Keith E., 232
Wilderness Society, 53
Wilson, James Q., 4